# THE BLACK

D0430418

# THE BLACK DEATH

*Natural and Human Disaster*
*in Medieval Europe*

## ROBERT S. GOTTFRIED

**THE FREE PRESS**
New York London Toronto Sydney

Copyright © 1983 by The Free Press
A Division of Macmillan Publishing Co., Inc.

All rights reserved. No part of this book may be reproduced or
transmitted in any form or by any means, electronic or mechanical,
including photocopying, recording, or by any information storage
and retrieval system, without permission in writing from the
Publisher.

THE FREE PRESS
A Division of Simon & Schuster Inc.
1230 Avenue of the Americas
New York, N.Y. 10020


First Free Press Paperback Edition 1985
Printed in the United States of America

paperback printing number

19  20

hardcover printing number

2 3 4 5 6 7 8 9 10


**Library of Congress Cataloging in Publication Data**

Gottfried, Robert S.
   The black death; natural and human disaster in Medieval
Europe.
   Includes bibliographical references and index.
   1. Black death—Europe. I. Title.
RC178.G3G67   1983   616.5′732   82-48745
ISBN-13: 978-0-02-912630-1
ISBN-10:    0-02-912630-4
ISBN-13: 978-0-02-912370-6 (Pbk)
ISBN-10:    0-02-912370-4 (Pbk)

*To
Philip James and Jane Louise,
the apples of my eye*

*Nature, the vicaire of the almyghty lorde.*

Geoffrey Chaucer,
*The Parliament of Fowls,* c. 1380

# Contents

# Contents

# Acknowledgments

As in the past, many scholars have generously given of their time to help me make up my deficiencies in interpretation and writing style. Among them are Michael Adas, Paul Clemens, James Green, John Gillis, Angeliki Laiou, Maurice Lee, William McNeill, William O'Neill, Traian Stoianovich, and Joseph Strayer. An early draft of Chapter 2 was presented before the Social History Group Seminar at Rutgers University and I have benefited from the members' suggestions. My editors at Macmillan, Colin Jones, Joyce Seltzer, and Eileen DeWald, consistently gave me good advice. The Rutgers University Research Council and the Charles and Johanna Busch Memorial Bio-medical Fund have supported my research, reading, and writing, and have enabled me to hire research and editorial assistants. Among these were Claire P. Griffin and Patricia R. Lanni. A grant from the American Council of Learned Societies was of great help during the last stages of writing. Without such scholarly, editorial, and financial aid I could not have written this book.

# Introduction

IN OCTOBER 1347 a Genoese fleet made its way into the Messina harbor in northeast Sicily. Its crew had "sickness clinging to their very bones."[1] All were dead or dying, afflicted with a disease from the Orient. The Messinese harbor masters tried to quarantine the fleet, but it was too late. It was not men but rats and fleas that brought the sickness, and they scurried ashore as the first ropes were tied to the docks. Within days, the pestilence spread throughout Messina and its rural environs and, within six months, half the region's population died or fled. This scene, repeated thousands of times in ports and fishing villages across Eurasia and North Africa, heralded the coming of the greatest natural disaster in European history—the Black Death.

The Black Death was a combination of bubonic, pneumonic, and septicaemic plague strains. It devastated the Western world from 1347 to 1351, killing 25%–50% of Europe's population and causing or accelerating marked political, economic, social, and cultural changes. People were astounded, bewildered, and terrified. "Father abandoned child, wife husband, one brother another, for the plague seemed to strike through breath and sight. And so they died. And no one could be found to bury the dead, for money or friendship."[2] People were in great horror of this seemingly inexplicable pestilence for which there were no remedies. As the Florentine humanist Petrarch wrote: "Oh happy posterity who will not experience such abysmal woe—and who will look upon our testimony as fable."[3]

The long-term effects of plague were even more profound. The Black Death was the first epidemic of the second plague pandemic, a series of cyclic outbreaks of the disease which recurred until the eighteenth century. European population declined steadily for at least a century after 1350; chronic depopulation characterized the fourteenth and fifteenth centuries. The old constitutional, governmental, and commercial institutions, the old philosophical notions, and even the systems of religious belief came under massive—and, frequently, successful—challenge. Aristocrats and churchmen, who had dominated the preplague world through control of property, were confronted by peasants and merchants newly prosperous from trade in agricultural and industrial goods and restless with their continuing role as the underlings in Europe's social structure. Preplague production, predicated on cheap, abundant human labor, was replaced by new methods that often were based on relatively sophisticated technology. In effect, the Black Death and the second plague pandemic intervened in the development of the Western world with as sudden and profound a force as any event in history.

Virtually all historians assign to the Black Death an important role in European history, but there is considerable debate on the nature, timing, and long-term effects of this role. Some scholars believe the changes the Black Death brought were short-lived, while others regard the Black Death as *a*, or even *the*, major turning point in the transition from medieval to modern Europe. Most early students of the subject subscribed to the latter perspective. In 1893, F. A. Gasquet wrote that the Black Death marked the end of the Middle Ages.[4] A cardinal, he blamed the disease for the decline of the Christian Church, especially monasticism. This perspective was also pressed by G. G. Coultan, an early exponent of social history. Coultan felt that there was a silver lining in the depopulation caused by plague, namely, greater per capita prosperity for the survivors, and that this wealth helped to bring about the Renaissance and the Protestant Reformation.[5] J. W. Thompson did not press the connection between the Black Death and the Renaissance and Reformation, but instead concentrated on the Black Death's psychological impact.[6] He compared its devastation with that of World War I, and found the former's impact to be deeper and longer lasting. The Black Death killed much of the "flower" of a generation and left many of the survivors in psychological and moral crisis. This perspective is espoused today by the prominent French medievalist Yves Renuoard. Furthermore, in a recent study by the Rand Corporation, the Black Death was ranked as one of the three worst catastrophes in the history of the world.[7]

In the 1930s, perhaps influenced by contemporary events, historians began to diminish somewhat the role of the great natural phenomenon. Some Marxists, like the Russian E. A. Kosminsky, believed that plague was but a part of a general crisis in the rural economy and society which centered around Europe's hierarchical social structure.[8] This view was shared by some non-Marxists. M. M. Postan, a pioneer in applying empirical methods to economic history, also lessened the role of the Black Death. He claimed that the crisis began in the mid-

thirteenth century and developed as population levels exceeded food
supplies.[9] Europe became successively poorer after about 1300; depopulation caused by plague, some gains in per capita income
nothwithstanding, merely accelerated the collapse of an already
crumbling society. Raymond Delatouche, a prominent French medievalist, deemphasized the Black Death on different grounds.[10] Delatouche claimed that the late medieval crisis was moral rather than economic. Its roots lay in the philosophical and religious tensions of the
thirteenth century.

This diminution of importance of the Black Death continued to
attract disciples after World War II. There were even new tacks. A
bacteriologist, J. F. D. Shrewsbury, argued that the plague bacillus,
*Yersinia pestis*, was not as virulent as most historians believed and
that, at least in the British Isles, the Black Death could not have
killed more than 20% of the population.[11] But the best postwar studies on the Late Middle Ages have been intensive, empirical works on
specific regions. The data they have yielded tend to support the sup-
positions of the Coultan-Thompson generation. Among the most
prominent of these recent scholars are the American David Herlihy
and the Frenchmen Élisabeth Carpentier, Éduoard Baratier, and Guy
Bois. They agree that there was a general late medieval crisis which
began with overpopulation in the thirteenth century, but believe that
plague was the most important part of the problem and caused the
most fundamental changes. Herlihy and Carpentier studied the Italian towns of Pistoia, in Tuscany, and Orvieto, in Umbria, and their
*contadi,* or surrounding countrysides.[12] Both concluded that, while
the Black Death itself was a tremendous blow, the most important aspect of plague was its cyclic recurrence. They stressed the elasticity
and resilience of humanity in response to any single disaster. But pandemic plague struck every few years, ensuring depopulation and giving continuing impetus to the changes of the Late Middle Ages. Both
Baratier and Bois, who did detailed studies of the French regions of
Provence and Normandy, came to the conclusion that successive
plague epidemics kept population low until the 1470s.[13]

This emphasis on pandemic plague has been incorporated into a
broad environmental and biological interpretation of the Late Middle
Ages. The environmental perspective, first advocated by the Scandinavian demographers E. Jutikkala and M. Kauppinen, more recently
stressed by a number of English historians, including J. D. Chambers
and John Hatcher, and nicely summed up by the Frenchmen J.-N.
Biraben and Emmanuel LeRoy Ladurie, presents the Black Death

and general demographic, social, and economic change in a broad ecological framework.[14] Biraben, for example, claimed that pandemic plague is affected by changing weather systems and rodent and insect life cycles. He did not ignore the crucial role played by man in the dissemination of disease, but avoided ascribing too much emphasis to trade routes and the state of transportation and communication.[15]

This book follows the environmental approach to plague, which distinguishes it from other recent studies of the Black Death, notably that written by Philip Ziegler.[16] The Black Death and second plague pandemic can be understood only in their epidemiological context, as part of a 300-year period of ecological crisis. This emphasis on exogenous environmental factors is not at the exclusion of general political, social, and economic problems. Rather, the desire is for a more balanced perspective that considers, say, how rodent communities and weather conditions, as well as merchant adventurers, spread epidemic disease. Similarly, in studying the declining crop yields of the late thirteenth century, it is important, where possible, to investigate changing levels of precipitation and nutrients in the soil, as well as the kinds of crops peasants were planting and how they were bequeathing their property.

There are many difficulties in writing a book about the Black Death and the second plague pandemic. One concerns the predominance of a number of deep-seated misconceptions. Many historians still emphasize the enormous death rate caused by the Black Death. However, human population is resilient enough to rebound from a single attack, even one as devastating as the Black Death. It was the successive blows of the second pandemic which produced the most pronounced changes. Other historians tend to lower plague mortality, claiming that the Black Death killed but 20% of Europe's population, rather than 30%, 40%, or even 50%. Yet 20%, especially when compounded by successive epidemics, is still greater than the mortality caused by any other phenomenon in European history. There are even some misnomers. A few professional historians continue to call the Black Death the "Black Plague." The epidemic of 1665 is usually called the "Great Plague," and with good reason. It may have killed 15% to 20% of western Europe's population, but neither it nor any medieval epidemic was called the "Black Plague." In fact, the term "Black Death" was not used in the Middle Ages, and probably was first applied to the epidemic of 1347–51 around 1550.[17] In medieval times, people referred to it as the "pestilence," a simple, graphic description which, by 1400, was used in a broad way to denote any disaster, epidemic or otherwise, that was afflicting society.

Another difficulty concerns evidence. Medieval records are often scanty, especially when dealing with natural phenomena. Chronicles provide descriptions of bad weather, but no data; there are a few late medieval natural histories and several agricultural manuals, but they do not deal with insect or rodent life cycles. Still, new methods of research have given historians considerable information about the environment of late medieval Europe. Dendrochronology (the measurement of tree rings), pollen analysis, and carbon half-life dating of archaeological remains now allow for reliable estimates of mean temperature and precipitation levels, diagnosis of degenerative diseases, and speculation as to the nutritional value of diet. Application of the methods of the social scientist, such as computer programming and sophisticated statistical analysis, have produced good demographic data. It is still necessary to speculate about many important things but, in the last decade, research has brought much new information to light. Such work enables me to bring a new perspective to the reader.

# CHAPTER 1
# A Natural History of Plague

LIKE ALL INFECTIOUS DISEASES, the Black Death has a natural history and can be properly understood only in that context. First, there is environment.[1] Anyone traveling through Europe today would find it hard to imagine what the continent looked like a thousand years ago. There were no sprawling urban and industrial complexes, the outstanding characteristic of the last century, and surprisingly few towns of any size. Towns were usually far apart, located next to the sea or astride great rivers. By the middle of the twelfth century, a few urban centers in Italy and the Netherlands, and perhaps Paris, had fifty thousand or more people, but most claimed a thousand or so inhabitants. Nine out of ten Europeans lived in still smaller settlements, nucleated villages or hamlets of a few hundred people, fifteen to twenty miles apart. Both town and village were small and cramped, with woefully inadequate sanitation and transportation facilities. Ironically, in the confines of their small but isolated settlements, most people lived close together and had little privacy.

Surrounding the villages were the fields, pastures, and woodlands from which most people squeezed their subsistence. By 1250 or so,

field and pasture had come to dominate Europe's landscape, but, until at least the mid-twelfth century, the extent and density of the
woodlands characterized the European environment. In the far
north—most of Scandinavia and Russia—the forests were coniferous,
consisting primarily of fir trees, with a smattering of birch and,
where the land was poorly drained and the elevation low, moors,
marshes, and tundra. The rest of Europe had deciduous forests. The
generally cold, wet, acidic-soil areas around the Baltic and North
Seas and throughout much of eastern Europe had beech trees surrounded by holly and other aquifoliacs. Central Europe was mostly
oak forest. Where the soil was alkaline, especially on both sides of
the Alps and the Carpathians, the oaks were mixed with alders.
Where the climate was wetter and the soil was more acidic, as in most
of central and northern France and central Germany, the oaks were
surrounded by birch and aspen. South of the Alps, in most of the
Mediterranean Basin, the sunlight was brighter, the temperatures
were higher, the rainfall was less frequent and less well-distributed
throughout the year, and the soil was sandy and acidic. The Mediterranean Basin had also been settled longer than northern Europe and
had a higher population density. Hence, it was less densely forested
than the North; but, even in the twelfth century, much woodland remained, particularly stands of conifers, such as pines and junipers,
which can tolerate sandy soils.

A second consideration in studying disease is causation.[2] All epidemics, plague included, are caused by parasites that have relations
with other, usually larger organisms. This process is a natural part of
human and animal ecology. A third factor, and one of paramount
concern to man, is toxicity. Epidemiologists generally distinguish between lethal and nonlethal diseases. Nonlethal infections are usually
"old" and well-established. Often, they are only mildly deleterious
to their hosts, thus ensuring a steady supply of victims. By contrast,
those spectacular diseases that periodically burst onto the historical
stage, killing large numbers of people, are caused by newer parasites
that have yet to establish an equilibrium with their hosts. An example
of an older disease is malaria; the plasmodium that causes it is debilitating, but generally not fatal. An example of a newer disease is pneumonic plague, which is 95% to 100% fatal. Both diseases have been
significant in the past, but because of the plague's enormous mortality, it has had far greater impact.

A fourth concern regarding infectious diseases—and, indeed, an
important way of distinguishing one from another—is their means of

transmission. One such mechanism is direct contact between people, usually via the respiratory system. Diseases so disseminated include influenza, diphtheria, measles, and pneumonic plague. Respiratory diseases are highly communicable, virtually impossible to prevent, and closely related to human population density. Consequently, they were common in the cities and towns of medieval Europe. A second mechanism of dissemination comprises enteric diseases, those spread through the digestive system; among them are dysentery, diarrhea, typhoid, and cholera. Like respiratory afflictions, enteric ailments were very common throughout the Middle Ages. They often reflected social conditions, especially poor sanitation. Because of this, and in contrast to respiratory diseases, enteric diseases can be eliminated rather easily through basic improvements in public health.

Diseases are spread in at least two other fashions. One is through venereal contact, the prime example being the treponema infections, especially syphilis, and gonorrhea. The causative organisms of venereal ailments are highly vulnerable when exposed, even in temperate environments, and were less frequent in the Middle Ages than were either respiratory or enteric diseases. A fourth group, however, was very common—diseases transferred to humans from animal hosts, with animals acting either as intermediaries, as with malaria or typhus, or as primary or secondary epizoötic victims, as with bubonic plague. The role of animals in the spread of diseases can be crucial: humans share 65 different diseases with dogs; 50 with cattle; 46 with sheep and goats; 42 with pigs; 35 with horses; 32 with rats and mice; and 26 with poultry.[3] While not as common as respiratory or enteric diseases, those transmitted by animals are usually more lethal, since most viruses and bacteria, the organisms that actually cause infection, gain in virulence as they pass through the chain of hosts.

In addition to their virulence, diseases facilitated by animal intermediaries are important for other reasons. They represent still another disease classification and interpretation in that their dissemination and frequency are based primarily on the animal hosts rather than on humans. Bubonic plague provides a good example. When a rodent population in which plague is enzoötic, that is, indigenous, begins to multiply and reaches a certain population density, there is a concentrated transfer among the rodents of parasites—fleas, in this case—and bacteria. The result is usually an epizoötic among the rodents, which sometimes leads to an epidemic of bubonic plague. Some scholars have suggested that communicable diseases are a basic part of the human environment and a function of the population density, and that civilization and disease travel hand in hand.[4] Accordingly, the incidence of a given epidemic would hinge on patterns of human settlement. This is indeed the case with respiratory, enteric, and venereal diseases, but it is not so with those diseases spread by animal intermediaries. The latter are primarily dependent on factors exogenous to civilization, such as climate and rodent and insect population density and ecology. There is great danger when studying the history of infectious diseases in being too anthropocentric and overemphasizing the human element. In many epidemic diseases, humans are most effective as carriers when entering new ecospheres, such as the Americas in the sixteenth century, where they brought smallpox and measles, rather than in areas of older inhabitation, such as Europe in the Middle Ages.

Another key characteristic in the development of infectious diseases is immunity. Humans have complex mechanisms for defending themselves against pathogens, the microorganisms that cause disease. Individual resistance varies with many factors, such as number of protective antibodies—the proteins generated in reaction to the disease toxins introduced into the bloodstream. Immunity is either innate or acquired; if acquired, it is either active or passive. Active immunity comes when the host generates his own defenses, passive when generated defenses are introduced. Passive immunity is often only temporary. In the Middle Ages, active immunity was particularly important in determining the extent and intensity of an epidemic. Some infections, especially respiratory types such as smallpox and measles, do not change a great deal in their etiology. Hence, survival from an initial attack confers a degree of immunity, limiting recurrence to those members of society born after the last epidemic. Diseases for which there was immunity had less of an impact on medieval Europe than did more complex, multiple infections such as dysentery, influenza, and plague, for which immunity is quite limited, if it exists at all.

Medieval infectious diseases were an inheritance from the classical world. Between about 500 B.C. and A.D. 550 there were extensive contacts between the animal populations and the civilizations of China, Central Asia, India, the Upper Nile, and the Mediterranean Basin. As a result, as William McNeill has argued, there was a general confluence of Eurasian and African disease pools which, by the sixth century A.D., brought to the Mediterranean Basin most of the important diseases that can survive in temperate climates.[5] To be sure, this proliferation of diseases took a long time. With a few exceptions, such as the Athenian Plague of the fifth century B.C., the classical world was remarkably free from major, deadly epidemics. This was fundamental to its steady population growth, which continued almost unabated until the second century A.D. But this biological peace was deceptive; in fact, the peripatetic character of ancient empires acted as a conduit and incubator for future disease patterns. An example was the reticulum of commerce and communications established by the Romans late in the first century B.C. This included their famed road system and, even more important, network of commercial sea routes. The sea routes converged on the Levantine Coast, then branched east across the northern Arabian Peninsula to the Arabian Sea, the Indian Ocean, and South Asia; and west to Italy, southern Gaul, and Iberia, whence goods proceeded inland via major river valleys such as the Rhone. Sea travel was relatively quick and, with good weather, all Mediterranean ports were just a few days apart. Thus, a person who seemed well on embarkation could fall sick en route, infect fellow passengers, and then spread the disease hundreds of miles from its point of origin. Further, cargoes were often bulky enough to conceal potential insect and rodent intermediaries. This, coupled with the linking of south and central Asia, the Middle East, the Nile Delta, and the European coast along the Mediterranean, brought about the fruition of disease pools.

From the second through the sixth centuries A.D., three new and lethal infections emerged from this disease pool, bringing an end to the ecological stability of the ancient world. The first began in 165 and persisted until 180, striking Italy and the western part of the Roman Empire. It seems to have been brought west by Roman legionnaires and probably marks the introduction into Mediterranean Europe of smallpox. Some authorities believe that smallpox was concomitantly present among the Germanic tribes beyond the Rhine-Danube frontier, but, even if this were so, the barbarians apparently did not transmit it to the peoples within the Empire, at least not before the third century.[6] Smallpox is one of man's most communicable diseases and can be very deadly to a population with no innate immunity. This was the case in the Roman Empire. The physician Galen estimated that between a quarter and a third of Italy's population died during the 15 years after it appeared.[7] But because the smallpox virus changes little and survival of an attack generally confers immunity, its role in the Middle Ages was limited to areas it had yet to visit and to those who never had had it—primarily children. Thus, it was as a killer of children that smallpox made its biggest mark in the medieval world.

Smallpox was joined in 251 by the second of the great epidemic diseases, marking the classical/medieval disease watershed. This disease was the "Antonine Plague," probably measles. It was described by St. Cyprian, bishop of the North African town of Carthage:

> Now that the bowels loosened into a flux exhaust the strength of the body, that a fever contracted in the very marrow of the bones breaks out into ulcers of the throat, that the intestines are shaken by the continual vomiting, that the blood-shot eyes burn, that the feet of some or certain parts of their members are cut away by the infection of diseased putrefaction that, by a weakness developing through the losses and injuries of the body, either the gait is enfeebled, or the hearing impaired, or the sight blinded.[8]

At its height, measles allegedly killed 5000 people a day in Rome, and it remained a major menace until about 260. Measles is like smallpox in many ways and the two diseases were not distinguished by European doctors until the sixteenth century. It is caused by a virus, transmitted via the respiratory system, and highly lethal to a population with little or no immunity. As is the case with smallpox, however, survival of a measles attack confers immunity from future visitations. Thus, it, too, was primarily a childhood affliction in the Middle Ages. Nevertheless, it is important not to diminish the effects of either disease, especially in their initial appearances. Measles depleted the population, hastened the desertion of many rural areas (particularly in the grain-producing regions of Sicily and North Africa), and cut the rolls of the Roman army and taxpayers. It caused at least a temporary reduction in East–West trade and, with smallpox, has formed the cornerstone of a major theory of the decline of the Roman Empire.[9]

Important as smallpox and measles were in the natural history of infectious disease, their combined role was dwarfed by the arrival in 541 of a third disease. This was plague, caused by a complex series of bacterial strains called *Yersinia pestis*.[10] Plague's etiology helps to explain its historical importance; *Y. pestis's* toxicity varies, but the disease is always highly lethal. Under normal circumstances, it lives in the digestive tract of fleas, particularly the rat fleas *Xenopsylla cheopis* and *Cortophylus fasciatus*, but it can also live in the human flea, *Pulex irritans*. Periodically and for reasons that epidemiologists still do not fully understand, the bacilli multiply in the flea's stomach in numbers large enough to cause a blockage, thus threatening the flea with starvation. The "blocked flea," while feeding, regurgitates into its victims large numbers of *Y. pestis* bacilli. This process is crucial to plague's progress; furthermore, *Y. pestis* cannot pass through healthy skin, but only through a break in the surface.

Dozens of rodents carry plague. Among them are tarbagons, marmots, and susliks in Asia, prairie dogs and ground squirrels in America, and gerbels and mice in Africa. Generally living in networks of tunnels just beneath the earth's surface, these rodents can be very numerous. In the Volga steppe in south Russia, an average of 325,000 susliks per four square miles has been estimated. In Europe, rats, especially the black rat, *Rattus rattus*, have been most important carriers. Black rats are quite sedentary and rarely move more than 200 meters from their nests. Because they live so close to humans, they are most dangerous to them. An excellent climber, *R. rattus* was well-suited to both the thatched roofs of peasant dwellings and the high roof beams and dark corners of urban houses. But, important as black rats were in the dissemination of plague, it is essential to emphasize that they were not the only secondary carriers. Along with the other rodents already mentioned, additional secondary vector hosts included virtually all household and barnyard animals save the horse, whose odor apparently repels even starving blocked fleas.

When *Y. pestis* is enzoötic, that is, endemic to a rodent population, it is called silvatic plague. Silvatic plague is crucial to human epidemics because its presence in a rodent population provides a reservoir, or focus, in which the disease can survive for extended periods of time. Reservoirs may help explain the cyclic occurrence of plague, which ultimately made it so important in the Middle Ages. *Y. pestis* is able to live in the dark, moist environment of rodent burrows even after the rodents have been killed by an epizoötic, or epidemic. Thus, if a new rodent community replaces the old one, the plague chain can be revived.

The fleas carrying *Y. pestis* turn to humans only after their supply of secondary hosts has diminished. Most secondary hosts can tolerate a modest proportion of *Y. pestis* in their bloodstreams, but when the bacilli multiply and invade the pulmonary or nervous systems, the secondary hosts succumb. The fleas then seek a new host—and sometimes that host is a human being. Humans, then, are not a preferred host for *Y. pestis*, but rather, the victims of an animal epizoötic. In effect, humans are victims of changes in insect and rodent ecology.

There are three principal varieties of plague—bubonic, pneumonic, and septicaemic. Bubonic is by far the most common and
therefore the most important of the three. Its incubation period from
the time of infection to the appearance of the first symptoms is generally about six days. The initial symptom, a blackish, often gangrenous pustule at the point of the bite, is followed by an enlargement of
the lymph nodes in the armpits, groin, or neck, depending on the
place of the flea bite. Next, subcutaneous hemorrhaging occurs,
causing purplish blotches and swelling in the lymphatic glands, from
which bubonic plague takes its name. The hemorrhaging produces cell
necrosis and intoxication of the nervous system, ultimately leading to
neurological and psychological disorders, which may explain the *danse*
macabre rituals that accompanied the Black Death. Bubonic plague is
the least toxic of all plague types, but it is still highly lethal, killing 50%
to 60% of its victims.

Pneumonic plague is unique in that it can be transmitted directly
from person to person. This is in part the result of pneumonic
plague's peculiar etiology, for it seems to occur only when there is a
sharp temperature drop and the infection moves into the lungs. After
the two-to-three-day incubation period, there is a rapid fall in body
temperature, followed by a severe cough and consolidation in the
lungs, rapid cyanosis, and the discharge of bloody sputum. The sputum contains *Y. pestis*, making transmission airborne and thus direct
from human to human. Neurological difficulties and coma follow infection, with death coming in 95% to 100% of the cases. Therefore,
while pneumonic plague is less frequent than bubonic, it is far more
virulent.

Like bubonic plague, septicaemic plague is insect-borne, but its
precise etiology and occasional appearance in selected epidemics have
not been adequately explained. It is known that in septicaemic plague
*Y. pestis* bacilli enter the bloodstream of victims in massive numbers.
A rash forms within hours and death occurs within a day, before the
buboes even have time to form. This type of plague is always fatal,
but it is very rare and, because it is present in the bloodstream in such
large quantities, it can be transmitted by the human flea, *P. irritans*,
and even by the human body louse.

There are peculiar environmental conditions that determine the
presence and virulence of plague epidemics. First, there are factors of
insect and rodent ecology. The appropriate fleas and rodents must
live near people. The flea must be blocked or *Y. pestis* will remain in
the digestive system; and the secondary host must die before the flea

moves on to a tertiary host. An epizootic rather than an enzootic condition must prevail among the secondary host population, and the tertiary host must be man rather than other large mammals. Climate also plays an important role. The rat flea *X. cheopis* is quite hardy; it can survive for between six months and a year without a rodent host in dung, an abandoned rat's nest, or even textile bales. But it is active only at temperatures of 15°C-20°C, with 90%-95% humidity. Cold limits the flea's activity, while heat retards its productivity, and humidity of less than 70% kills it. These climatic factors limit most plague outbreaks to particular seasons in different parts of the Western world. In western Europe, for example, it generally comes in late summer and early autumn. It is important to stress that an outbreak of plague occurs only in confluence with a variety of environmental conditions.

Plague may be the most virulent of the human infectious diseases. But, historically, its frequency is even more important than its virulence. Plague comes not in isolated epidemics, but rather, in pandemics. A pandemic is a linked series of epidemics that strike in cyclic fashion. It occurs when *Y. pestis* has been established in the local rodent population, as discussed above, and is itself determined by climatic and ecological conditions. Once a pandemic is present, plague epidemics will recur in intervals of between 2 and 20 years. Hence, epidemics will strike at least once in every generation and act as a regular population check. Plague is unique among epidemic diseases in its deadly combination of virulence and frequency.

*Y. pestis* is native to particular parts of the world. These permanent reservoirs, called "inveterate foci," include central Asia, Siberia, the Yunan region of China, parts of Iran and Libya, the Arabian Peninsula, and east Africa. Europe probably has never had an inveterate focus. But because of its commercial connections and the geographical configuration of the Eurasian land mass and the Mediterranean Basin, it was always proximate to such reservoirs. Plague has taken two forms in Europe. The first was what epidemiologists call "temporary foci," reservoirs of prolonged plague persistence, like the pandemics already mentioned. When ecological and etiological conditions among the rodent and bacterial populations changed, the temporary plague foci disappeared. The second form was that of a locus of brief duration. Such loci were simply incidents of epidemics which did not become established among the local insect and rodent populations. These included epidemics of septicaemic plague—attacks so virulent that they killed off virtually everyone and thus provided no reservoir for the future—and epidemics brought to ports by ships and limited in their dissemination.

Medieval Europe was struck by two plague pandemics. It is likely that the first came down the Nile from east Africa to lower Egypt, and thence into the relatively populous eastern Mediterranean Basin.[11] The first epidemic of this pandemic has been called "Justinian's Plague" after the Byzantine emperor reigning at the time of its outbreak. In 541, Justinian was trying to reconquer the western parts of the old Roman Empire from its new Germanic overlords. The Byzantine court historian, Procopius, wrote:

> During this time there was a pestilence, by which the whole human race came near to being annihilated. Now in the case of all other scourges sent from Heaven some explanation of a cause might be given by daring men, such as the many theories propounded by those who are clever in these matters; for they love to conjure up causes which are absolutely incomprehensible to man, and to fabricate outlandish theories of natural philosophy, knowing well that they are saying nothing sound, but considering it sufficient for them, if they completely deceive by their argument some of those whom they meet and persuade them to their view. But for this calamity it is quite impossible now to express in words or conceive in thought any explanation, except indeed to refer it to God. . . .
>
> It started from the Egyptians who dwell in Pelusium. Then it divided and moved in one direction towards Alexandria and the rest of Egypt and in other directions; it came to Palestine on the borders of Egypt and from here it spread over the whole world, always moving forward and traveling at times favorable to it. For it seemed to move by fixed arrangement, and to tarry for a specified time in each country, casting its blight slightingly upon none, but spreading in either direction right out to the ends of the world, as if fearing lest some corner of the earth might escape it. For it left neither island nor mountain ridge which had human inhabitants; and if it passed by any land, either not affecting the men there or touching them in indifferent fashion, still at a later time it came back. . . .
>
> With the majority it came about that they were seized by the disease without becoming aware of what was coming either through a waking vision or a dream. And they were taken in the following manner. They had a sudden fever, some when just roused from sleep, others while otherwise engaged, without any regard to what they were doing. And the body showed no change from its previous color, nor was it hot as it might be expected when attacked by fever, nor indeed did any inflammation set in, but the fever was of such a languid sort from its commencement and until evening that neither to the sick themselves nor to a

physician who touched them would it afford any suspicion of danger. It was natural, therefore, that not one of those who contracted the disease expected to die from it. But on the same day in some cases, in others on the following day, and in the rest not only in the particular part of the body which is called the groin, that is, below the abdomen, but also inside the armpits, and in some cases besides the ears, and at different points on the thighs came a large swelling or bubo.[12]

In a sixth century context, Justinian's Plague was very nearly "worldwide," striking central and south Asia, North Africa and Arabia, and Europe as far north as Denmark and as far west as Ireland, where mortality proved especially severe. Only eastern Asia seems to have escaped. In Constantinople, the center of the Byzantine Empire, the plague was at its most virulent from autumn 541 until spring 542. During a four-month span it allegedly killed 200,000 of the city's people, perhaps 40% of the total population.[13] It had a devastating effect in Italy, southern France, the Rhine Valley, and Iberia, where it lingered until autumn 544. When Justinian's Plague had finally spent itself, between a fifth and a quarter of Europe's population south of the Alps had perished. In political terms, it dealt a crippling blow to Byzantine plans to conquer the western Mediterranean, and perhaps so weakened Byzantium as to set up its defeat by the Arabs a few generations later. From the perspective of the history of infectious disease, it marked the arrival in Europe of a third pandemic disease in a 400-year period, and the last one to come to the West from the lands abutting the Indian Ocean for almost a millenium.

Justinian's Plague established a temporary focus of *Y. pestis* among European fleas and rodents, ensuring that subsequent epidemics of the pandemic would recur in 10-to-24-year cycles for the next 200 years.[14] Plague returned from 558 to 561, again beginning in Egypt, spreading throughout the eastern Mediterranean Basin to Constantinople, and then traveling west through the Italian ports of Ravenna and Genoa into southern France. It came again from 580 to 582, and from 588 to 591, the latter spreading from Spain to southern France and Italy, the reverse of the usual pattern of dissemination. There is some evidence that these third, fourth, and fifth plague epidemics were exacerbated by accompanying sieges of smallpox. The sixth plague epidemic occurred from 599 through 600. In Italy and southern France, it was the most lethal epidemic after Justinian's Plague, killing perhaps 15% of the population.

After 599–600, successive epidemics of the first plague pandemic were less virulent, but about as frequent. Large parts of Mediterranean Europe were afflicted in 608, 618, 628, 640, 654, 684–86, 694–700, 718, and 740–50. More localized plague epidemics struck Sicily and Calabria in 746, and Naples and southern Italy in 762. In both instances, the epidemics remained restricted, suggesting that they were introduced by foreign ships and that Y. pestis was no longer enzoötic among the indigenous rodent populations—the latter perhaps the result of a mutation in the bacillus or a change in rodent and insect ecology. By the late eighth century, the first plague pandemic had come to its end in Europe.

The first pandemic, although restricted mainly to the Mediterranean Basin and consisting primarily of bubonic plague, left an indelible mark on early medieval Europe. Because it was recurrent, it helped to keep population levels below those of 541 before the plague. The demographic historian J. C. Russell has estimated total population loss from 541 to 700 at 50% to 60%.[15] Contemporaries were baffled by the new disease, as would be their counterparts in the fourteenth and fifteenth centuries. Explanations of its causation were usually taken from Biblical exegesis, and high mortality was attributed to divine judgment. Pilgrimages and visible demonstrations of piety increased, and the Christian Church seems to have gained in influence during the pandemic. There is little statistical evidence that can be used to measure the pandemic's impact on economy and society, but it must have disrupted trade routes and patterns, at least during plague flare-ups, and changed patterns of food production and distribution. It was a major retardant during Europe's Dark Ages.

From the late eighth through the mid-fourteenth century, Europe was remarkably free from most epidemic diseases.[16] There were isolated, often severe, infections, such as the unidentifiable epidemic of 870, which swept through western Europe killing perhaps 10% of the populations of England and France. Most infectious diseases in this period were endemic, or linked closely to famine, malnutrition, or plant diseases, such as recurring epidemics of ergotism, also called St. Anthony's disease, which struck from the mid-tenth through the mid-eleventh centuries. With the exception of a few isolated coastal epidemics, plague would not strike again en masse until 1347, and smallpox and measles were restricted to younger members of society. Since, in medieval demographic terms, childhood diseases were relatively unimportant, their effect on overall population levels was limited. At the same time, influenza and typhus, scourges of the late fifteenth and sixteenth centuries, had not yet made a significant impact. In part because these major constraints on population were curbed, the period between the ninth and fourteenth centuries corresponded with medieval Europe's most extended era of demographic and economic expansion.

The most important infectious disease in Europe from the tenth through the thirteenth centuries was leprosy, or Hansen's Disease.[17] It is a chronic infection that develops slowly over a number of years and, by itself, rarely kills its victims. It does, however, produce for the afflicted decades of pain and suffering, and renders them vulnerable to respiratory and enteric ailments. Leprosy is not especially contagious, but because it so horribly mutilates and scars its victims, it always has been dreaded. Extremities and facial features slowly rot away, with the face becoming an almost formless mass. Compounding this horrible visage is a foul odor coming from gangrenous parts, all combining to make the disease and its victims quite horrifying.

Medieval society was unable to provide preventive or curative treatment for the leper; its best alternative was isolation. Upon diagnosis, the leper was counted among the dead, and a quasi-requiem mass was sung for his soul. Earth was shoveled on his feet, symbolizing departure from the mainstream of society, and the patient was removed to a leper hospital where, isolated from the rest of society, including friends and family, he lived out his days. Most medical authorities considered that the disease was caused by divine judgment and felt that mortal men could therefore never develop an effective cure. One of the few dissenters to this opinion was the thirteenth century English physician Gilbertus Anglicus. Having observed a number of lepers over several years, he concluded that the ailment was not easily communicable and was primarily a nervous affliction that might be treated in the same fashion as other nerve-related diseases. But even Gilbert was generally bereft of concrete ideas, suggesting only a few ways to balance the "body humors," that being a favorite medieval medical cure inherited from the Greeks. Isolation was the most practical—and, in many ways, the most humane—treatment.

Leprosy was not a great killer. Its demographic impact was rather limited and did not compare with that of plague or smallpox. Instead, it was an important cultural phenomenon, entering the psyche, art, and religion of Europe. The Christian Church regarded lepers as unclean, and it became known as the "disease of the soul." Because of their forced isolation from society, lepers' legal identities became muddled. In many northern Italian cities, canon lawyers were called upon to discuss the alienation of lepers' property, and in several Rhineland towns, including Trier and Mainz, elaborate sets of rules were drawn up to guide lepers through their everyday routines. They were barred from all churches, markets, shops, and other public places. They could not wash or drink from any civic water source, and had to wear distinctive clothing. The leper was made to touch everything with a rod and could not enter inns or taverns. Sexual intercourse, even with spouses, was strictly forbidden. No public building could be touched without gloves, and shoes had to be worn at all times. Lepers were even required to stand downwind of those ordinary folk who chose to address them.

The incidence of leprosy seems to have increased from the eighth through the thirteenth centuries, reaching a peak early in the fourteenth century, and then disappearing almost entirely by 1400. Several theories have been offered to explain its rise and fall. The rise is usually connected with concomitant movements among the general population; increases in the latter yielded more potential and actual leprosy victims. The decline of leprosy is much harder to explain and has elicited several theories.[18] One explains the disappearance by the Black Death; as the great plague swept away a third to a half of Europe's population, it took an even higher proportion of the already weakened lepers. Subsequent plague epidemics of the second pandemic had a similar effect until, by 1400, most of Europe's lepers had died. A second theory credits advancing medical analysis. Leprosy, with its characteristic skin eruptions, manifests itself in a fashion similar to that of many common skin diseases. Some modern authorities believe that high medieval chroniclers and physicians simply called all or at least most people with any skin diseases lepers without regard to whether they had the real thing, smallpox, measles, or just a severe rash or case of acne. By the late fourteenth century, physicians and even surgeons and apothecaries had become more sophisticated and discriminating in their diagnoses. Leechbooks and pharmaceuticals identified and typed a wide variety of skin conditions, and were more accurate when identifying Hansen's Disease *per se*.[19]

A third theory explaining the decline of leprosy emphasizes the rise in incidence of pulmonary tuberculosis. In some circumstances, immunity reactions to tuberculosis provide a measure of resistance to Hansen's Disease. McNeill has offered that pulmonary tuberculosis, with its rapid means of transmission, afflicted more people than leprosy, which is not very contagious.[20] Hence, survivors of tuberculosis gained a degree of immunity from leprosy. A fourth theory credits improved hygiene, especially in urban areas, while a fifth theory emphasizes the increased consumption of vitamin C. Whatever the precise cause, with the exception of a few isolated regions in Norway and Poland, the incidence of leprosy declined markedly, and many of Europe's leper houses closed down, changed their focus toward other ailments, especially plague, or became retirement homes or almshouses.

Europe's relatively disease-free era ended abruptly in the mid-fourteenth century. Population had increased about 300% from the tenth to the mid-thirteenth century to 75–80 million, higher than it had been for close to a thousand years.[21] Militant imperialism had extended the boundaries of the Christian West into Russia, Iberia, and Palestine. Internal European trade and travel had improved considerably with the opening of new Alpine passes, the establishment of a direct sea-link between the Italian and Netherlandish cities, and the integration of the Baltic and North Sea hinterlands with the rest of the continent. Most important in epidemiological terms, closer connections were being forged between Europe, Asia, and Africa. To ease a bullion shortage, Italian merchants turned to Arab middlemen for access to sub-Saharan gold supplies. As demand for luxury goods and spices rose, more ships and caravans journeyed to south and central Asia. Much of this trade was carried on through Middle Eastern intermediaries, but, from the twelfth century onward, Europeans played a large and ever-growing role. In all, contacts between East and West flourished as never before. These contacts, so positive for commerce, changed the balance and pattern of infectious diseases. By the end of the twelfth century, Europe's disease pool was stable.[22] Smallpox, measles, malaria, leprosy, and a few other diseases had established a tentative equilibrium within Europe's population. Plague, the greatest epidemic killer, had disappeared. But, in the thirteenth century, climatic changes began to alter the insect and rodent ecology of Eurasia, and Mongol tribesmen began their conquest of central Asia. These factors would combine with the new political, social, and economic forms which were developing in Europe—in part, at least, because of the absence of plague—to forever change the course of Western history.

# CHAPTER 2
# The European Environment, 1050–1347

T HE DYNAMIC ELEMENT behind the development and expansion of the High Middle Ages, as the period from the tenth through the thirteenth centuries is generally called, was steady, unabated population growth. Scholars have debated this population increase which followed nearly 700 years of decline or stagnation, and although they disagree on its relative importance, a consensus on causes has emerged. First, a number of agricultural and technological innovations in the tenth and eleventh centuries produced a food surplus.[1] These included new crops; the spread of a three-field planting scheme; a new harness that facilitated the use of horses, rather than oxen, as draft animals; and new sources of power, such as windmills and watermills. Second, eleventh and twelfth century Europe was politically stable for the first time since the Carolingian period in the eighth century, the result of nascent royal power and resurgent aristocratic governmental and military power. This stability put an end to two hundred years of invasion. And, third, Europe's disease pool had reached an equilibrium of sorts; as has been recounted, the High

Middle Ages was remarkably disease-free. The result was an increase in population from about 25 million in 950 to about 75 million in 1250. In some regions, the rate of increase was even greater. In certain areas of France, for example, population rose at a rate of over 1% per annum, an enormous figure in a premodern society.[2] In some frontier areas, growth rates were even higher; many scholars believe that populations in eastern Germany rose in these centuries by as much as four or even five fold.[3]

Concomitant with, and in part spurred on by, continuous demographic growth were important changes in society and economy. A guiding theory of high medieval society was "trifunctionality"—a tripartite, hierarchical division of class. The theory was first advanced by several eleventh-century French clerics—in particular, Adelbero of Laon and Gerard of Cambrai—who saw their own interests closely tied in with those of the reigning Capetian monarchs, who ruled over a highly structured and stable society.[4] The first class, or order, was the *oratores*, or clergy. Their role was to obtain divine grace for everyone through prayer and admirable activities; in practice, because many clerics were literate and well-educated, the *oratores* also functioned as society's bureaucrats, or clerks. The second order was the *bellatores*, the military elite whose role was to provide protection, while the third was the *laboratores*, everyone else, who supported the two elites. In the eleventh century, the *laboratores* were primarily *agricolae* and *rusticae*, or rural agricultural workers, but, from the twelfth century on, an increasingly important minority of *bourgeoisie*, or workers and merchants from towns, developed. Trifunctionality was to provide an orderly, interdependent, and harmonious society, its equilibrium guaranteed by God's lieutenant on earth, the king. Proponents of the scheme claimed that it was part of a divine design, and supported it from the one means of mass communication of the day—the pulpit.

Because most of Europe's wealth came from the produce of the land, even after the urban expansion of the twelfth and thirteenth centuries, aristocrats and rural workers occupied special positions. The rural workers were peasants and lived within the manorial system. By the eleventh century, manorialism had taken full form. Peasants, almost always unfree customholders, or serfs, held land controlled by the *bellatores*, or military aristocracy, from whose ranks a king was drawn. Despite the claims of the proponents of trifunctionalism, until about 1200 most kings were little more than *primus inter pares*, with real political power resting with the local landlords.

The lords fought, arrayed in chain-link armor and on horseback. Hence, they needed time and resources to refine their martial skills and pay the high costs of mounted warfare. A servile and immobile peasantry best filled these needs, and it was for this reason, along with their inability to protect themselves, that most of Europe's peasants were unfree.

Peasants did not own the land that they farmed.[5] Rather, they held it of the lords, generally under three conditions. First, the peasants paid the lords rent for the arable, the land actually farmed in the open fields, and for the houses and gardens they held in the manor village. Second, peasants owed a labor obligation on those parts of the arable called the *demesne*. The lord would keep the produce of the *demesne*, but would never farm it himself. Rather, the peasants provided free labor. Another aspect of the labor service was boon work. This was extra service spent working the *demesne* during harvest time, and occasionally was required before peasants were allowed to harvest their own crops. Third, peasants owed their lords "banalities," a potpourri of lesser obligations. These included periodic taxes on inheritance rights and marriage banns, and milling fees.

The nature of these obligations began to change in the mid-to-late twelfth century. First came a new way of discharging rent obligations. In the eleventh and early twelfth centuries, most peasants paid their rents "in kind," that is, in food or other material goods. By 1200, however, many were paying in cash or some sort of specie. This was acquired from the sale of surplus agricultural goods, usually to townsfolk, the rise of towns being another product of the prolonged population growth.

A second tenurial change came with the total, or more frequently, partial freedom of a substantial portion of the peasantry. Freedom could be obtained in one of two ways. First, using cash procured through the sale of foodstuffs, peasants could buy commutation— that is, exemption from labor services. It is important to stress that freedom meant being quit of labor services, not rent. The lord still held the land as tenant-in-chief and the peasant had to pay recompense for its use.

The second way to obtain freedom was through assarting, the physical expansion of the arable. It was undertaken throughout Europe in the eleventh, twelfth, and thirteenth centuries, and was particularly frequent across the North European plain through the drainage of fens and marshes, the damming and diking of the North and Baltic Sea Coasts, and the cutting, burning, and general clearing of the primeval deciduous and coniferous forests. Some assarting was undertaken on the fringes of well-established manors in long-settled areas, but much of it was a frontier movement done at the borders of Christendom. Lords would become owners, or at least tenants-in-chief, of these new lands, but, as always, it was the peasants who did the actual work. The only way most peasants would migrate to the frontier was if they were given the land in free tenure—that is, if they only had to pay rent, something many of them could acquire only piecemeal if they stayed around their birthplaces. Netherlandish peasants, experienced at farming low, wet areas, were in particular demand. Many of them carved farms out of the wilderness of north-eastern Europe in the twelfth and thirteenth centuries, much as North American pioneers did in the eighteenth and nineteenth centuries. Northeastern Europe was ideally suited to cereal farming. Once cleared, drained, planted, and harvested, it became a major granary, particularly for the towns of the Rhineland and the Low Countries.

Local assarting, the extension of the arable around well-established manors, was less romantic, but perhaps more important, than the great frontier movement. Peasants who stayed at home and had large families also wanted more land, but looked to the remaining local scrub, meadow, and woodland rather than to the open spaces of the East. Adjacent lands were simply added to existing fields. Further, much of this land could be had as freehold. Since it had not been cultivated in the recent past, there were few customary obligations attached to it. Since the lords had received nothing before the land was cleared, they were usually happy to get a flat rent fee for it and forego traditional labor obligations. Something, after all, was better than nothing. Hence, many peasants who did not join the pioneering movements or did not have the capital to buy commutation still won a partial freedom on the lands they had assarted. It is important to reiterate that all of these "free" peasants, even the pioneers, continued to pay rent, since none actually owned the lands they farmed. They were, however, relieved of the most onerous of their obligations—unpaid labor.

The produce from the new farmlands provided a food surplus. Although Europe's population continued to grow apace, most scholars believe that food supplies, especially in cereals, increased at an even faster rate. The agricultural innovations of the tenth and eleventh centuries, applied to the rich virginal soils, pushed seed yields (the number of seeds harvested from the one originally sown) from a paltry 2 or 3 to 1 to a more respectable 5, 6, 7, or even 8 to 1.[6] Carbohydrates remained the staple of European diet in the twelfth and early thirteenth centuries; protein, especially from animal sources, was relatively scarce. Most North European peasants began their day with a breakfast of porridge, lunched on bread and perhaps cheese and ale, and dined on a pottage. This was supplemented by bits of herring, greens, bacon, milk, and cider; beef, venison, poultry, or pork was added only on a few selected feast days. Throughout the Mediterranean Basin, diet was somewhat different in kind, but not in nutritional structure. Wine, mutton, and derivatives of olive oil were occasional treats, but grain products formed the bulk of the diet. Still, per capita caloric consumption was probably higher than it had been for centuries. Europe was growing in every sense.

There were other major changes in the manorial system by the late twelfth century. Many lords, having granted commutations, abandoned direct cultivation of their estates. Supervising grumbling or unwilling workers was difficult, and even a lord and his entourage could eat only so much food. Given the rise of food markets which accompanied the new agricultural surplus, it was often simplest for the landlords to take the entire manor and "farm it out"—that is, to include the *demesne* as part of the general field system that the peasants cultivated entirely for their own profit and to substitute cash payments for labor services. In effect, the lords became *rentiers*, taking fixed incomes from their holdings rather than cultivating them directly.

These changes in Europe's rural economy spurred the development of an efficient economic organization which, among other things, provided incentive for personal material gain. Before the mid-twelfth century, the manorial system was ineffective and wasteful. Peasant farmers who held land at fixed fees and were not able to adapt easily to new market conditions had little opportunity to increase their profits. The economic and tenurial changes of the twelfth and thirteenth centuries, however, altered all of this. Growing population and rising per capita food consumption encouraged increased production. A premium was now placed on skillful cultivation, since any food surplus could be sold at some profit. A market economy had developed throughout rural Europe by the 1180s.

The fruition of Europe's rural economy helped to give rise to a veritable urban revolution.[7] The combination of food surplus and population increase meant that fewer people had to live directly off the land. There was increasing specialization of nonalimentary production, particularly in areas with direct access to great rivers or the sea—overland transportation of bulk goods like foodstuffs was generally too slow and hazardous to be profitable—and in areas of less-than-optimum farmlands. In effect, established towns grew along with rural settlements, and new towns were founded and flourished—most notably in northern and central Italy, the Netherlands, and northern Germany. Old trade routes were redoubled and new ones were created. Goods from Asia and the Middle East were carried by Italian merchants to markets all across Europe. A mercantile and industrial group, or bourgeoisie, developed, with liquid capital rather than land as their principal asset. In Italy, a sophisticated banking, credit, and insurance system evolved and, by the early thirteenth century, it was possible to attract investors to ventures because profits were very high and the risks were comparatively low. Parts of Europe, especially the towns of Flanders and Tuscany, even developed quasi-capitalistic, entrepreneurial industry. Economic development was so pronounced that many scholars call the era the age of "Commercial Revolution."

Government, too, expanded from the eleventh through the early thirteenth centuries.[8] A richer populace meant new sources of funds for kings, lords, and merchant princes. Growing tax revenues were used in much of Europe to build nascent bureaucracies, staffed increasingly with lay officials, and to hire professional soldiers. In much of western Europe, strong kings emerged and challenged the aristocracy for political power, while in Italy and the Netherlands townsmen asserted their sovereignty. There were tremendous cultural gains—so much so that the proliferation of knowledge beginning around 1080 has been called the "Twelfth Century Renaissance."[9] By the early thirteenth century, the intellectual movement had swelled beyond "rebirth." Learning had become so extensive and complicated that higher education, like economic activity, became specialized and was institutionalized in universities.

Nothing better sums up the character and extent of the eleventh-, twelfth-, and thirteenth-century growth than the actual physical expansion of the Christian West.[10] In eastern Europe, it was called the *Drang nach Osten*, or drive to the East—the incorporation under German auspices of many Slavic peoples into the larger European community. In Iberia, French, Norman, and Spanish knights began the *Reconquista*, the reconquest of a part of Europe which had been under Islamic control since the eighth century. And Christian soldiers from all over Europe took part in the Crusades, the military expeditions to wrest control of the Holy Land from the Turks. The *Recon-*

*quista* and the Crusades brought enormous cultural advantages to European civilization. Western soldiers came into contact with intellectually and materially superior civilizations and brought back goods and ideas that helped to facilitate European growth, which became self-perpetuating.

In the first half of the thirteenth century, medieval Europe reached the apex of its development. An extended period of international peace had begun. Holy Mother Church enjoyed widespread influence; Innocent III (1198–1216) was perhaps its greatest pope. The Franciscan and Dominican orders enjoyed great prestige, and magnificent Gothic cathedrals stood as a monument to Christian authority. Governmental authority was more widespread than ever, and social status and personal relationships were governed increasingly by wealth rather than birthright. In general, it was an era of rising expectations.

In the mid-thirteenth century, things began to change. Many of these changes were socially induced, but others were environmental—the most important being changes in the weather. In recent years, many historians have assigned to climatic change a seminal role in influencing premodern society. In an economy such as that of medieval Europe, in which most of the wealth came from the produce of the land, this was certainly the case. Glacial and pollen evidence suggest an improvement in Europe's weather between 750/800 and 1150/1200.[11] Paleoclimatologists have labeled this period "the early medieval warm" or, more commonly, "the little optimum," in contrast with "the big optimum" of prehistory. During the late eighth century, the Alpine glaciers began to retreat. Pollen studies suggest that beech forests along the glacier Fernau and in the Ardennes region of northern France expanded to their A.D. 200 borders. In Germany, a number of deciduous species that had vanished after 200 reappeared, and cores of foraminifera were deposited along its North Atlantic Coast. All these phenomena were indicative of the warming trend during the period 750/800 to 1150/1200; the mean temperature of this era probably exceeded that of the period 350/400 to 750/800 by more than 1°C. The entire era 750/800 to 1150/1200 was characterized by milder winters and drier summers.

The little optimum has been credited with facilitating many of the political, social, and economic trends of the High Middle Ages. Some scholars, again noting the overriding importance of agrarian activities in the medieval economy, believe the little optimum contributed to the great increase of foodstuffs between the ninth and twelfth centuries. Others credit it with the era's growing sea and land travel, expanding trade and urbanization, and even the entire Commercial Revolution.

By the late twelfth century, the four hundred years of the little optimum were drawing to a close. From 1150/1200 to 1300/1350, it got colder and wetter. The Alpine glaciers Fernau, Vernagt, Aletsch, and Grindelwald all advanced for the first time since the eighth century, with the tree line retreating in their path. Radiocarbon data from Aletsch's peat bogs show that they reached a maximum retreat from 1200 to 1230; those from Grindelwald reached their apex in 1280, while the others peaked between 1215 and 1300. Another glacier, Allalin, in the Saaser Visp Valley in Switzerland, was a major pasture area in the eleventh and twelfth centuries. Archival records from livestock farmers show that the northern pastures, which had been used for hundreds of years, had to be abandoned because of the advancing glaciers and could not be used again until late in the fourteenth century.

Additional evidence of the new cold era comes from Scandinavia. As the little optimum proved to be a period of expansion in the Far North, abetting the general population growth of the eleventh, twelfth, and thirteenth centuries, and leading to the Viking era and the settlement of Iceland and Greenland, the thirteenth and fourteenth centuries were an era of contraction. Ice floes drifted far to the south, blocking traditional North Atlantic shipping lanes. The most direct westerly routes from Norway to Iceland and Greenland had to be given up, with the crucial Bergen-to-Reykjavik route increased by 400 miles. At certain junctures in the fourteenth century, Norwegian ships could not even supply the Icelanders with foodstuffs, and the Icelanders had to reorient their trade south to the British Isles. For the Greenland settlements, the dislocations proved fatal. Many of the West Coast fjords were blocked completely twelve months a year. One Greenland farm after another had to be abandoned as the growing season grew ever shorter. A famous text describing the problem survives from a Norwegian priest, Ivar Baardson, who served as steward to Greenland's bishop of Gaarder from 1341 to 1364: "From Snefelness to Iceland to Greenland, the shortest way had always been the following: two days and three nights, sailing due west. In the middle of the sea are reefs called Gunbierneshier. That was the old route, but now the ice has come from the north, so close to the reefs that none can sail by the old route without risking his life.''[12] The Baltic Sea froze twice, in 1303 and 1306–1307. The water levels in the Mediterranean and Caspian Seas rose markedly, and the Thames River in England froze twelve times between 1400 and 1480. This period of colder, wetter weather is called the "Little Ice Age" by paleoclimatologists. Europe's weather was as inclement as it had been during the Dark Ages, and perhaps as bad as at any time since the Great Ice Age of prehistory.

The greatest effects of the Little Ice Age were in agriculture. It is worth reemphasizing that medieval Europe was an overwhelmingly rural society, dependent for the vast bulk of its wealth on the produce of the land. Detailed local studies have shown that a good autumn harvest came when summer and autumn of the previous year were dry, winter was either average or severe, and summer dry.[13] A bad harvest came from one of two circumstances: either when the fall of the previous year was very wet, soaking the fields, followed by wet winter and summer; or when the previous autumn was wet, the winter average and the summer dry. Too much cold and too much precipitation washed away topsoil, killed seedlings, blanched wheat, allowed weeds to flourish, and paved the way for famine. Ironically, too little precipitation in southern Europe could mean insufficient nutriment for crops and, when coupled with strong winds, the blowing away of topsoil. In general, the colder, wetter weather was disastrous for agriculture.

Europe's environmental problems were exacerbated by a variety of social ills.[14] Fertility levels remained high and population continued to increase throughout the thirteenth century, but by 1250 the expansion of arable had virtually come to an end. Almost all the best land in Europe had been assarted, so that the lands being brought under plow were of increasingly marginal quality. The food surplus began to shrink. Fields were planted more intensively than ever and, in some places, fallow—and occasionally even pasture—lands had to be planted. Fodder crops were abandoned. The curtailing of pasture meant an end of animal husbandry in some regions, which, in turn, meant the elimination of an important source of protein—a nongrain food hedge against crop failure—and a dearth of manure for fertilizer. Because wheat produced the highest yields per seed, more peasants turned to its exclusive cultivation. Around 1250, Europe entered a cycle of poverty similar to that of many Asian societies. Growing population and a finite amount of land produced a monoculture of wheat; if the wheat crop failed, given the lack of alternatives, people would starve.

Things got worse after 1250.[15] Living standards stagnated and then began to drop. The wheat monoculture led to overcultivation and soil exhaustion, as evidenced in the drop in seed yields. Data from the estates of the bishop of Winchester, in southern England, a major grain-producing area, show the astounding decline in agricultural productivity. Wheat yields (that is, seed harvested to seed planted) fell from about 5 to 1 early in the thirteenth century to as low as 1½ to 1 by 1330. Barley went from as high as 10 to 1 to as low as 2 to 1, with an average of a bit more than 3; and rye from close to 4 to 1 to less than 2 to 1. These yields, as dismal as those during the Dark Ages, made the labor of planting barely worth the effort; and they were made continually worse by colder, wetter weather. By the end of the thirteenth century, Europe was in the throes of a classic Malthusian subsistence crisis.[16] Population growth was outstripping food production, and Europe was getting poorer and poorer.

The agricultural woes of the peasantry were accompanied by new tenurial problems. As mentioned, during the halcyon years of the late twelfth and early thirteenth centuries, many peasants substituted cash payments for part, or even all, labor obligations. At the same time, some lords simply farmed out their entire estates, including their *demesnes*, for a fixed sum. Because of this and assarting, many peasants were cultivating more land than their ancestors could have imagined. But rising prices, especially food prices, caused by increasing population brought changes. Many lords found it hard to live on old, fixed rents. Further, with food prices so high—up as much as 70% from 1150 to 1250—there were great profits to be made if the lords harvested the produce of their *demesnes* and marketed it directly. Hence, after 1250, many lords stopped taking cash payments and began to enforce old labor obligations. Many peasants found themselves spending an ever-growing portion of their time doing free work at precisely the point at which they needed to concentrate their efforts on their own arable—and, indeed, on all the arable they could farm. To make matters even worse, when the peasants needed additional grain, they were often forced to buy supplies from the lord—the very grain produced by their own labor.[17]

In light of the growing economic difficulties, why did the peasant population continue to increase? In part, it grew because of the absence of major, exogenous, killing diseases; mortality rates were relatively low. But in part, population continued to increase because of high fertility levels, the result of early first marriage.[18] Age of first marriage, especially for women, is important because in the Middle Ages most births came within wedlock, and women had a finite period, probably between ages 16 and 40, in which they were fecund. If marriage came at, say, age 25, about a third of this fecund period would be eliminated, thus curtailing the number of births. In preindustrial Europe, age of marriage was usually determined by the availability of land. During the great expansion of the twelfth and early thirteenth centuries, assarting meant that people could marry earlier, hence raising fertility rates. By 1250, land was harder to get. But most scholars believe that relatively early ages of first marriage, probably in the early twenties for women and mid-twenties for men, continued. It is hard to say why these trends persisted in the face of new social and economic conditions. But custom of at least a century's duration and general inertia must have been important factors.

To sum up, Europe got colder and wetter after 1250. Population continued to grow steadily even as the amount of arable remained constant. As a result, existing arable was overcropped and seed yields began to drop. Heavy demand for the existing arable caused rents and entry fines—the payments by tenants as a condition of their holding—to rise steadily, and vacant holdings—a fairly common phenomenon before 1200—to become virtually nonexistent. Landholding size dropped gradually and then precipitously, and many younger sons were of necessity disinherited and forced into wage work in an era of notoriously low pay for agricultural workers. For the lord who held the land, the century after 1250 was an era of economic prosperity; for the peasants who worked it, it was an era of unqualified disaster.

In normal years, when harvests were adequate, the peasantry managed to squeak by, albeit on ever-diminishing margins and incomes. But the potential disaster of a crop failure always loomed and, as weather conditions continued to deteriorate in the late thirteenth century, Europe was struck by a series of famines.[19] The 1290s was an extremely rainy decade; in some areas, crops literally rotted in the fields. In the harvest years of 1291, 1292, and 1293, wheat failed in England and reached only about half its 1280s' levels in France and Germany. The next two harvests produced adequate yields, but there was another shortfall in 1297, this time in parts of the Mediterranean Basin as well as north of the Alps. There are no data available from which European mortality might be estimated, but most experts agree that it was at least 5% higher than normal. None of the individual famines of the 1290s struck every corner of the Continent, and northern Germany, the Low Countries, Poland, and Iberia seem to have emerged relatively unscathed. Even in England and France, where the effects were most severe, the famines appear to have had minimal psychological impact. Demographic and social patterns underwent few significant changes, and the population/production crisis continued to worsen.

Conditions deteriorated even more between 1300 and 1347. A succession of very wet seasons caused a series of crop failures and food shortages which would not come entirely to an end until after the Black Death. In 1304 and 1305, famine struck northern France and the Netherlands. In 1309, excessive rainfall brought about the first continentwide famine in over 250 years. In France, it persisted through 1310. The weather continued to be bad; every year from 1310 to 1319 had above-average precipitation. The rains, high population, heavy dependence on wheat, and cultivation of much marginal arable combined to produce the worst decade of famine in European history. The excessive humidity caused trees and bushes to overgrow, rivers to swell, and crops to rot in the fields. In France, every harvest from 1308 to 1319 was below the average of the period 1300–05; in Germany, this would be the case between 1312 and 1320, and in England, from 1313 to 1320. By 1314, even the grain-producing regions of northeastern Europe began to experience shortfalls. Townsfolk in the Netherlands, southern Germany and northern Italy had difficulty acquiring food. And from England, Holland, France, and central Germany came the first simultaneous references to widespread hunger and starvation.

The harvest of 1315, though bad by thirteenth century standards, was still the best in five years, and some observers believed the famines had come to an end. They were wrong. In 1316, the wheat crops failed once again all across the continent, and conditions became worse than ever. Using 1310 as a base year, wheat prices in the London Cheap, the principal grain market in the city, stood at 5 shillings, 7 pence per quarter (a common measure, usually about 8 bushels)—and this was after 20 years of steady inflation. By July 1316, a quarter sold for 40 shillings. By comparison, it sold for 44 shillings in the market town of Leicester, and 26 shillings in villages in Suffolk, one of the more fertile parts of England. Further, all of this occurred *before* the disastrous autumn 1316 harvest. After it, wheat prices rose another 75% *and* this was in England, ordinarily a grain exporter, where average food prices were lower than those in most continental markets. Elsewhere, things were far worse. In France, from 1310 to 1314, wheat yields dropped 50%, to about 4 bushels per seed. In 1315, they dropped to 2.5 bushels per seed, and, by 1316, to virtually 1 to 1. The chronicler Guillaume de Nages wrote:

> We saw a large number of both sexes, not only from nearby places but from as much as five leagues away, barefooted and maybe even, except for women, in a completely nude state, together with their priests coming in procession at the Church of the Holy Martyrs, their bones bulging out, devoutly carrying bodies of saints and other relics to be adorned, hoping to get relief.[20]

The years 1315-17 were the most severe for Europe's urban areas. Netherlandish merchants could not buy grain from traditional sources in England, France, and the Baltic Sea hinterlands. Fish prices in Holland rose over 500%, and surplus food stocks, accumulated with great care over a number of years, were exhausted. In Ypres, Flanders, 2800 bodies, approximately 10% of the town's pre-1310 population, were buried in the first six months of 1315. By 1317, at least 17% to 20% of Ypres's population had perished, a figure comparable to the mortality the town would suffer a generation later during the Black Death. In Ghent, Bruges, Louvain, and the Dutch towns, mortality from the famines probably ranged between 10% and 15%.

The major Italian cities had developed elaborate methods of provisioning themselves. By the fourteenth century, most of them had gained control over their *contadi*, or surrounding countrysides, from which the bulk of their foodstuffs came.[21] Great port cities such as Venice and Genoa used their merchant and naval fleets to garner imports; in Venice, there was even a grain commission that regulated food prices. Yet the early fourteenth century food crisis struck Italy as well. The Florentine chronicler Giovanni Villani wrote:

> The famine was felt not only in Florence but throughout Tuscany and Italy. And so terrible was it that the Perugians, the Sienese, the Lucchese, the Pistolese and many other townsmen drove from their territory all their beggars because they could not support them. . . . The agitation of the [Florentine] people at the market of San Michele was so great that it was necessary to protect officials by means of guards fitted out with an axe and block to punish rioters on the spot with the loss of their hands and their feet.[22]

By 1320, the large urban centers of Italy probably had lost up to 10% of their total population.

In the Rhineland, chroniclers reported the need to post troops at gibbets in Mainz, Cologne, and Strasbourg. Ravenous people were rushing the gallows, and cutting down and eating the corpses. However apocryphal the reports of cannibalism might be, there are many more substantial records of the dearness of grain during the great famines. English chroniclers stressed that horsemeat, normally scorned even by peasants, was too expensive for all but the aristocracy. The rest of the populace was reduced to eating dogs, cats, and "unclean things."[23] All livestock prices save those of draft animals rose so high that in February 1316 a royal proclamation was issued which attempted to fix alimentary prices. But the proclamation failed because it "ordained that the ordinance regarding livestock, fowl and eggs should not stand because few were found on account of the dearth and lack of victuals." People paid any price for food.

Adding to the general misery was a series of related enteric diseases, probably typhoid fever, dysentery, and diphtheria, which increased the already inflated mortality. In all, heriots (the death duties paid by tenants' heirs to their lords) from estates in England increased 10%–12% in 1316. All classes were afflicted and, in 1317, normal, everyday social operations throughout Europe began to grind to a halt. Alms collections stopped and the number of vagabonds and thefts increased markedly. In Kent, a third of all thefts in 1316-17 involved foodstuffs; in a Midlands session of peace, 15% of all crimes brought before the court involved thefts of food.[24]

In 1317 and 1318, harvests throughout Europe improved, and conditions gradually got better. But a new catastrophe, animal murrains, began. From 1316 to 1322, a series of livestock epidemics devasted what remained of Europe's cattle population. The next two years, 1322 and 1323, proved to be a period of respite, but they were followed by a succession of sheep murrains in 1324 and 1325. Coupled with additional grain harvest failures in 1321 and 1322, the murrains extended Europe's problems for another eight years.

The agrarian crisis of 1309–25 had profound effects on European society and economy. From 1316 to 1322, human population was reduced rather markedly, as higher mortality caused demographic decline, ranging from 10% to 25%. Every grain crop except oats, which often thrive in conditions of heavy rainfall and high humidity, produced yields far below average. But crop yields would eventually come back; more crucial and damaging was the depletion of European livestock. For example, on Inkpen Manor in Berkshire, England, there were 468 sheep in 1313. By 1317, there were only 137. On the three Huntingdonshire estates of Ramsey Abbey, also in England, the number of cattle in the same time span fell from 54 to 6, 47 to 2, and 65 to 9.[25] Recovery, especially in the crucial sheep's-wool market, was a long time in coming since many landlords lacked the capital to invest in new breeding stock. In many cases, it took generations before herds reached their thirteenth-century levels.

Devastating as they were in the short term, however, the famines of the 1310s and 1320s produced little long-term demographic change. Postfamine marriage and fertility levels remained high, and population began to rise almost immediately.[26] By the mid-1330s, Europe's subsistence crisis had been renewed. In northern France, famine occurred in the following years: 1330–34, 1344, 1349–51, 1358–60, 1371, 1373–74, and 1390, with Paris experiencing additional shortages in 1323 and 1325. In southern France, 1329, 1335, 1337, and 1343 were famine years. All over the kingdom, conditions were made worse by the Hundred Years' War with England, fought largely in French territory. In England, famine struck in 1335 and 1344; Germany and eastern Europe were affected in 1336 and from 1346–48, at which time a series of enteric diseases also ravaged the population. Southern Europe suffered as well. Both Iberia and the north Italian cities had major famines in the mid-1330s and the early and late 1340s; conditions were so bad by 1347 that Sienese paupers, turned out by their own town fathers, showed up at the gates of Florentine almshouses.

While Europe's subsistence crisis was most obvious in agriculture, it was evident in many other things as well. Invariably, markets for industrial products suffered. Population levels by the 1340s were almost as high as they had been at the turn of the fourteenth century, but pauperization cut into the spending power of all but the elite. Demand from great lords for luxury goods remained high, but many gentlemen and bourgeois suffered along with the peasants as food costs took an ever-higher proportion of their incomes. Europe's banking system was also shaken. In the 1340s, both of Italy's principal banks, the Bardi and the Peruzzi, almost collapsed. This was primarily the result of defaults by the kings of England and France, whose solvency had in turn been affected by the plight of their subjects. There were exceptions to this general crisis. Some trade, particularly that between the Italian and Netherlandish towns, expanded, but it is important to remember that agricultural products must have accounted for 75% to 80% of all trade goods. Eventually, falling agricultural productivity affected all commercial activity and accelerated declining standards of living.

Europe's subsistence crisis must be understood within a social context.[27] The old bonds of the trifunctional system were crumbling. Despite the commercial, financial, and industrial slowdown, the bourgeoisie was in a stronger position than it had been in the twelfth century. Townsmen had both liquid capital—with which they could buy exemptions, favors, privileges, and titles from lords and kings—and the literary and mathematical skills necessary for governmental service. By contrast, the position of the clergy was less secure. Their dominant role in government and education was being challenged by the bourgeoisie. The Babylonian Captivity, the residence of the pope away from Rome in Avignon, the intellectual and theological doubts raised by empiricists such as Duns Scotus and William of Ockham, and the growing independence of national churches in England, France, and Iberia all served to weaken Holy Mother Church.

The most profound social changes occurred among the groups directly dependent upon the produce of the land—the aristocracy and the peasantry. As noted, in financial terms, most magnates prospered throughout the thirteenth and early fourteenth centuries. Prices for their produce and rents from their lands were higher than ever before. But the aristocrats also faced deep-seated problems. They owed their existence to their role as a mounted military force, which necessitated the expense of keeping horses and armor and long hours of practice to master difficult techniques of combat. They provided protection for defenseless peasants, who in turn worked and supported their lords. Life was not easy for the peasants, but at least they had a degree of certainty in their lives—principally, that they would be able to pass their holdings on to their children. In the fourteenth century, all of this changed. New weapons and methods of military organization challenged the nobility's supremacy on the battlefield. Mercenary armies, using pikes and longbows, took the measure of knights in the field, while artillery in the hands of kings threatened knights in their castles. As royal power grew in the West and municipal authority increased in parts of Italy, the Netherlands, and Germany, the peasants could look to new figures for protection. There were no more infidel or pagan armies, save in parts of southeastern and far eastern Christendom, from whom the lords had to protect the peasants; indeed, to many peasants, it was the lords who represented the greatest threat to stability and security.

But, for the peasants, the chief issue, as always, was the productivity of the land. After 1250, harvests decreased in size, while long-forgotten labor services and banalities were resurrected. Some peasants made adjustments. Nonpartible primogeniture, the inheritance of family holdings exclusively by the eldest son, became the rule in many parts of Europe. Yet average holding size in the common fields still shrunk from 1250 to 1348, and most younger sons stood no chance whatsoever of obtaining enough property to marry and support a family. Indeed, by the 1330s many eldest sons began to find themselves in similar positions. In the past, the peasant had been guaranteed the right, so to speak, to be a peasant; after 1250, this was becoming more and more difficult. The old manorial system was crumbling, and the lords, who seemed now to be doing little of real benefit, were getting richer. In 1347, the bonds and structure of European society, intricately developed through 400 years, were coming apart.

# CHAPTER 3
# The Plague's Beginnings

Sometime in the late thirteenth or early fourteenth century the ecological balance of Eurasia was violently disrupted. A result was the spread of *Y. pestis* and plague from a permanent locus, the Gobi Desert, east into China, south into India, and west across central Asia to the Middle East and the Mediterranean Basin. This marked the onset of the Black Death and the coming of the second plague pandemic.

There are several theories that try to explain the Black Death. One, developed in part by William McNeill, assigns a crucial role to the nomadic rulers of the Mongol Empire.[1] Begun in the late twelfth century by Genghis Khan and still powerful in the fourteenth century, the Mongol Empire was important because it served as the link between less mobile Eurasian societies in China, India, the Middle East, and Europe. The Empire was bound together by highly mobile Mongol horsemen, who formed a network of military and governmental communications spanning Asia from Russia to Persia and from the Punjab to Manchuria. By the late thirteenth century, the Empire had reached the Yunan region in southern China. The Yunan is today an inveterate focus of plague, and many scholars believe that it has been

33

such since the sixth century A.D., when *Y. pestis* came from east Africa during the first pandemic. McNeill and others argue that, by the early fourteenth century, Mongol horsemen and supply trains had picked up the infected insect or rodent hosts of *Y. pestis* and carried them back to Mongol headquarters at Karakorum, in the Gobi Desert. Local Gobi rodents were then infected and they and Mongol horsemen carried it throughout the far-flung Empire in the same fashion that they had brought plague into the desert. There are variations on this theory; many scholars believe that the Gobi region was itself an inveterate focus of *Y. pestis*. In either circumstance, the domination of much of Eurasia by the Mongols was crucial to the spread of plague.

A second interpretation recognizes the importance of the Mongols, but claims that environmental, rather than human, factors were most important in plague's origins and spread.[2] The environmental theory relies on the climatic changes outlined in Chapter 2. As the prevailing Eurasian wind patterns changed, western Europe, dominated by Atlantic breezes, became much wetter; by contrast, sirocco winds from the Sahara blew hot, dry air into the already hot and dry central parts of Asia. The environmentalists believe that this gradual dessication, which began in the mid-thirteenth century and continued into the early fourteenth century, caused Mongol and Turkic nomads to move their flocks—the most important part of their pastural economies—east and west in search of greener pastures. At the same time, central Asian wild rodents—marmots, susliks, tarbagons, ground squirrels, and the like—also moved in search of food and water, infecting local rodent populations with *Y. pestis* and thus extending the second plague pandemic.

Both theories are compelling, and the truth no doubt lies in some combination of the two. The importance of Mongolia, however, is paramount. The rodents and men of the steppes and desert were clearly the initial carriers of plague. The nomadic tribesmen seemed even to have a sense of the connection between plague and rodent intermediaries, and developed a series of customs to prevent the spread of *Y. pestis*. The trapping of marmots, usually the principal host to the flea *X. cheopis*, was generally forbidden; they could be shot, but only at a safe distance. Animals that moved slowly were untouchable, and there were widespread taboos about using furs from certain types of rodents. Whatever the precise cause or chronology, an epizoötic, and then an epidemic, of plague erupted in the Gobi Desert sometime in the late 1320s.

News of natural disasters in Asia began to filter back to the West from travelers early in the 1330s.[3] A series of droughts and earthquakes from 1330 to 1333 and subsequent flooding in 1334 caused widespread famines, which were worsened by swarms of locusts that destroyed what remained of the crops. These adverse ecological blows continued into the 1340s and, at some point—perhaps as early as 1331—were joined by plague. The Chinese records are vague. An unspecified epidemic broke out in the province of Hopei in 1331 and allegedly killed 90% of the population, but both the mortality and the description of the disease cast doubt on whether it was the Black Death. The first unimpeachable references appear in 1353, when chroniclers claim that two-thirds of China's population had died since 1331.[4] Whatever the precise dates and circumstances, by the mid-fourteenth century, the Black Death had struck China and, by 1393, after successive cycles of plague epidemics, the Chinese population had dropped to about 90 million from a thirteenth-century high of over 125 million.

The westward spread of the Black Death is better documented. Between 1330 and 1346, plague probably infected the Western world in two ways. The first was strictly ecological. Dislodged central Asian rodents infected local animal, and then human, populations—a gradual, but very comprehensive, process. The second was the work of man—the elaborate East–West trading system established in the twelfth and thirteenth centuries.[5] There were three principal arteries of this East–West trade. The first was an overland path through northern China and across central Asia to the trading entrepôts along the northern shore of the Black Sea. This route was traversed primarily by caravans, which were protected by the Mongol Peace, a guarantee enforced by the Mongol khans. The second path was primarily by sea and involved the lucrative spice trade from south Asia. Ships sailed west across the Indian Ocean into the Persian Gulf, whence goods were transported by caravan across the northern Arabian Peninsula to the Levantine Coast. The third route also was primarily by sea and emanated from south Asia. Goods were carried across the Indian Ocean, around the southern Arabian Peninsula, past Yemen, and into the Red Sea. There, they were taken overland to Gaza or the ports of the Nile Delta.

At the end of each route were Italian merchants, primarily Genoese in the Black Sea and Venetians and Pisans in the Mediterranean, who carried the goods by ship to Italy, southern France, and Catalonia, where they were taken overland into northern Europe. In 1291, the intra-European routes of this system were facilitated when Genoese ships sailed for the first time through the Straits of Gibraltar, north into the Atlantic, through the English Channel and into the North Sea ports of the Netherlands. By the fourteenth century, the entire system was relatively quick and efficient. *Y. pestis* could be carried either by the fleas and rats aboard the trading ships or, in the case of pneumonic plague, by the merchants themselves. By the 1340s, the Eurasian commercial network was sufficiently fluid for an epidemic to pass through it before the disease's carriers fell victim themselves.

Historians debate which of the three trading routes was most important in the spread of the Black Death. It is likely that the overland route through central Asia was most crucial, but the other two also played an important role in plague's spread, if not in its origins. For ships on these sea-based routes brought infected Asian black rats, plague's most prolific carriers, to the West.

The first records of the Black Death's westward movement are from 1339.[6] Archaeological evidence shows that substantial portions of a Nestorian Christian community near Lake Issyk Kul, in the Tien Shan region of central Asia, died from bubonic plague. Narrative records show that later in the year plague reached Belasagun, Talas, and perhaps Samarkand, along the rivers Jaxartes and Oxus in Transoxiana. By 1345, it was at Sarai, a major trading center astride the Lower Volga. By 1346, it reached Astrakhan, the Caucasus, and Azerbaijan, and rumors of its devastation began to reach the ports of the Mediterranean. One chronicler claimed: "India was depopulated; Tartary, Mesopotamia, Syria, Armenia were covered with dead bodies; the Kurds fled in vain to the mountains. In Caramania and Caesaria [in Asia Minor] none were left alive."[7]

To most Westerners, Tartary and the Orient were remote areas inhabited by pagans and infidels. Strange things happened in such exotic places and there was no reason to think that similar disasters would strike the West. But in September 1345, the Black Death did come close to home. It reached the Crimea, along the northern coast of the Black Sea, where Italian merchants had a number of trading colonies.

Traditionally, the entry of the Black Death into Europe has been assigned to the Genoese settlements at Caffa. A street brawl between Christian merchants and the local Muslim residents degenerated into a war and, after some initial skirmishes, the Muslims sought help from the local Tatar lord. This lord, a Kipchak khan named Janibeg, raised a large army and forced the Genoese to fortify their quarters in town. The Tatars laid siege to Caffa, but, in the course of the attack, plague erupted among their army. It decimated the besiegers and prompted Janibeg to share his woe; he ordered his surviving troops to load plague victims on catapults and toss them over Caffa's walls and into the citadel. Rotting bodies proliferated in the town, and the Black Death spread throughout. Finally, the Genoese were forced to flee. They took to their ships, sailed back to Italy, and introduced the Black Death into the Mediterranean Basin.

There are many implausible aspects to this traditional account. The first concerns the source, the Piacenzan chronicler, Gabriele de Mussis.[8] He did not leave his home in Italy during the Black Death and seems to have picked up his story from returning sailors, not always a reliable source. More important, plague's complex etiology and the necessity of insect and rodent hosts or live human victims with pneumonic plague casts doubt on the role of catapulted bodies, however numerous they might have been. It is more likely that the urban Caffan rodent population was infected by its rural counterpart. But however accurate the particulars of Mussis's account, the story does tell a great deal about the mechanism of at least one of the plague strains which made up the Black Death. It moved overland until it reached the terminus of the trade route from Asia. Once there, it moved across the open sea in merchant ships and inland up rivers and across major highways; then it returned to attack areas it had initially bypassed. The importance of trade routes in facilitating the spread of the Black Death is shown by plague's progress in Christian Russia. Traveling north across the steppes from the Crimea, it had little direct contact with the Tatars. The Black Death would not get there until late 1350 or early 1351, and then it came from eastern Europe, not directly across the grasslands. In effect, the Black Death traveled not "as the bird flies," but via the circuitous loop of commercial routes.

The Black Death came to Constantinople late in 1347. Overlooking the Golden Horn and controlling the passage between the Black Sea and the Mediterranean, Constantinople was the capital of the Byzantine Empire. It was one of the largest Christian cities in the world, with a population of well over 100,000 and perhaps as many as 250,000. Although not as impressive or important as it had been earlier in the Middle Ages, Constantinople was still a major commercial center and an important port of call for most Mediterranean merchants. The emperor, John Cantacuzenos, believed that the Black Death was divine punishment for aid the Byzantines and Genoese had given to Muslims in capturing the Christian town of Romanis in Asia Minor. He described the impact of the plague in the eastern Mediterranean: "The plague attacked almost all the seacoasts of the world and killed most of their people. For it swept not only through Pontus, Thrace and Macedonia, but even Greece, Italy and all the islands, Egypt, Libya, Judea, Syria and spread throughout the entire world.[9]

As Cantacuzenos suggested, the Black Death spread from Constantinople throughout the rest of Byzantium and the eastern Mediterranean Basin. The historian Nicephoros Gregoras, who survived the Black Death in Constantinople, wrote:

> it invaded the Aegean Islands. Then it attacked the Rhodians . . . and those colonizing other islands. The calamity did not destroy men only but many animals living with and domesticated by man. I speak of dogs and horses [most authorities believe that *X. cheopis* will *not* attack horses] and all species of birds, even the rats that happened to live within the walls of the houses.[10]

Nicephoros' mention of rats is fascinating indeed, but he does not seem to have realized their overriding importance. Neither he nor any other Byzantine chronicler, physician, or theologian brought them up when discussing the Black Death's origins and causes.

It is difficult to measure quantitatively the impact of the Black Death on the Byzantine Empire. Recent research on peasant communities in Macedonia shows that there, as in much of the Christian world, the Black Death struck an already declining population.[11] Political instability and constant civil wars, military incursions by the Serbs and the Ottoman Turks, and economic domination by the Italians were all crucial in the decline. But the Black Death accelerated this drop in population and was by far the single most important blow. The Venetian observer who claimed that 90% of Constantinople's population perished surely exaggerated, but his impression provides a vivid image of plague's impact.

Italian merchants also brought the Black Death to the Muslin Mediterranean.[12] It probably reached Alexandria, the principal port of Egypt, in late autumn 1347. In its first few weeks, the Black Death killed between 100 and 200 people each day. Then, as the weather got colder, the plague got worse. Chroniclers tell of blood-spitting victims, a sign of deadly pneumonic plague, and mortality ran as high as 750 per day. By spring 1348, the death toll may have reached 1000 a day. Alexandria's population before the Black Death was probably about 100,000; it is not possible to compute the exact percentage of those who died of plague, but the city did not approach its preplague population until the sixteenth century. Other places in the Nile Delta were also devastated. Damietta, an important fishing port, was especially hard hit. Gardens and fruit trees were allowed to dry up and fishermen stayed in port for weeks on end. In other Delta villages, the death rate was so great that law courts were suspended and wills could not be probated. In Bilbais, for example, bodies were piled in mosques and shops, and roads were littered with decaying cadavers. Some roads had so many bodies piled along their sides that bandits took to utilizing them to conduct ambuscades.

From the Delta, the Black Death moved up the Nile, reaching Cairo by spring 1348 at the latest. Like Constantinople, Cairo was one of the largest cities in the world; with its extensive suburbs, it may have had 500,000 people. Throughout the rest of 1348, mortality in the city averaged at least 300 a day and, at peak periods of infection in late spring and early autumn, the daily death count may have reached 7000. One source even claims as many as 20,000 deaths on particular days. Everything was in chaos. There was a shortage of coffins, so the dead were borne on wooden planks. Funeral processions wound through the city continuously and, by autumn 1348, there were no more shrouds available in the city. Preachers and gravediggers also were in short supply, leading to mass burials in large, open trenches. As in the Delta, there were so many dead that mosques and shops were piled high with bodies. Prices rose and begging in the streets became widespread.

Ibn Taghrī Birdī, writing about a funeral during the plague epidemic of 1429 in Cairo, could easily have described a processional during the earlier visitation:

> The child of an individual in our service . . . died, and we went out with him to the oratory. The boy was less than seven years old, and when we set him down to pray over him among the dead, a large number of others were brought, until their numbers were beyond counting. Then prayer was said over them all, and we went to take up the dead body, but found that someone else had taken him and left us another one of about the same age. His family took him up but did not become aware of it; I, however, perceived this and told a number of others; but we did not inform his parents of it and said: "Perhaps the one who took him will give him the best interment; there is no profit in talking about it—there would only be an increase in grief." But when the boy had been buried and the proprietors of the funeral office took up the bier they cried out and said: "This is not our bier; this is an old one and its furnishings also are worn out."[13]

In all, 200,000 Cairenes died, representing a third to two-fifths of the city's overall population; this death toll was greater than the total population of any Christian city, with the possible exceptions of Constantinople and Venice.

From Cairo, the Black Death spread throughout the Middle East. By February 1349, it had reached Aswan, along the Upper Nile. The following summer, in the nearby town of Asyūt, only 116 of 6000 people paid taxes. To the east, across the Sinai, the town of Gaza was struck in spring 1348. Gaza was the major market town in an important agricultural region, yet the food markets were closed for two months as a result of the plague. Gaza served as the gateway for plague into Palestine and Syria. A Cairene traveler in Jerusalem wrote the following account:

> I asked him [a Jerusalemite] the reason for this [a feast], and he informed me that he had vowed during the epidemic that, if it was lightened and a day passed without having to pray for any dead, he would arrange a feast. He then said to me: "Yesterday, I did not pray for any dead, so I will give the promised feast." I found that those who I had known among the sheiks of Jerusalem had almost all ascended to God Almighty.[14]

In late 1348, the Black Death reached Antioch, a major commercial seaport with a preplague population of about 40,000. It is possible that plague was introduced not only from Palestine, but also through trading vessels from Constantinople, Cyprus, or Alexandria. Mortality may have exceeded 50% of the total population, and many residents were so frightened that they fled to the lands north of the city, where the Black Death had not yet arrived. Their flight, accompanied by the relentless movement of infected rodents, facilitated the spread of the Black Death. Some of the fleeing Antiochers died en route, and their horses returned to Antioch. Greedy townsfolk then followed the horses back to their former owners and stripped the victims of all their valuables. By early 1349, the Black Death had reached Damascus, one of the greatest cities in the Mediterranean Basin. Before the plague, it had between 80,000 and 100,000 inhabitants. Mortality from the Black Death was very high. At its peak, plague killed about 2000 people a day, and population fell to about 50,000, a loss of between 38% and 50%.

Good descriptions of plague's effect in other parts of the Islamic world are available. From Egypt and Palestine, the Black Death spread throughout the Arabian Peninsula, eventually reaching Islam's holiest city, Mecca. There are no reliable body counts, but all commentators agree that the death toll was very high. Interestingly, the presence of the Black Death in the sacred city provoked an important theological debate. The Prophet Mohammed had claimed that deadly diseases would never reach his Holy City. When plague did come, many Islamic scholars said it was because of the presence in Mecca of nonbelievers, a position that seemed to satisfy most of the Muslim faithful.

From the Muslim Middle East, the Black Death spread to North Africa, both overland and by ship from Egypt. It is likely, however, that the plague also came from the Christian parts of the Mediterranean Basin. Tunisia and Libya, in particular, had very close relations with Italian merchants from Pisa, Genoa, and Sicily. Under any circumstances, Tunis, probably North Africa's largest town, was struck in spring 1348. The historian Ibn Khaldūn estimated that, in May and June 1348, 1000 people perished each day. He believed that of all the peoples of North Africa, only the nomadic Berbers of the western desert escaped demographic disaster. His friend, the poet Abū I-Qāsim ar-Rahawī, wrote:

> Constantly I ask God for forgiveness
> Gone is life and ease
> In Tunis, both in the morning and the evening
> And the morning belongs to God as does the evening
> There is fear and hunger and death
> Stirred up by the tumult and pestilence.[15]

By 1349, the entire Islamic world had been engulfed by the Black Death. About a third of the general population and perhaps 40% to 50% of those living in towns had died. The effect was summed up by Ibn Khaldūn, both of whose parents perished:

> Civilization both in the East and the West was visited by a destructive plague which devastated nations and caused populations to vanish. It swallowed up many of the good things of civilization and wiped them out. It overtook the dynasties at the time of their senility, when they had reached the limit of their duration. It lessened their power and curtailed their influence. It weakened their authority. Their situation approached the point of annihilation and dissolution. Civilization decreased with the decrease of mankind. Cities and buildings were laid waste, roads and way signs were obliterated, settlements and mansions became empty, and dynasties and tribes grew weak. The entire inhabited world changed. The East, it seems, was similarly visited, though in accordance with and in proportion to [the East's more affluent] civilization. It was

as if the voice of existence in the world had called out for oblivion and restriction and the world responded to its call. God inherits the earth and whoever is upon it.[16]

In the Christian parts of the eastern Mediterranean Basin, the effects of the Black Death were as bad as those in the Muslim world. After spreading the plague to Constantinople and throughout Byzantium, Italian ships carried *Y. pestis* to the island of Cyprus in late summer or early autumn 1347. Cyprus had suffered a series of natural disasters in 1347, including an earthquake and several tidal waves, but the Black Death was far worse. So high was mortality and so frightened were Christian Cypriots that they assembled all their Muslim prisoners and slaves and slaughtered them, lest the Muslims inherit the island in the wake of massive Christian deaths.[17] When a merchant ship from Rhodes came to Cyprus in November 1347, the captain found no one in port and decided to go elsewhere. Somehow, however, fleas and rats infected with plague managed to get aboard. Plague broke out on the Rhodian ship and, after the ship landed in Antioch, spread throughout Syria.

It was from another Mediterranean island, Sicily, that the Black Death entered western Europe.[18] The Genoese fleet reached Messina, the principal port in Sicily, early in October 1347. The Franciscan friar, Michael of Piazza, told of its effect. The Genoese were forbidden to stay but, as recounted in the introduction, they docked long enough to spread the plague. Within a few days, the Sicilian rodent and human populations had been infected and, by the middle of the month, the Black Death had spread throughout the island. It would be tedious to recount in detail the misfortunes of the Sicilians; they were depressingly similar to those suffered in the Byzantine Empire, the Middle East, and North Africa. Yet one incident does stand out. The town of Catania, about 55 miles south of Messina, is the second port on the island's eastern coast. A few sick Messinans made their way to the nearby town and were treated kindly by the Catanians. Many were even hospitalized, apparently at local expense. But the Catanians soon realized the virulence of the disease and the possibility that the very people they were helping might be carriers. According to Michael of Piazza, "they refused even to speak to any from Messina, or have anything to do with them, but quickly fled at their approach."[19] A quarantine was imposed, but, as would be the case throughout Europe, it was designed to exclude people and not the rodents who were plague's principal disseminators. By the end of October, Catania was infected and, by early November, all of Sicily was stricken with the Black Death.

By December 1347, the Black Death had spread to southern Italy and much of southern Europe. Because Italy was the commercial center of the Mediterranean Basin, the Black Death entered from dozens—perhaps hundreds—of ports and fishing villages. This was important, for when plague was introduced into a region from a number of different points, it proved to be particularly deadly. The 1340s had been a difficult period. Northern and central Italy were the most urbanized parts of the West; the economies of the towns there depended on commerce, industry, and finance. The famines and food shortages of the early fourteenth century brought soaring food prices, which left people with less money to buy finished goods. This, combined with the insolvencies besetting many of Italy's banks, brought widespread political and social tensions. More than any other place in the West save France, Italy was in crisis before the Black Death. Still, the plague brought difficulties that no one could have imagined.

The principal points of entry in central and northern Italy were the great ports of Pisa and Genoa. Genoa was struck in late 1347.[20] Its population had been falling since 1315, but it was still around 100,000; testamentary evidence suggests a decline of 30% to 40%. Pisa, a town of perhaps 40,000, also lost between 30% and 40% of its population; more importantly, it served as the springboard for plague in Tuscany, Italy's most prosperous and heavily urbanized region.[21] One of the first inland towns to be struck was Prato.[22] A rich market town 40 miles from the sea, it had a preplague population of between 10,000 and 15,000. Notarial records of a wealthy merchant, Francesco di Marco Datini, suggest plague mortality of 40%. Depopulation brought a pronounced labor shortage and a subsequent boom in the slave trade. The traditional source of slaves for Italy was Circassia, many of whose inhabitants were light-skinned, light-eyed, and fair-haired. Most of them were Muslim, which prompted the Christian Church to allow their enslavement under the theory that their masters would have the opportunity to convert them to the "true" faith. But this boom was short-lived; like the rest of the Near East, Circassia was depopulated by the Black Death, leaving fewer people to be enslaved. The Datini records show that Italian merchants began to look to new areas, particularly Africa south of the Sahara Desert, an almost plague-free region from which Arab traders got their slaves. Thus, European interest in Africa was renewed and the black slave trade began.

Like Prato, Pistoia was an important market center.[23] It was centrally located astride major commercial routes, with six highways converging on it, and served as a major communications and cultural center. It was therefore a prime candidate to receive the Black Death early and severely. Like Genoa and Pisa, Pistoia's population had declined from the famines of the early fourteenth century; it had dropped from 30,000 in 1240 to about 24,000 in 1348. But this general, rather gradual crisis was dramatically exacerbated by the Black Death. As soon as plague came in May 1348, a quarantine was imposed. Pistoian authorities believed, probably correctly, that the infection came from Pisa and Lucca, the latter a financial and textile-producing center to the southwest. Visits to, and visitors from, both places were banned, as were imports of textiles and foodstuffs. Crowds were not allowed to gather; even at funerals, attendance was limited to family members. When plague did come, church bells were stilled, lest their ringing disturb the afflicted. All was to no avail, however, and mortality was about 40%.

The Black Death came to Orvieto in April or May 1348 with the entourage of the Ambassador of Perugia, still another Tuscan town.[24] The records of Orvieto's medical community, which was quite sophisticated for the time, show how poorly equipped even the most advanced fourteenth-century communities were when dealing with plague. There was a single municipal physician, a single municipal surgeon, and 15 to 20 private doctors, all serving a population of 12,000 to 15,000. There were three hospitals—one public and two private—and a series of sanitation laws designed to curb industrial pollution. It was a comparatively good system, but it proved to be useless against a new, complex, lethal, and highly contagious disease such as plague. The Black Death raged throughout the spring and summer, during which time the weather may have been too warm to sustain bubonic or pneumonic plague. References to victims dying within 24 hours of infection suggest the presence of the deadly septicaemic strain, as does the general abatement in September and October, normally the peak season for bubonic plague. Mortality was so severe in summer that there appears to have been a substantial "die-off" before the optimal autumn season. Chroniclers claimed that 500 people perished each day; if this is correct, 3% to 4% of Orvieto's population died daily. This may well be exaggerated, but municipal records show that virtually no doctors could be found throughout the summer. So many notaries were killed that hundreds of business transactions became hopelessly entangled and had to be renegotiated after the epidemic. In all, close to half the population died.

The Black Death elicited different responses in different places. In Orvieto, it brought a religious revival. In 1349, at popular behest, the town fathers added 50 new religious dates to the municipal calendar. In 1350, which was a jubilee year, civic authorities abandoned traditional curfews and kept the town's gates open day and night so that pilgrims on their way to Rome might always be accommodated. There were more tangible displays of popular piety as well. Construction of a new cathedral was continued apace and, in the 1360s, hastened, despite a severe postplague depression in Orvieto's economy, a labor shortage, and soaring construction costs.

The rest of Tuscany suffered, too. Siena, 30 miles south of Florence, was one of Europe's most important banking centers.[25] The chronicler Agnolo di Tura (The Fat) wrote a vivid description of the Black Death:

> The mortality in Siena began in May. It was a cruel and horrible thing; and I do not know where to begin to tell of the cruelty and the pitiless ways. It seemed that almost everyone became stupified by seeing the pain. And it is impossible for the human tongue to recount the awful truth. Indeed, one who did not see such horribleness can be called blessed. And the victims died almost immediately. They would swell beneath the armpits and in their groins, and fall over while talking. Father abandoned child, wife husband, one brother another; for this illness seemed to strike through breath and sight. And so they died. And none could be found to bury the dead for money or friendship. Members of a household brought their dead to a ditch as best they could, without priest, without divine offices. Nor did the death bell sound. And in many places in Siena great pits were dug and piled deep with the multitude of dead. And they died by the hundreds, both day and night, and all were thrown in those ditches and covered with earth. And as soon as those ditches were filled, more were dug. And I, Agnolo di Tura . . . buried my five children with my own hands. . . . And so many died that all believed it was the end of the world.[26]

Agnolo believed that 52,000 Sienese died, surely an inflated figure since the town's population in 1348 could not have exceeded 60,000. But mortality was very high in any case, and about half of Siena's population succumbed.

Florence was one of Europe's most beautiful, illustrious, and prosperous cities, but it, too, had undergone food shortages, bank failures, and political crises in the first half of the fourteenth century.[27] By 1348, it had about 80,000 inhabitants, down between 25% and 50% from 1300. The chronicler Giovanni Villani claimed that the Black Death reached Florence in late 1347, killed about 4000 people, and then diminished in virulence through the winter of 1348. In the spring, it struck with renewed fury. The classic description was written by the famous humanist Giovanni Boccaccio:

> In . . . 1348 the deadly plague broke out in the great city of Florence. . . . Whether through the operation of the heavenly bodies or because of our own inequities, which the just wrath of God sought to correct, the plague had arisen in the east some years before, causing the death of countless human beings. It spread without stop from one place to another until, unfortunately, it swept over the west. Neither knowledge nor human foresight availed against it, although the city was cleansed of much filth by chosen officers in charge and sick persons were forbidden to enter it, which advice was broadcast for the preservation of health. Nor did humble supplication serve. Not once but many times there were ordained in the form of processionals and other ways for the propitiation of God by the faithful, but in spite of everything, towards the spring of the year the plague began to show its ravages in a way just short of miraculous. It did not manifest itself as in the east, where, if a man bled at the nose he had certain warning of inevitable death. At the onset of the disease, both men and women were affected by a sort of swelling in the groin or under the armpits, which sometimes attained the size of a common apple or egg. Some of these swellings were larger and some were smaller, and all were commonly called boils. From these two starting points the boils began in a little while to spread and appear generally all over the body. Afterwards, the manifestations of the disease changed into black or lurid spots on the arms, the thighs and the whole person. In many ways, these blotches had the same meaning for everyone on whom they appeared. . . . Such was the cruelty of heaven and to a great degree of man that between March [1348] and the following July it is estimated that more than 100,000 human beings lost their lives within the walls of Florence, what with the ravages attendant on the plague and the barbarity of the survivors towards the sick. Who would have though before the plague that the city held so many inhabitants?[28]

While Boccaccio's estimate of Florentine morbidity is too high, scholarly estimates range from 45% to an incredible 75% of Florence's total population. As much as a third of the city's population might have died in six months, and the immediate impact was enormous. Shops and factories closed, and prices for foodstuffs and basic commodities soared as the market system that brought goods in from the surrounding countryside collapsed. The wealthy fled the city, doctors and apothecaries charged exorbitant fees for their services, and nearly empty streets resonated with the sound of carts and wagons assigned to pick up the dead. Boccaccio describes the scene in lurid terms:

> It was common practice of most of the neighbors, moved no less by fear of contamination by the putrefying bodies than by charity towards the deceased, to drag corpses out of the houses with their hands . . . and to lay them in front of the doors, where anyone who made the rounds might see them, especially in the morning, more of them than he could count; afterwards, they would have biers brought up. . . . Nor was it once or twice only that one and the same bier carried two or three corpses at once, but quite a considerable number of such cases occurred, father and son, and so forth. And times without number it happened that, as two priests bearing the cross were on their way to perform the last office for someone, three or four biers were brought up by the porters in the rear, so that whereas the priests supposed that they had but one corpse to bury, they discovered that there were six to eight, or sometimes more. Nor for all their number were the obsequies honored by either tears or lights or crowds of mourners; rather, it was come to this, that a dead man was then of no more account than a dead goat would be today.[29]

Like their Sienese neighbors, many Florentines adopted an Epicurean attitude, drinking, reveling, and spending money. Parents abandoned children, husbands left wives, and sick relatives were forsaken. A group called the *becchini* appeared. They were usually men of lower social rank, often themselves afflicted with plague, who carted the dead and performed other tasks that no one else cared to do. Some of the *becchini* apparently turned to extortion, rape, assault, and even murder. They would force their way into the houses of the sick and threaten to carry away those still healthy unless certain demands were met. The *becchini* helped to keep the streets deserted. The chronicler Stefani claimed that the only sounds that could be heard came from carts—those of the rich, fleeing with their belongings, and those of the charnel crews, coming for the dead.

The experience of two other Italian cities, Venice and Milan, further illustrates the diverse effects of the Black Death. Venice was probably the largest and richest city in Europe.[30] Unlike most other towns in the Mediterranean Basin, it prospered right up to the onset of the Black Death. It had a preplague population of 120,000 to 150,000. Venice's prosperity was based on commercial success, particularly its dominance over trade in the eastern Mediterranean. It had a stable, conciliar, oligarchic government and a generally peaceful corps of industrial workers who were calmed by the highest wages in Europe. The oligarchy controlled production and marketing in several key industries, including shipbuilding and glassmaking, and put together an impressive schedule of trading ventures. The Venetians even had a maritime empire that included parts of the Black Sea, the Levant, Dalmatia, and several important Mediterranean islands. Like Orvieto, Venice had an elaborate system of sanitation and public health, including civic physicians and hospitals. With such an efficient governmental and medical organization, Venice was better prepared than any place in Christendom to deal with the plague. But plague proved to be as deadly in Venice as it was virtually everywhere else, and the city's most distinguished historian, F. C. Lane, wrote that the Black Death "dominated several centuries of Venetian demographic history."

Venetian galleys from Caffa probably brought plague late in 1347. It was most severe through the following winter and spring, killing close to 600 people a day. In March, Doge Andrea Dandolo and the Great Council established a sophisticated quarantine and prevention system. Certain barges were designated to ferry victims to special islands in the lagoon, and all dead were laid at least five feet deep in the earth. A general quarantine of up to 40 days was imposed on incoming ships, with violators facing penalties of death. Changes were made in the way medical professionals were allowed to operate. Surgeons, previously considered to be little more than craftsmen, were allowed to practice in the same fashion as university-trained physicians, a response to a condition in which "nearly all doctors withdrew on account of fear and terror." Such attempts to upgrade sanitary and medical systems were admirable, but, given the etiology of plague, doomed to failure. In Venice, where records were better kept and official figures more accurate than in any other town in Italy, Lane estimated that 60% of the total population died in the 18-month period beginning in December 1347.

Milan was the principal city on the Lombard plain.[31] It controlled much of the overland Alpine trade with northern Europe and had close to 100,000 people in 1348. Like Genoa, Florence, Rome, and Venice, it was one of the major cities of Italy. Milan differed from the other centers, however, in the nature of its government. Its ruler was an absolute despot, a member of the Visconti family whose powers were more extensive than those of any contemporary ruler. When news of the Black Death reached Milan, the Viscontis and their advisers acted quickly. Municipal authorities walled up those houses in which plague victims were discovered, isolating in them the healthy as well as the sick. So popular did this become that many householders followed suit, in some cases killing members of their own families. Given the plague's most common means of transmission, such measures should have had limited effect on mortality. Yet, Milan's death rate was less than 15%, probably the lowest in Italy save a few Alpine villages. But Milan was exceptional. Generally, Italy, Europe's commercial nexus, suffered as severely as it did because of its many points of entry for different strains of plague. Conservative estimates of mortality are about 33%, but many scholars believe that it reached 40% or even 50%. Taking into account the famines of the early fourteenth century, it is likely that the Italian population was reduced by 50%–60% from 1290 to 1360.

From Italy, the Black Death spread across the western Mediterranean Basin. By January 1348, it had reached Marseille, a principal French port. One authority claimed that it killed 50,000 people, a figure far too high since it probably exceeded Marseille's entire population.[32] Nonetheless, the January inception date suggests pneumonic plague, raising the possibility of a death rate of 50% to 60%. Montpellier, the largest town in southern France, with a population of around 40,000; Narbonne, the second largest town, with perhaps 25,000 to 30,000 people; Carcasone; Toulouse; Montauban; and Bordeaux, the latter oriented toward the Atlantic rather than the Mediterranean—all were infected by summer 1348. Mortality in these towns averaged about 40% of the total population, but in select subpopulations it was even higher. In Montpellier, for example, only 7 of the 140 Dominican friars survived. At Marseille, the chroniclers claim that all 150 Franciscans perished or fled.

A careful study has been made of the effects of the Black Death at Perpignan.[33] Just north of the Spanish border, sandwiched between the Pyrenees and the Mediterranean, Perpignan had between 12,000 and 15,000 inhabitants. No figures for total mortality are available, but good data exist for select groups. Of 125 notaries, 45 survived. Only 1 of the 9 municipal physicians survived, and 16 of the 18 barber-surgeons died. Perpignan had a large Jewish community, from whom Christian neighbors were wont to borrow money. In January 1348, there are records of 16 such loans. In February, there were 25 and, in March, 32. In the first 11 days in April, there were 8, a bit low, but close to the norm. Then came the Black Death. There were three more loans in April and not another financial transaction until the middle of August.

Avignon, about 50 miles north of Marseille on the Rhone River, was the seat of the papacy in 1348.[34] It was a congested but beautiful city with a highly transient population that could have fluctuated between 20,000 and 50,000. As a result of the papal residence, it was a very wealthy city and the center of considerable ecclesiastical, financial, and commercial activity. The Black Death probably appeared in winter 1348; as in Marseille, the inception date suggests the possible presence of pneumonic plague, an hypothesis borne out by extremely high mortality. Between February and May, up to 400 people a day died. In one six-week period, 11,000 people were buried in a single graveyard, at least 1 out of every 3 cardinals died, and total mortality probably exceeded 50%. Pope Clement VI behaved coolly and responsibly, as did most of the Avignonese clergy, but they had reason to panic; mortality among the clergy in general and those of Avignon in particular was among the highest in Europe. The English chronicler Henry Knighton claimed that 65 Carmelite Friars died in Avignon during the first week of the Black Death. Clement issued several bulls, urged calm, relaxed the rules for absolutism, and, after initially encouraging asceticism and processionals, condemned the latter when they became too large and got out of hand. He issued bulls protecting the Jews and excoriating the flagellant movements which sprang up in central Europe, and solicited responsible medical opinion. Eventually, as mortality peaked late in spring, Clement took the advice of his doctor, Guy de Chauliac, and fled the city. He took refuge near the town of Valence, also along the Rhone, and returned to Avignon as soon as plague had subsided there.

Rural southern France was infected from the port towns, both by fleeing people and by the inexorable advance of rodent epizoötics. In southern France, as in Italy, the Black Death exacerbated a bad situation. The famines of the early fourteenth century and the battles of the Hundred Years' War, many of which were fought there, had impoverished much of the countryside. In the county of Nice, for example, up to a third of the population had perished between 1300 and 1348. But, as was the case everywhere else, the Black Death was the worst disaster.[35] The province of Languedoc was perhaps the hardest hit. In Albi, a market district to the east of the Garonne River, evidence from a tax called the *compoix* shows a drop in the number of taxpayers from 10,000 in 1343 to 5000 in 1357. Of course, no one likes to pay taxes, and the decline in taxpayers might not be concomitant with a 50% population decline. But in the rather large village of Mar-sillargues, which had a preplague population of about 1000, mortality from the Black Death was 50%. This was also the case in the township of Ganges, in the Cevannes along the Herrault River. In 1339, Ganges had over 300 electors in its local assembly; by 1350, there were less than 140 electors.

In all of Languedoc, one of the wealthier provinces in France, close to 50% of the population was killed during the Black Death, and the overall effect was disastrous. The market for agricultural products bottomed out, dealing a fatal blow to the specialized cash crops that had been one of the area's economic staples. Viticulture, for example, began a retreat that lasted well into the sixteenth century. Even the most basic agricultural activity, the cultivation of ce-real crops, suffered from reduced demand. Languedoc, a region heavily dependent on its rural economy, suffered a condition histo-rians call *Wustüngen*—the abandoning of arable and, in some cases, even of entire villages due to the depopulation brought by plague.[36] Furthermore, the devastation of Languedoc was not exceptional. In Provence, a wealthy region along the Rhone Valley, mortality from the Black Death was about 50%, with the death count in selected dis-tricts rising as high as 70%. Provence, too, suffered from *Wüs-tungen*, and the Black Death proved to be the most severe in a series of demographic setbacks that began in the late thirteenth century.

Like Italy, Iberia suffered the misfortune of receiving the Black Death from disparate sources.[37] There were at least three avenues of entry. First, plague came from the south, across the Straits of Gibral-tar from the Moorish caliphates of North Africa to those of southern Iberia. Second, it came from the north, across the Pyrenees to the Basques-speaking villages. Third, and probably most important, merchant ships from Italy brought the Black Death to the Balearic Is-lands and then to the major ports of the west coast, Barcelona and Valencia. Like France, Iberia had been rent by incessant wars; when the Black Death erupted, the Christian Aragonese and Portuguese were at war, and the Castilians were fighting the Muslim Granadans. The army of Alfonso XI of Castile was besieging the fortress of Gi-braltar when the Black Death struck both sides. Alfonso refused to leave his troops, came down with the plague, and died in March 1350, the only crowned head in Europe to die of the pestilence.

Gibraltar was one of the last places in Iberia to get the Black Death; the first reported cases were in spring 1348. Since there are no definitive data for Spain and Portugal, it is hard to measure precisely the Black Death's demographic effect. Barcelona and Valencia were two of the largest towns in Spain, with preplague populations of perhaps 50,000 and 30,000, respectively; estimates of mortality for each range between 30% and 40%. For Aragon, Catalonia, Granada, and Portugal, plague mortality was about 30%. For Castile, parts of which were sparsely inhabited uplands, mortality seems to have been between 20% and 25%. Throughout Iberia, local institutions of justice and law enforcement broke down, and looters and criminal bands became ubiquitous. In a few instances, pilgrims to the shrine of St. James Compostela, one of Christendom's holiest shrines, were robbed or beaten. Royal authorities responded quickly and, like their clerical counterparts in Avignon, acted calmly and responsibly. Legislation was passed to control wages and prices, and transfers of food were arranged in order to alleviate local shortages. Pedro IV of Aragon even established a quarantine, a noble if ineffective attempt to isolate the Black Death to parts of his kingdom.

Royal efforts were also made to protect the Jews.[38] Iberia had one of the Mediterranean's largest and most successful Jewish populations and, despite sporadic incidents of anti-Semitism, the Jews had been treated better there than in any other part of the Christian world. Jews served in large numbers as royal tax collectors, physicians, apothecaries, interpreters, and managers of great estates throughout the Iberian Peninsula. The Black Death ended this toleration and began an era of virulent anti-Semitism, which ended with the elimination of the once prominent and prosperous Jewish community. Many Christians believed that the Jews brought on the Black Death by poisoning supplies of drinking water. This was an old idea. For example, in 1321 in Languedoc, a number of lepers had been accused of fouling the drinking supplies; as they were being executed, several cried out that they had been encouraged in their deed by Jews. This idea became current again in 1348. In the German town of Neustadt, after being broken on the rack, a Jewish physician named Balovignus confessed that he had indeed poisoned local wells. He claimed that a Jewish boy had been sent to him by the chief rabbi of Toledo, Spain. The boy had carried a powder which, on pain of excommunication, Balovignus was to use to contaminate the wells. This he did, after warning his co-religionists. Word spread from Germany, and pogroms erupted wherever there were Jews. Many Spaniards did not need the excuse of the wells. The general breakdown of law and order made Jews especially vulnerable, particularly if they were wealthy. The kings of Castile and Aragon moved quickly to protect their Jewish subjects, but it took two years to reestablish normal police and judicial authority. By that time, Iberia's Jewish community had been decimated to one-quarter its former size.

By 1350, the Black Death had run its course in the Mediterranean Basin. Between 35% and 40% of the overall population had perished. The crisis brought on by the plague was summarized by the Florentine chronicler Villani:

> Having grown in vigor in Turkey and Greece and having spread thence over the whole Levant and Mesopotamia and Syria and Chaldea and Cyprus and Rhodes and all the islands of the Greek archipelago, the said pestilence leaped to Sicily, Sardinia and Corsica and Elba, and from there soon reached all the shores of the mainland. And of eight Genoese galleys which had gone to the Black Sea only four returned, full of infected sailors, who were smitten one after the other on the return journey. And all who arrived at Genoa died, and they corrupted the air to such an extent that whoever came near the bodies died shortly thereafter. And it was a disease in which there appeared certain swellings in the groin and under the armpit, and the victims spat blood, and in three days they were dead. And the priest who confessed the sick and those who nursed them so generally caught the infection that the victims were abandoned and deprived of confession, sacrament and medicine, and nursing. . . . And many lands and cities were made desolate. And the plague lasted till _____ [39]

Villani purposely left a blank near the end of the sentence. He planned to fill in a date after the Black Death disappeared, but he was unable to do so. Villani died in the *annus terribilis* of 1348.

# CHAPTER 4
# The Plague's Progress

F ROM SOUTHERN FRANCE, the Black Death spread northward along river valleys such as the Rhone and across major overland trade routes. France was the most populous Christian kingdom, with between 18 and 24 million inhabitants. Northern France was part of the great European plain, one of the world's most fertile wheat belts. Despite the famines of the early fourteenth century and the depredations of the Hundred Years' War, it had as high a rural population density as any place in the West. As northern and central Italy exemplify the impact of the Black Death on urban areas, so France provides a good example of plague's effect in the countryside.

The Burgundian village of Givry is one of the few places in Europe for which parish registers survive before the sixteenth century.[1] In 1340, the registers show a population of between 1200 and 1500; from 1338 to 1348, an average of 30 people died each year, a rather low figure for a preindustrial community. But, in 1348, this changed. In a 14-week period, 615 deaths were recorded, suggesting that overall mortality from the Black Death was about 50%. Even better descriptive and statistical information comes from the duchy of Normandy.[2] In most Norman villages, a black flag was flown on church

54

steeples to warn everyone of the presence of the Black Death. La Graverie, La Léverie, and St. Marie Laumont were villages along the Vire River. Half the population of St. Marie died between July and September 1348. In La Léverie, the lady of the manor died, but she could not be buried because the local priest had disappeared and no cleric from any of the surrounding parishes would enter the village. At La Graverie, "the bodies of the dead decayed in putrefaction on the pallets where they had breathed their last." A systematic study of late medieval Normandy has shown that, by 1348, like Languedoc, the duchy was in the midst of a general crisis begun by the famines of the 1290s and 1310s and exacerbated by the Hundred Years' War. But these crises paled beside the Black Death. The peak period for plague mortality was late spring and summer 1348; overall, about 30% of Normandy's people perished.

Northern France had several important towns, where, evidence suggests, the Black Death was more severe than in the country-side. In Caen and Rouen, the two largest towns in Normandy, plague mortality was between 40% and 50%. In Tournai, an important tex-tile town on the Netherlandish border, the local bishop was one of the first to die. As in Normandy, the Black Death was at its worst in late summer:

> Every day the bodies of the dead were borne to the churches, now five, now ten, now fifteen, and in the parish of St. Brice, sometimes twenty or thirty. In all parish churches the curates, parish clerks and sextons, to get their fees, rang morning, evening, and night the passing bells, and by this the whole population of the city, men and women alike, began to be filled with fear.[3]

The Black Death came to Paris in late spring 1348, probably from the trade routes running north from Lyons and the Rhone Valley. Paris was the largest city in northern Europe, with a population esti-mated at between 80,000 and 200,000. As in Normandy, the death count rose through the hot summer months, suggesting the presence of septicaemic plague. Mortality peaked in late autumn and early winter, indicative perhaps of the pneumonic strain. During the peak months of November and December, it was reported that 800 people died each day. The effects of the Black Death in Paris were summed up by Jean de Venette, a Carmelite friar and master of theology at the University of Paris. He wrote:

> So high was mortality at the Hotel Dieu [Paris's principal hospital] that for a long time more than 500 dead were carried daily with great devo-tion in carts to the cemetery of the Holy Innocents in Paris for burial. A

very great number of the saintly sisters of the Hotel Dieu who, not fearing to die, nursed the sick in all sweetness and humility, with no thought
of honor, a number too often renewed by death, rest in peace with
Christ, as we may piously believe.[4]

Interesting evidence comes from the accounts of the parish of St.
Germain l'Auxerrois. From 1340 through May 1348, 78 people be-
queathed legacies to the parish churches. From June 1348 through
January 1349, the total rose to 419.[5] Overall, close to a third of
Paris's inhabitants probably died during the Black Death. The city
offered many attractions and considerable economic opportunities,
and immigrants swelled its population as soon as the plague had
gone. But, as had been the case in the great cities of Italy, the general
disruption was enormous. In all, the chaos the Black Death brought
to France was well described by Jean de Venette:

> In A.D. 1348, the people of France and of almost the whole world were
> struck by a blow other than war. For in addition to the famine . . . and
> to the wars . . . pestilence and its attendant tribulations appeared again
> in various parts of the world. In the month of August 1348, after Ves-
> pers, when the sun was beginning to set, a big and very bright star ap-
> peared above Paris, towards the west. It did not seem, as stars usually
> do, to be very high above our hemisphere, but rather, very near. As the
> sun set and night came on, this star did not seem to me or many other
> friars who were watching it to move from one place. At length, when
> night had come, this big star, to the amazement of all of us who were
> watching, broke into many different rays, and, as it shed these rays over
> Paris towards the east, totally disappeared and was completely annihi-
> lated. Whether it was composed of airy exhalations and was finally re-
> solved into vapor, I leave to the decision of astronomers. It is, however,
> possible that it was a presage of the amazing pestilence to come, which,
> in fact, followed very shortly in Paris and throughout France and else-
> where, as I shall tell. All this year and the next, the mortality of men
> and women, of the young even more than the old, in Paris and in the
> kingdom of France, and also, it is said, in other parts of the world,
> was so great that it was almost impossible to bury the dead. . . . The
> plague lasted in France for the greater part of the years 1348 and 1349,
> and then ceased. Many country villages and many houses in good towns
> remained empty and deserted. Many houses, including some splendid
> dwellings, very soon fell into ruins. Even in Paris several houses were
> thus ruined.[6]

From northern France, the plague continued to spread steadily
and relentlessly into Picardy and then the Low Countries, where it
continued to defy explanation, categorization, or stereotype. Boccac-

cio and many other fourteenth-century commentators, including the Sorbonne medical faculty, felt that the Black Death was most severe in the towns and advised flight to the countryside. Such advice was often well-founded, for the heavily urbanized parts of central Italy suffered mortality of over 50%, while parts of rural northern France lost around 30%. But the Black Death was a complex combination of bacterial strains; sometimes it took only the bubonic form while, at other times, the bubonic, pneumonic, and even septicaemic forms appeared simultaneously. This helps to explain why mortality patterns in parts of the Netherlands—after northern and central Italy, Europe's most urbanized region—did not follow Italian or northern French patterns. The towns of Ghent, Bruges, Ypres, Brussels, and Antwerp, in the counties of Flanders and Brabant, were major textile manufacturing centers with populations of between 20,000 and 60,000.[7] Yet plague mortality was "only" about 20% to 25%, not much more than it had been during the great famines of the 1310s. By contrast, the county of Holland, one of the most rural and least densely settled parts of the Netherlands, suffered losses of 30% to 35%—losses so great that the reclamation of lands along the Zuider Zee came to a halt after 300 years of diking, draining, and damming.

Like the county of Holland, Scandinavia was overwhelmingly rural and agricultural, was sparsely settled, and suffered very high mortality from the Black Death.[8] In some areas, more than 50% of the total population died. This may have been the result of the cold northern climate, which facilitated pulmonary complications and, hence, pneumonic plague. Tradition has it that the Black Death entered the Far North through the Norwegian port of Bergen, probably in May 1349. Bergen was one of the largest towns in Scandinavia and a major commercial center of the Hanseatic League, a trading confederation made up principally of German-speaking towns ringing the Baltic Sea. In May, a London wool ship was spotted drifting around Bergen harbor. Plague had broken out and killed all the ship's crew before it reached port. The ship finally ran aground and was boarded by municipal authorities, but before they could impose a quarantine, the Black Death had spread ashore, just as had been the case in Messina. This account may be apocryphal, but it captures the terror and havoc that followed in the wake of plague. By the end of 1350, the Black Death had spread through Scandinavia, its impact reflected in the lament of Magnus II of Sweden: "God for the sins of men has struck the world with this great punishment of sudden death. By it, most of our countrymen are dead."

Even more grisly and macabre than the Bergen incident was the progress of the Black Death in Greenland, the westernmost outpost of Christendom.[9] Beginning in the tenth century, small groups of Norwegians and then Icelanders had migrated westward; by the twelfth century, they had established settlements on Greenland's east and west coasts. Heavily reliant on provisions from Scandinavia, the Greenlanders probably got the plague from supply ships. Most scholars believe that the Black Death moved from Bergen to Iceland, to the Hebrides, the Orkneys, the Shetlands, and the Faroes, and then to Greenland, probably in winter 1350. There are no population records for Greenland from before or after the Black Death, and only a few scattered records of plague's devastation. But when Norwegian ships put into the western settlements in the early fifteenth century, the sailors saw only wild cattle roaming through deserted villages. In Scandinavia proper, the Black Death probably killed 45% to 55% of the population. In Iceland, the death toll may have reached 60%, and in Greenland it combined with deteriorating climatic conditions to bring Christian settlement to an end altogether.

The best information about the Black Death in northern Europe comes from the British Isles.[10] Gascon ships brought plague to the small Dorset port of Melcombe Regis in southwestern England in September 1348. Gascony was an English possession for much of the fourteenth century, and its principal town, Bordeaux, was the hub of a flourishing wine export trade. Thus, it was inevitable that once the Black Death reached southern France it would make its way to Britain. The initial contact at Melcombe Regis was followed by many others in the Southwest, including the ports of Bristol, Southampton, Plymouth, and Exeter. Bristol and Southampton were also important terminals in the Anglo-Italian trade, suggesting that plague may have come from Italian, as well as French, sources. London, England's capital, largest town, and principal port, had trade connections throughout Europe and was infected with the Black Death by late autumn 1348. Like Italy, England afforded plague multiple points of entry and, thus, suffered particularly heavy mortality.

The best description of the arrival of the Black Death in England was written by Henry Knighton, a canon of St. Mary-of-the-Meadow Abbey in the East Midlands town of Leicester:

> Then the dreadful pestilence made its way along the coast by Southampton and reached Bristol, where almost the whole strength of the town perished, as it was surprised by sudden death; for few kept their beds more than two or three days, or even half a day. Then this cruel death

spread on all sides, following the course of the sun. And there died at Leicester, in the small parish of Holy Cross, 400; in the parish of St. Margaret's, Leicester, 700; and so in every parish, in a great multitude. Then the bishop of Lincoln sent notice throughout his whole diocese, giving general power to all priests, both regulars and seculars, to hear confessions and give absolution with full episcopal authority to all persons, except only in the case of debt. In such a case, the debtor was to pay the debt, if he were able, while he lived, or others were to be appointed to do so from his goods after his death. In the same way, the Pope gave plenary remission of all sins to all receiving absolution at the point of death, and granted that this power should last until Easter next following, and that everyone might choose his own confessor at will.[11]

Another chronicler, Geoffrey the Baker, claimed that plague reached Bristol by the middle of August, a date verified by Knighton. Bristol was England's second largest town, but was small by Continental standards, with a population of 10,000 to 12,000. Among selected groups, 50% of the beneficed clergy and 30% of the patriciate, or elite ruling class, were killed. Since many members of both groups fled Bristol on hearing of the plague, this figure is even more sobering. The Black Death lingered for twelve months, was most severe in spring 1349, and began to slacken in autumn. Overall estimates of plague mortality in Bristol range between 35% and 40%.[12] So great was the immediate effect that 20 of the town's craft guilds were forced to shorten the lengths of their apprenticeships, and 15 guilds had to design new quality control regulations, so low had the level of craft skills fallen.

England was primarily rural—about 90% of its population lived in communities with less than 1000 inhabitants—and the effects of the Black Death can be seen best by looking at its villages and manors. Rural records are quite extensive. Many manors had three distinct sets of records: account rolls—annual or biennial reports of payments and arrears of peasant obligations taken by the lord's managing agents; surveys and extents—periodic, large-scale investigations undertaken to determine precisely what the lord owned and was owed; and court rolls—records from monthly and biannual courts held by the lord so that the peasants could renew their obligations and air their grievances. Such detailed information, especially that from the court rolls, provides a "microscopic" perspective of plague's impact.

The duchy of Cornwall lies in the southwestern corner of England.[13] In the middle of the fourteenth century, much of it belonged

to Edward the Black Prince, the eldest son of King Edward III and a
hero of the Hundred Years' War. Cornwall had a mixed economy of
cash-crop farming, husbandry, and mining, and prospered in the
early fourteenth century. Still, while the Cornish population was
greater in 1348 than ever before, the region was thinly settled compared to the grain-producing rural regions. This is important because
the Cornish experience during the Black Death shows how impervi-
ous plague was to human settlement patterns. While local ecological
conditions almost always affected the severity of plague in a given
area, density of human population was important only when the
pneumonic strain was present.[14]

The Black Death came to Cornwall in late winter 1349 from Bristol, Exeter, and Plymouth. There are no data from which total plague
mortality can be calculated, but the bishop of Exeter, in whose jurisdiction Cornwall fell, left records of the granting of benefices, that
is, the appointment of new rectors for parishes. These records survive
unbroken from 1272 through the 1340s. The period 1339–49 averaged
just over four grants per year. By contrast, from March 1349 to
March 1350, there were 85 grants, more than 20 times the previous
decennial average, with the peak coming between Easter and Mich-
aelmas (29 September) 1349.

Manorial records provide additional and more personal references to the effects of the Black Death. The accounts of Rillaton
Manor show that the reeve, John de Rill, died from plague on 12
March 1349. William Carnek, the bailiff of Helston-in-Kirrier Manor
died on April 11, and Lucas Cerle, reeve of Liskeard Manor, was too
weak to continue his duties by the end of March. In effect, much of
the management of the rural economy was lost to the plague. Tin
mining, a staple of the Cornish economy, virtually stopped. The
amount of tin presented for coinage in 1351 was less than one-fifth
the amount presented before the Black Death. Manorial mills, a crucial source of power, fell into disuse. Throughout the duchy there was
a widespread increase in vacancies (holdings for which there were no
tenants) and an accompanying decay in rentals. This drop in rents
was a setback for the lords of the manors, but even more serious was
the deterioration of land and buildings during the vacancies. Considerable capital expenditures were necessary to make them suitable
once more for farming.

The West Midlands were more typical of English and northern
European rural society than was Cornwall. This extremely fertile area
was one of the West's principal wheat-producing areas. Cuxham

Manor, 12 miles south of the town of Oxford, is considered by many authorities to have been a model rural estate.[15] In 1349, the lord of Cuxham Manor was Merton College, Oxford, one of the principal centers for the study of the physical sciences in Europe. The Black Death came in March 1349. Since 1311, Robert Oldham had served as bailiff of Cuxham. Plague killed him late in March but, faithful servant to the end, his last hours were spent in making up the lord's accounts. Oldham was succeeded by his son John, who died in April. John was followed by Thomas atte Green. Thomas died in June. A fourth bailiff died in July, and a fifth either died or fled by July 1350. By 1360, Merton College ceased trying to exploit Cuxham directly and instead farmed out the entire manor to leasehold tenants.

There were marked social and economic effects from the plague, including labor shortages and difficulties, a dramatic increase in wages paid for virtually every service, and even a change in the types of crops sown. Less wheat and oats were planted, a response to severely diminished human and animal populations, and more vetches and barley were planted, a sign of diversification of diet and increasing demand for ale. Customary labor, that is, unpaid service to the lord, was so scarce that, despite the high wages, hired day laborers had to be brought in to work the *demesne*. At Cuxham, as in Cornwall, there was a great increase in the number of vacancies. All the homesteads on the north side of the village stream were abandoned, the result of a two-thirds drop in total population. The 1377 Poll Tax lists only 38 inhabitants over age 14, down from 100 in 1348. Further, this figure might well include postplague immigration, since all twelve of the Cuxham villein tenants were dead by December 1349. A final effect can be seen in the drop of manorial profits. From 1291 to 1349, they ranged from £25 to £65 per annum, and averaged over £40. In 1354–55, the only year in the decade following the Black Death for which they were recorded, profits tumbled to less than £11. For the rest of the fourteenth century they never exceeded £20 in any given year, and in the fifteenth century they were never more than £18.

Halesowen Manor, also in the West Midlands, was just southwest of Birmingham and about 60 miles northwest of Cuxham.[16] It was a large parish of about 10,000 acres, situated in broken, hilly terrain and consisting of a complex of twelve hamlets scattered around a central market village. It is hard to pinpoint preplague parish population, but the excellent records for 1348 suggest about 675 people, only 14 less than the peak population recorded the year before the great famine of 1315–16. The Black Death arrived in May 1349 and was most severe through the balance of that spring and summer. By the end of August, four special court sessions had been convened just to register plague deaths and, for the next six months, most activity at subsequent court sessions dealt with problems the Black Death had wrought. Among male tenants, the group for which the best data survive, mortality was almost 46% by the end of 1349. This figure was matched in other English villages. For example, on Alvechurch Manor in Worcestershire, also in the West Midlands, 44% of all tenants died; on Redgrave Manor in Suffolk, in eastern England, mortality exceeded 50%.

England has excellent ecclesiastical records from the plague years. In January 1349, the bishop of Bath and Wells wrote a letter to his parish priests summing up affairs in the diocese:

> The contagious pestilence of the present day, which is spreading far and wide, has left many parish churches without parson or priest to care for the parishioners. Since no priests can be found who are willing, whether out of zeal or devotion to exchange for a stipend, to take pastoral care of these aforesaid places, nor to visit the sick and administer to them the sacraments of the church, we understand that many people are dying without the sacrament of penance. [Therefore] . . . persuade all men, in particular, those who are now sick or should feel sick in the future, that, if they are on the point of death and cannot secure the services of a priest, then they should make confession to each other . . . or if no man is present, then even to a woman.[17]

Mortality among the clergy in England seems to have been even higher than that among the lay population. In Somerset, the diocese just south of Bath and Wells, admissions to new benefices rose over 500% from November 1348 to January 1349.[18] In Oxford, 43% of the beneficed clergy died. In Bicester, about 13 miles northeast of Oxford, 40% of the beneficed clergy perished, while in Wycombe, in Buckinghamshire, it was an astonishing 66%. There is also some information about Oxford students, most of whom took at least minor clerical orders. When the Black Death struck, probably early in 1349, most of the student body and faculty fled and the colleges shut down. Two Oxford dons, Richard Fitzralph and John Wyclif, gave inflated but nonetheless very telling statements on plague's effect. Fitzralph claimed that the university had 30,000 students enrolled in 1348, and only 6000 by 1350, while Wyclif said the figures were 60,000 and 3000, respectively. Both estimates are far too high, since Oxford had 1000 to 1500 students, but they give vivid evidence of the psychological impact of the Black Death. A modern study of mortality among the theology faculty puts the death toll at less than 10%, but this is probably because so many of the dons fled.[19] Mortality among theology students, despite flight, was close to 30%, and it was between 35% and 40% among the less mobile townsfolk of Oxford. As for those who fled, one can only assume that many of them ended up padding the tolls in the towns, villages, and hamlets in which they sought refuge.

The dioceses in Lincoln and York covered much of northern England.[20] A series of superb bishops' registers allows for a detailed, statistical study of clerical mortality during the Black Death. Plague began in Lincoln in February 1349 and was most severe in the following April and May. In nine deaneries in the archdeaconry of Huntingdon, 35% of the beneficed clergy died. By comparison, from 1347 to 1349, rather typical years, mortality was less than 8%, and, in 1350, when things had begun to return to normal, mortality was less than 2%. In York, 40% of the clerics died, perhaps a reflection of York's colder climate and attendant pulmonary complications and pneumonic plague. It must be remembered that the beneficed clergy were an elite, by and large better-educated and more mobile than the lay population. While there is no clear-cut evidence that education and mobility actually gave an advantage in avoiding plague, they certainly did not hurt. Hence, high plague mortality among the clergy suggests at least as high, and perhaps even higher, plague mortality among the general population.

Winchester, in southern England, had a population of between 5000 and 8000 people.[21] It had gradually declined from the eleventh century, but remained one of the richer towns in the kingdom. The Black Death came in late 1348. By January 1349, churchyard cemeteries were full, and new ground had to be consecrated. But even the new space proved to be inadequate and, to the dismay of the bishop, many townsfolk buried their dead in a common pit outside the town walls. Eventually, population decreased to such an extent—at least 50% below the preplague level—that part of High Street, the principal commercial thoroughfare in town, was consecrated as a burial ground. Winchester was left with a physical reminder of the Black Death. Its cathedral never received two planned towers, and a temporary west facade was shored up and made permanent when high postplague costs curtailed a more ambitious plant. By the time of the 1377 Poll Tax, the population of Winchester had dropped below 3000.

Records from the estates of the bishop of Winchester provide another example of the effects of the Black Death in rural England. Farnham Hundred was about 10 miles south of London. It contained ten separate villages and was in the middle of one of the richest and most populous parts of England. Reeves' accounts from the estates show a population of about 3500 in 1348. Heriots, the payment at the death of a tenant to the lord in the form of the best chattel of the holding, and *defetus per pestilentium*, or vacancy records, indicate that the Black Death came in autumn 1348 and persisted through summer 1349. Of 740 family heads, 185, or about a quarter, perished. Through the rest of 1349 another 101 died, making total plague mortality almost 39%.

The Black Death arrived in London by late September 1348. It came from the west and the south, via roads from Bristol and Southampton, and probably directly from ships sailing up the Thames to London Bridge. With about 50,000 inhabitants, London was by far England's largest town, the only one on a par with the great cities of the Continent.[22] Earlier in the fourteenth century, overcrowding had caused a breakdown in its sanitation and public health system. By 1348, things had improved a bit, mostly through royal initiative, but the Fleet, London's principal stream flowing into the Thames, was so choked with sludge, garbage, and human and animal waste that water barely flowed. Surely, the filth, poor sanitation, and overcrowding—50,000 people in one square mile—facilitated plague mortality associated with pneumonic strains.

The walls of fourteenth-century London were crumbling, but with the Thames running along its south side and the Tower covering its east side, the city could have been isolated from much of the surrounding countryside. This apparently was what London officials tried in vain to do. As in Orvieto, both existing public health laws and quarantine measures hastily adopted to combat the Black Death were designed to reduce industrial pollution, dispose of human waste, and keep out human visitors. The latter, in particular, was doomed to failure since the Black Death came in the fall, suggesting the bubonic strain brought by rats and fleas. It lingered throughout autumn 1348 and developed into pneumonic plague in the winter. From February 2 until April 2, over 2000 people were buried in a single cemetery, and the worst was yet to come. From June through September, civic reports listed an average of 290 deaths each day. Three of the seven major benefices of Westminster Abbey fell vacant in June and July. John Stratford, the archbishop of Canterbury, died in May 1348. His successor, John Offord, died in May 1349, before he was invested; and his successor, the famous Oxford don Thomas Bradwardine, died in August. Scheduled to convene in Westminster in autumn 1349, Parliament never assembled. The Black Death lingered until late spring 1350 and killed between 35% and 40% of London's population—a figure that some scholars would raise as high as 50%. Since London offered excellent opportunities for social and economic advancement, and was a magnet for immigrants, its population probably began to rise as soon as the plague had subsided. Still, the city would not have 50,000 people again until early in the sixteenth century.

Of all England's regions, the most severely afflicted was East Anglia.[23] Although in some ways it was a microcosm of the larger kingdom, in other ways it was very different. One of the principal differences was economic orientation, the result of its geographic situation. East Anglia was cut off from much of England on its west side by fens and marshes, and was surrounded on the north and east by The Wash and the North Sea. Generally poor roads added to the difficulties of overland travel. As a result, East Anglian merchants relied on sea transport for their principal trade commodities, wool and woolen cloth, and they forged close ties with their Continental counterparts. It was probably through ships plying the Netherlandish trade that the Black Death first came to East Anglia in spring 1349. It is likely that this was exacerbated by the later addition of plague strains from London and Essex. Hence, East Anglia received the Black Death from several sources and experienced extraordinary plague mortality.

From May through September 1349, a period of only five months, contemporaries claimed that a third of the local population died. In Cambridgeshire, three villages from which good evidence survives suffered losses of 53%, 57%, and 70%. At Cambridge University, the devastation was far worse than at Oxford; 16 of 40 resident scholars died between April and August. Sudbury, an important market and ecclesiastical center, had 107 market stalls in 1348. By 1361, there were only 62. Bishop Bateman of Norwich, whose diocese covered most of East Anglia, spent 1349 riding about the district, a step ahead of the plague. In June, he fled Great Yarmouth for Norwich; from there he went south to Ipswich, west to Bury St. Edmunds, southwest to Sudbury, and finally north to his rural estates in Hoxne.

The best evidence comes from East Anglia's principal towns, Norwich and Bury St. Edmunds. Norwich was the de facto capital of the region and had perhaps 10,000 to 12,000 inhabitants in 1348, making it the second or third largest town in England.[24] The Black Death came in January 1349, at some point probably took the pneumonic form, and lasted until spring 1350. About half the beneficed clergy and 40% to 45% of the secular population died. Four parish churches ceased to function because there were no priests to say mass and few parishioners to hear it. So great was the shortage of clergy that Bishop Bateman, when he stopped fleeing, founded Trinity Hall at Cambridge University for the purpose of training more priests.

Bury St. Edmunds was a prosperous town of over 7000 people.[25] It had a diversified commercial and industrial economy, and was built around one of the wealthiest abbeys in Europe. Abbey records show the effects of plague. On 19 January 1351 Pope Clement VI granted Abbot William of Bernham permission to ordain as priests ten monks under age 25, since the high mortality brought on by the Black Death had resulted in a shortage of monks. The report claimed that 40 monks or half the abbey's total, perished during the plague. According to the 1377 Poll Tax, the general population totaled about 4200, a decrease of over 40%. For the surrounding villages that depended on Bury's marketplaces, the toll was even higher, an astonishing 60%. It is likely that for all of East Anglia, plague mortality approached 50%, ranking it with Tuscany and parts of Scandinavia as the European areas most devastated by the Black Death. To reiterate, two conditions seemed to engender extraordinary plague mortality: entry into a region at many different junctures, which gave rise to multiple plague strains; and a particularly cold or damp climate, which gave rise to pulmonary complications that could degenerate into deadly pneumonic plague.

The Black Death was almost as severe in the rest of Britain. Knighton's comments about heavy mortality in Leicester and Leicestershire have already been noted. Mortality for the beneficed clergy was 48% in Newark, Nottinghamshire; 57% in Stow, Lincolnshire; 56% in Lincoln town; and 58% in Doncaster.[26] North of the River Tweed, the Scots delighted in the woes of their "auld" enemy. An army was raised in summer 1349 to take advantage of the English weakness, but it never marched. By July, the Black Death had reached Scotland. The best account is that of the chronicler John of Fordun:

In the year 1350 there was in the kingdom of Scotland so great a pestilence and plague among men . . . . as, from the beginning of the world even unto modern times, had never been heard of by men. . . . For to such a pitch did the plague wreak its cruel spite that nearly a third of mankind were thereby made to pay the debt of nature. Moreover, by

God's will, this evil led to a strange and unwonted kind of death, inso-much that the flesh of the sick was sometimes puffed out and swollen, and they dragged out their earthly life for barely two days.[27]

Good information survives on the effects of the Black Death in Wales. Plague patterns in Wales are important because parts of it are very mountainous, providing another environment in which the effects of the Black Death can be measured.[28] Plague came from the Severn Valley in March 1349. Within two weeks, rents began to fall; for example, in the lordship of Abergavenny, in south central Wales, rents dropped to a third of their preplague levels. In certain villages, it was even worse. At Wereyth, preplague rents totaled almost £14 every year. By 1350, they had fallen to less than £2. In Trefgaythel, preplague rents were about £4 per annum; by 1350, they were a mere six shillings "because of the mortality."

The Black Death reached northern Wales by spring 1349 and lasted into the autumn. Mills were rendered valueless "for lack of grinding, because there was no grain, and this because of the pesti-lence."[29] There were no revenues from courts, markets, or fairs. The lead mines of Holywell were closed because there were no miners left. The village of Ruthin is one of the few places in Wales where court rolls survive. Through April and May 1349, life went along in the usual fashion, and there were no records of deaths. But, in the second week of June, seven people died. By the end of the month, at least 77 people—more than a third of Ruthin's entire population—had per-ished.

The Black Death reached Ireland by early spring 1349, probably via ships from Bristol and Chester. It was at its worst in the ensuing summer, when it killed the archbishop of Dublin, probably the most important churchman in Ireland. Irish sources are scattered and it is not possible even to estimate total plague mortality. Nonetheless, one of the best impressions of the Black Death was left by the Irish Minorite, John Clyn of Kilkenny:

I, as if among the dead, waiting till death do come, have put into writing truthfully what I have heard and verified. And that the writing may not perish with the scribe and the work fail with the laborer, I add parch-ment to continue it, if by chance anyone may be left in the future, and any child of Adam may escape this pestilence and continue the work thus commenced.[30]

Another hand continued the chronicle: "Here it seems that the au-thor died."

The Black Death came to Germany across the Alps from Italy, and across the Rhine from the Netherlands and France.[31] Chroniclers are prone to exaggerate, but such exaggeration is useful in providing an impression of the experience of contemporaries. Many German observers claimed that but one out of ten townspeople survived. Others reported that 11,000 died in Münster, and 90,000 in Lübeck, the largest of the Hansa towns. Both are obvious overstatements; the figure for Lübeck is probably four times greater than the town's overall population. But the impressions remain vivid.

There are more accurate estimates.[32] In Bremen, along the River Wesel, the town council drew up a list of the dead; it had the names of 6966 people killed by plague, plus 1000 others for whom the cause of death was not specified. In a population of at most 12,000 to 15,000, this meant half to two-thirds plague morbidity. In Hamburg, the second most important Hansa port, 12 of 34 master bakers, 18 of 40 butchers, 27 of 50 town officials, and 16 of 21 town council members died. In Lübeck, the most important port, 11 of 30 councillors, 2 of 5 town clerks, and 27% of all property owners perished. Wismar, about 35 miles east of Lübeck along the Baltic coast, lost 42% of its town clerks. In Luneberg, a few miles southwest of Hamberg, mortality among clerks was 36% and, in Reval (now called Talinn), at the eastern end of the Baltic, it was 27%. In Magdeburg, along the Elbe, only three monks in the town's Franciscan friary were left alive. It is hard to be precise about morbidity in northern Germany since there is virtually no evidence from the rural hinterlands dominated by the Hansa. Nevertheless, urban data suggest a figure of 25% to 30%.

Other parts of Germany suffered less. In Alsace, Lorraine, and Bohemia, mortality was "only" about 10%. The Black Death also killed about 10% of the population of Nuremberg, perhaps the lowest death toll in any major city in the Western world.[33] An important cog in the trans-Alpine trade, Nuremberg had between 15,000 and 20,000 people in the early fourteenth century. It is difficult to isolate the environmental factors that contributed to Nuremberg's fortune, but the town was noteworthy for its steller system of public health. The streets were paved and regularly cleaned. Trash and garbage could not be dumped in the streets, but had to be bagged and carted away. Pigs were not allowed to roam the city, and personal cleanliness was held in high regard, an unusual attitude in late medieval Christendom. Bathing money was part of many workers' weekly wages, and municipal employees washed regularly. Nuremberg had 14 public baths and a rigorous system of inspection to make certain that they were clean and did not serve as brothels, as they did in many other towns. By the fifteenth century, it also had six municipal physicians, several private ones, and many more apothecaries, surgeons, and midwives—in all, a formidable medical community. These medical professionals calculated that dead bodies, poor ventilation, and the close quarters so common in medieval towns brought plague. This led to government regulations, in particular, the decision to bury cadavers outside the town walls. Priests were told to keep sermons short and disperse congregations early. The clothing and bedding of the dead were destroyed, while their rooms were fumigated. The air in such rooms was "purified," that is, filled with incense, since good smells were believed to help get rid of disease. Of course, smells have nothing to do with the spread of plague and, given the crucial role of fleas and rats in its dissemination, it would be a mistake to attribute too much to sanitation. The failure of Venice's excellent sanitation to stem the deadly effect of plague has been discussed. Still, Nuremberg's exceptional system of public health might have helped to prevent at least the deadly pneumonic strain.

Mortality in Germany, then, was lower than that in the Mediterranean Basin, France, the British Isles, and Scandinavia. Despite this, two distinct phenomena closely identified with the Black Death— flagellism and pogroms against the Jews—emerged in Germany. Flagellism was not peculiar to Germany or the mid-fourteenth century.[34] It appeared late in the tenth century at the approach of the millenium (the thousand-year anniversary of the birth of Christ), the time at which many people believed that Christ would return and signal the coming of the new age. Flagellism also cropped up in Iberia, France, and the Low Countries during the Black Death, and probably began in Hungary in 1348. But its most intensive manifestation was in the German Rhineland. There are two excellent descriptions. The first is by Jean de Venette:

> While the plague was still active and spreading from town to town, men in Germany, Flanders, Hainault and Lorraine uprose and began a new sect on their own authority. Stripped to the waist, they gathered in large groups and bands and marched in procession through the crossroads and squares of cities and good towns. They formed circles and beat upon their backs with weighted scourges, rejoicing as they did so in loud voices and singing hymns suitable to their rite and newly composed for it. Thus, for 33 days they marched through many towns doing penance

and affording a great spectacle to the wondering people. They flogged their shoulders and arms, scourged with iron points so zealously as to draw blood.[35]

The second is by Jean Froissart:

the penitents went about, coming first out of Germany. They were men who did public penance and scourged themselves with whips of hard knotted leather with little iron spikes. Some made themselves bleed very badly between the shoulder blades and some foolish women had cloths ready to catch the blood and smear it on their eyes, saying it was miraculous blood. While they were doing penance, they sang very mournful songs about nativity and the passion of Our Lord. The object of this penance was to put a stop to the mortality, for in that time . . . at least a third of all the people in the world died.[36]

The movement spread quickly across central Europe. Flagellants proceeded in bands of 50 to 300; they moved in long, snakelike processions, two by two, in groups of a few hundred. The band of flagellants walked with men in the front and women in the rear, chanting hymns. They dressed in cowled white robes emblazoned with red crosses on the front and back, and some carried crosses as well. Each band's leader was called "master" or "father." He heard confessions and, to the horror of the clergy, imposed penance and granted absolution. Each member swore absolute obedience to the master for the duration of the procession, usually 33⅓ days, which symbolized Christ's years on earth. The flagellants could not bathe, shave, or change their clothing; they could not sleep in soft beds and, although they were permitted to wash their hands once a day, it had to be done in a kneeling position, as a demonstration of humility. There were still more restrictions. Flagellants were forbidden to speak, even to one another, without the permission of the master. Sex was proscribed, and any male flagellant who said even a word to a woman had to kneel before the master and do penance. The master then beat him, chanting all the while, "Arise by the honor of pure martyrdom and henceforth guard yourself against sin."

When flagellants came into a town or village, they made their way to the most prominent local church. There they formed a circle. The men took off their outer clothing and put on loose skirts, which fell from their waists to their feet. Next, they began their standard rite. The penitent flagellants marched around in a circle, took a crucifix position, and were scourged. Sometimes the penitents would flagellate themselves, singing hymns, celebrating Christ's passion and the glories of the Virgin Mary. Generally, the master and two assistants stood in the center of the circle supervising the process and making sure that no one slackened in their enthusiasm. Three times during the rite all would fall down "as though struck by lightening" and lie prostrate, sobbing. The master would walk among them, asking God for mercy on all sinners. Then the flagellism would continue.

Each day, at least two complete rites were conducted. If a woman or priest entered the circle or interfered with the process in any way that had not been approved of in advance by the master, the entire flagellism had to start anew. If the master felt that the two "normal" flagellisms had not been done with sufficient zeal, a third might be ordered. Most seem to have been done quite thoroughly; occasionally the iron spikes from the scourges stuck in the flesh and had to be removed. Blood spurted out, and the flagellant's body would sometimes swell and become infected. Still, each flagellant was expected to perform every day.

Most people in the Rhineland were well-disposed to the flagellants and turned out in great numbers to watch them. Even neutral observers agreed that the effects of the processions were overwhelming. Spectators sobbed, cried, howled, and tore at their hair. The flagellants were seen as martyrs who atoned for the sins of the world and, hence, helped to avert further suffering from the plague and future visitations. Most villagers and townspeople regarded a visit by the flagellants as a privilege and an honor, and turned out to welcome them. Church bells were rung, usually without the sanction of the clergy, who saw their own positions being undermined, and local people opened their homes, fed the flagellants, and gave them candles for their rites. In some German towns, municipal councils even drew on public funds to help them. Much of this reflected the general dissatisfaction with the clergy, who were seen as corrupt and incapable of assuaging the pain of the Black Death in any way. By contrast, the flagellants appeared honest, novel, and pure of heart. They claimed to be able to ward off the devil, as well as plague, and people brought them their sick so that they might be cured. Their hair and nail clippings, as well as drops of blood, were regarded as sacred relics. Everyone pressed close to touch them, and there are even records of some villagers bringing corpses so that the flagellants could resurrect them.

Throughout most of 1348, the flagellants remained well-organized and straightforward in their goals, and were seldom challenged by lay or church authorities. But, in late 1348, some members in the movement began to get out of hand. There were reports of corruption, false promises, and sexual transgressions. Despite promises to the contrary, the Black Death still raged and, in much of Germany, was worse than ever. Perhaps more important, the whole movement turned into a "bloodthirsty pursuit of the millenium."[37] The Black Death was an ideal spur to millenarianism, and several natural disasters that occurred in 1348, including a number of earthquakes, seemed to provide physical evidence of the demise of the world. Many Germans believed that the Emperor Frederick Barbarossa would be resurrected, would drive out the clergy, and would force the rich to wed the poor. Christ would come, the Black Death would end, and a new age would dawn. Most flagellants became millenarians and began to add a challenge to established lay authorities in their bloody rites. Gradually, noble and bourgeoise elements left the movement; artisans and then peasants followed suit. By early 1349, the recessionals were dominated by marginal elements, including increasing numbers of vagabonds and criminals.

It was at this point that authorities began to lose sympathy and then to crack down on flagellants. In areas with strong central control, such as England, France, and the Iberian kingdoms, flagellism had always been restricted and was easy to eliminate. But in Germany, where central authority was weak and local lords usually went unchallenged, flagellism was most influential; accordingly, it was there that a crackdown was most necessary. The first step came at the beginning of 1349 when Pope Clement VI asked the faculty of the Sorbonne for its opinion on flagellism. Jean de Venette wrote that Clement

> acted on the advice of the masters of theology . . . who said that this new sect had been formed contrary to the will of God, to the rites of Holy Mother Church, and to the salvation of all their souls. That indeed this is true appeared shortly. For Pope Clement VI was fully informed concerning this fatuous new rite by the masters of Paris through emissaries recently sent to him, and, on grounds that it had been damnably formed, contrary to law, he forbade the flagellants under threat of anathema to practice in the future the public penance which they had so presumptuously undertaken. His prohibition was just, for the flagellants, supported by certain fatuous priests and monks, were enunciating doctrines and opinions which were beyond evil, erroneous and fallacious.[38]

On 20 October 1349 Clement issued a bull condemning flagellism and urging its repression. He sent letters to various civil authorities, including the kings of England, France, and Castile, and most of the German prelates and lay lords. By 1350, the movement had been almost completely eradicated.

One of the things the flagellants preached was anti-Semitism.[39] Persecution in southern Europe, particularly in Iberia, has already been discussed. In central Europe, especially in the Rhineland, it was much worse and had far-reaching effects. Again, Jean de Venette provides the most incisive commentary:

> the Jews were suddenly and violently charged with infecting the wells and water, and corrupting the air. The whole world rose up against them cruelly on this account. In Germany . . . they were massacred and slaughtered by Christians, and many thousands were burned everywhere, indiscriminately. The unshaken if fatuous constancy of the men and their wives [that is, the Jews] was remarkable. For mothers hurled their children first into the fire that they might not be baptized, and then leapt in after them to burn with their husbands and children. It is said that many bad Christians were burned who in a like manner put poison into wells. But in truth, such poisonings, granted that they actually were perpetrated, could not have caused so great a plague nor infected so many people.[40]

The medical faculties of the Universities of Paris and Montpellier, the two most distinguished medical schools in fourteenth century Europe, declared that all charges lodged against the Jews were false. Faculty members pointed out that Jews usually partook of the same water as their Christian neighbors, yet suffered approximately the same plague mortality. Pope Clement also refused to assign blame to the Jews. He even issued a bull ordering the clergy to protect local Jewish communities and pointed out that "most of the [flagellants] or their followers, beneath an appearance of piety, set their hands to cruel and impious works, shedding the blood of Jews, whom Christian piety accepts and sustains." In many places, authorities protected the Jews, but this was not so in Germany, where the absence of strong centralized authority allowed extremists to do as they wished.

In Switzerland, authorities promulgated a concerted and well-organized anti-Semitism that bordered on genocide. It began in September, 1348, when the town council of Zurich expelled all the town's Jews. Much worse was to follow. In Basle, also in Switzerland, all the city's Jews were gathered on an island in the Rhine and immolated. As an afterthought, the Basle town council passed a law prohibiting new Jewish settlement for 200 years. In Strasbourg, the town council tried to protect local Jews from the wrath of the citizenry. In response, the powerful merchants guild opposed and then deposed the old councillors, replacing them with new anti-Semitic members. In February 1349, the new council burned all 2000 Jews; as the ashes smouldered, many Strasbourgers sifted through the bones to try to find any valuables not melted in the fire. Through the spring and summer of 1349, the violence escalated. In some towns, the massacres took place as the Black Death raged; in others, the mere news of the plague's approach was enough to set off pogroms. In spring 1349 the large Jewish community at Frankfurt-am-Main was destroyed, followed by the annihilation of those in Mainz and Cologne. Mainz had more them 3000 Jews, probably the largest and wealthiest of all the northern European Jewish communities. They had a long and proud tradition. When attacked, the Jews rallied and fought back; in the first battle, over 200 Christians were killed. But the following day, drawing on nearby environs for reinforcements, the Christians stormed the ghetto again and overwhelmed the defenders. All the Jews were killed.

Similar pogroms took place in Brussels, Solothurn, Zofingen, Stuttgart, Landsberg, Burren, Memmingen, Lindau, Freiburg, Ulm, Gotha, Eisenach, Dresden, Worms, Baden, Erfurt, and Speyer. At Speyer, Jewish bodies were loaded into wine casks and floated down the Rhine. By the end of 1349, most of the violence had waned in the Rhineland, where the Black Death was beginning to wind down, but it picked up anew in the Hansa towns of the Baltic Coast and in much of eastern Europe, where the effects of plague were just beginning to be felt. The overall impact of what can only be called a holocaust was calamitous. By 1351, 60 major and 150 smaller Jewish communities had been extirpated, and over 350 separate massacres had taken place. The effect, an important legacy of the Black Death, was to encourage the eastward movement of the remaining northern European Jewry to Poland and Russia, where they remained for close to 600 years.

One of the reasons that surviving Jews moved east was the protection offered by King Casimir of Poland. It is difficult to discern why Casimir was so enthusiastic in his welcome of the Jews and so vigorous in his protection. He had a Jewish mistress and seemed well-disposed in general to Jews. Perhaps too he was anxious to have the commercial skills which some of the immigrants could offer, or was just a firm believer in justice. But his largesse might also have been due to the comparatively smaller role of the Black Death in eastern Europe. There is less information for the Slavic parts of the northern

world then for the other regions in Europe. Only some literary descriptions survive and there are virtually no sources which give reliable statistical information save those from a few Hansa towns in the
eastern Baltic. Indeed, it is not even clear when the Black Death arrived in the East. The Mark of Brandenburg, on the eastern fringe of
German-speaking Europe, did not get the plague until January 1351,
and it is unlikely that any part of Slavic Europe had it before spring
1350. Poland lost about a quarter of its population to the plague, a
very large figure to be sure, but one smaller than those in the southern and western parts of the continent. In some places, plague morbidity was lower still. Bohemia, for example, may have had a morbidity figure of "only" 15%, making it one of the least severely afflicted
regions in the Western world. Hungary was infected more severely
than its Slavic neighbors, losing perhaps a third of its people, but this
was clearly exceptional. Overall, the figures for mortality from the
Black Death in eastern Europe were probably between 20% and 25%.

Scholars have suggested a number of reasons for eastern Europe's
comparatively mild experience with the Black Death.[41] It was less
densely settled than parts of the West, but this was probably not crucial. Population density facilitated the spread of pneumonic plague
but it had minimal importance in the spread of bubonic, the most
common strain of the Black Death. Eastern Europe was surely as
densely settled as Scandinavia, Scotland, Wales, or Ireland, whose
climates were comparable but whose plague mortality was much
higher. The lower mortality in eastern Europe was almost certainly
the result of ecological and environmental differences. By spring 1351
the Black Death had been in Europe for two-and-a-half years. Given
the dynamism and mutability of *Y. pestis*, it is possible that the bacillus had begun to change to a slightly less virulent form. Bohemia is
ringed on all sides but the east by mountains, which had fewer potential rodent hosts for plague than did the plains. Some mountainous
regions such as North Wales had suffered severe plague morbidity in
1349–50, but if the plague bacillus had later weakened somewhat,
fewer rodent intermediaries might have made a difference. Hungary,
by contrast, is situated on a plain with abundant rodent species, and
this may account for its higher death toll. Whatever the exact reasons
for the differentials in plague mortality, most scientists rule out the
possibility of any innate or passive immunity to plague in Eastern Europe.

There is a final irony to the progress of the Black Death across
northern Europe. It was from the southern steppes of Russia that the

plague first worked its way into the West in 1346. But *Y. pestis* seems not to have crossed the steppes directly into the northern forest areas, controlled by the Duke of Muscovy and other Christian rulers. Rather, the Black Death made its way into Russia via the long, circuitous route from Caffa to Italy, through France, and across Germany, Poland and Lithuania; it probably did not reach Russia until late autumn 1350 or early 1351. Plague was not new to Russia in the mid-fourteenth century, for it was one of the few noncoastal parts of Europe in which periodic plague epidemics had struck between the first and second pandemics. For example, there had been an epidemic in the town of Smolensk, on the Dnieper River, which the chroniclers claimed had killed 32,000 people, a figure far too great since it was probably three times the entire town population.[42] An epidemic in Kiev in 1290 was said to have killed 7000 people in two weeks, still too inflated a figure to be taken at face value, but useful for the impression it must have made on contemporaries. As with the rest of eastern Europe, there are no reliable data for plague morbidity in Christian Russia. But chroniclers agreed that the Black Death was the worst epidemic on record, striking towns and countryside with equal fury, and allegedly destroying the entire populations of two towns. In Russia, as virtually everywhere else, the Black Death was the greatest demographic disaster ever.

# CHAPTER 5
# The Immediate Consequences

B Y THE END OF 1351 the Black Death had run its course. It is not possible to give a definitive figure for plague mortality, but all of Eurasia and that part of Africa north of the Sahara were afflicted; the most current estimates of morbidity in Europe range between 25% and 45%. Contemporaries were of a like mind.[1] In 1351, agents for Pope Clement VI calculated the number of dead in Christian Europe at 23,840,000. With a preplague population of about 75 million, Clement's figure accounts for mortality of 31%—a rate about midway between the 50% mortality estimated for East Anglia, Tuscany, and parts of Scandinavia, and the less-than-15% morbidity for Bohemia and Galicia. And it is unerringly close to Froissart's claim that "a third of the world died," a measurement probably drawn from St. John's figure of mortality from plague in the Book of Revelations, a favorite medieval source of information.

There were immediate and pronounced consequences from such enormous population losses, the first and most obvious of which were on human behavior and psychology. The shock was immense, and the mechanics and commonplaces of everyday life simply stopped, at least initially. When plague came, peasants no longer ploughed, merchants closed their shops, and some, if not all, churchmen stopped offering last rites. Many of the responses were described by Boccaccio in *The Decameron*:

Because of such happenings and many others of a like sort, various fears and superstitions arose among the survivors, almost all of which tended toward one end—to flee from the sick and whatever had belonged to them. In this way each man thought to be safeguarding his own health. Some among them were of the opinion that by living temperately and guarding against excesses of all kinds, they could do much toward avoiding the danger; and in forming a band they lived away from the rest of the world. Gathering in those houses where no one had been ill and living was more comfortable, they shut themselves in. They ate moderately of the best that could be had and drank excellent wines, avoiding all luxuriousness. With music and whatever other delights they could have, they lived together in this fashion, allowing no one to speak to them and avoiding news of either death or sickness from the outer world.

Others, arriving at a contrary conclusion, held that plenty of drinking and enjoyment, singing and free living and the gratification of the appetite in every possible way, letting the devil take the hindmost, was the best preventative of such a malady; and as far as they could, they suited the action to the word. Day and night they went from one tavern to another, drinking and carousing unrestrainedly. At the least inkling of something that suited them, they ran wild in other people's houses, and there was no one to prevent them, for everyone had abandoned all responsibility for his belongings as well as for himself, considering his days numbered. Consequently, most of the houses had become common property and strangers would make use of them at will whenever they came upon them even as the rightful owners might have done. Following this uncharitable way of thinking, they did their best to run away from the infected.

Meanwhile, in the midst of the affliction and misery that had befallen the city, even the reverend authority of divine and human law had almost crumbled and fallen into decay, for its ministers and executors, like other men, had either died or sickened, or had been left so entirely without assistants that they were unable to attend to their duties. As a result, everyone had leave to do as he saw fit.

Many others followed a middle course, neither restricting themselves in their diet, like the first, nor giving themselves free rein in lewdness or debauchery like the second, but using everything in sufficience, according to their appetites. They did not shut themselves in, but went about, some carrying flowers in their hands, some fragrant herbs, and others divers kind of species which they frequently smelled, thinking it good to comfort the brain with such odors, especially since the air was oppressive and full of the stench of corruption, sickness, and medicines.

Still others, of a pitiless though perhaps more prudent frame of mind, maintained that no remedy against plagues was better than to leave them miles behind. Men and women without numbers, encouraged by this way of thinking and caring for nobody but themselves, abandoned the city [Florence], their houses and estates, their own flesh and blood even, and their effects, in search of a country place—it made no difference whether it were their own or their neighbor's. It was as if [they believed that] God's wrath in seeking to punish the inequity of men by means of plague could not find them out wherever they were, but limited itself to doom only those who happened to be found within the walls of the city. They reasoned as though its last hour had struck, and therefore no one ought to be there.

Although the members of the different factions did not all perish, neither did they all escape. On the contrary, many in each group sickened everywhere, and since they themselves had set the example to those who had been spared, they were abandoned to their lot altogether.[2]

Of all these reactions, the Epicurean response, perhaps because of a macabre attraction for the dissolute, seems to stand out. Indeed, the pursuit of pleasure is the theme of *The Decameron*. The setting of the stories is fourteenth-century Florence; ten young people fleeing from the Black Death take turns telling tales, most of them bawdy and irreverent, to amuse themselves. Through all of plague's devastation, the revelers accept and observe the basic tenets and trappings of Christianity, and in many ways follow the rules of good Christian conduct. They are of the upper classes and do not question the hierarchy and order of temporal life. They do not seem to doubt the ultimate truth of the Christian faith and the dogmas of the church. Yet, the accepted Christian trifunctional scheme has changed somewhat. While none of the characters question God's omnipotence, many believe that their future is determined, not by their own actions—one of the tenets of the Roman Church—but by fate, luck, and chance. Good fortune was keenly sought as a sign of divine blessing. Bocaccio's characters valued qualities far different from those esteemed by most of their predecessors. Piety, martial or mechanical skills, scholarly intelligence were not emulated; rather, wit and cleverness were venerated as essential to success. The cuckold, not the cheat, the liar, or the coward, was reviled; the seducer, not the pious schoolman or brave knight, was admired. Rewards and triumph went to the active, to those who helped themselves. The Black Death, at least among a substantial portion of the most vigorous members of society, brought not so much a stoic acceptance of pain and suffering as it did a desire for an active, temporal life.

The Decameron is not the only example of popular literature reflecting the new values. Within a generation, Geoffrey Chaucer's Canterbury Tales, which expressed a perspective on life and values similar to that of The Decameron, had as much impact on the English reading public as Boccaccio's tales had had in Italy.[3] The new psychology was persistent. A century later, in France, the works of François Villon embodied the same spirit and espoused the same values.[4] Villon was a common criminal and vagrant, yet he was a brilliant poet; he used the traditional preplague forms and motifs, but his tone and attitudes were those of the new era. He was bitter and savage in his criticism, and he could be devastatingly sarcastic. Villon was superstitious, fascinated with death, afraid of the pains of hell, but hellbent on enjoying life and experiencing as much as he possibly could. It would be an oversimplification to explain late medieval hedonism solely in terms of the Black Death and the second pandemic, but to plague must go a substantial portion of the responsibility.

Epicureanism seems to have been especially strong among the most influential members of society, particularly the aristocracy and the intelligentsia, and its persistence made for a profound and prolonged moral crisis. Some scholars believe that such a crisis was well underway in 1347 and may have begun with the subsistence economy of the mid-thirteenth century; but all believe that the Black Death, as in so many other concurrent crises, made this one far more pronounced than it had been. Much of the old corporate cooperation and camaraderie were swept away, replaced in many cases by a strong strain of individualism. In some places, this would develop in constructive ways: witness the humanism of late-fourteenth- and fifteenth-century Italy, or the pietism and mysticism of the Rhineland and the Netherlands at about the same time. But, in the decade after the Black Death, individualism generally was directed towards self-aggrandizement and the pursuit of leisure and pleasure. The collective institutions and the old communality—both rural and urban—so characteristic of the twelfth and thirteenth centuries, were shattered. Old social, religious, and even familial bonds were relaxed. Restoring these bonds was the challenge that faced the people of the late fourteenth and fifteenth centuries.

Among the psychological changes brought by plague was a new sense of time, especially among the bourgeoisie.[5] Traditionally, merchants and churchmen had had a different sense of the temporal. To the churchman, time was infinite, the domain of God. To the merchant, time was finite, a function of distance—for example, the number of days it would take for a ship to sail from Genoa to Bruges—or of changing seasons—for example, the number of days before the Alpine passes would become impassable. Time was money, an attitude that caused considerable consternation among the clergy and prompted theologians to condemn the practice of usury. They argued that usury and all commercial ventures were suspect because they assumed control over the future, a mortgage of time which was reserved for God.

The Black Death changed this; it brought a sense of urgency, especially in urban areas. The work day was extended and night work became common as merchants sought greater profits and workers, higher wages. For example, in Ghent and several other Flemish towns, as the Black Death diminished in late 1349, textile laborers demanded that they be allowed to determine their hours. Clocks and the rhythmic chimes of bells became more important than ever. In 1355, the royal governor of Artois authorized the people of Aire-sur-la-Lys to build a belfry whose bells would sound the hours for textile workers and merchants. Conditions were similar throughout the urban areas of Europe. In Italy, a Florentine humanist thought every library should have a clock. One of the most cogent comments about time was made by the humanist Leon Battista Alberti in his dialogue on family life:

> GIANOZZO: There are three things which man may say properly belong to him; his fortune, his body, . . .
> LIONARDO: And what may the third be?
> GIANOZZO: Ah! A very precious thing indeed! Even these hands and these eyes are not so much my own.
> LIONARDO: Incredible! What is it?
> GIANOZZO: Time, my dear Lionardo.[6]

By the end of the century, "merchant's time," rather than "the traditional conception of time in Christian theology," became the rule.[7]

Such psychological changes had a pronounced effect on late medieval religion. The depth of both Christian and Muslim religious feeling in the West was one of the foundations of society. Followers of both faiths counted the hereafter more important than life on earth and, given the difficulties and brevity of earthly existence, salvation became paramount. The clergy claimed to be the conduit to salvation and thus held a special position. The Black Death—that sudden, precipitous, painful, and omnipresent killer—intensified the medieval preoccupation with death, judgment, heaven, and hell. Death seemed nearer, and salvation more important, than ever, and the clergy were put to a real test. If, in one fashion or another, they acted responsibly and were able to relieve the anxiety—and, in some cases, hysteria—of their flocks, their position would be strengthened. If not, the faithful would follow another path to heaven.

Generally speaking, both Islamic and Christian holy men failed the test. Muslim theologians, following long-standing doctrine, offered their followers three tenets.[8] First, the faithful should not flee the Black Death, but rather, should stay and accept Allah's will. Second, death by plague was martyrdom, a mercy for the true believer and a punishment for the infidel. Third, in a direct rebuttal of over a thousand years of accepted wisdom, the theologians denied the general medical opinion that plague was a contagious infection transmitted from person to person. They stated that it was foolish to flee from the Black Death because it was God, not men, who disseminated the disease. And there was another reason to reject the advice of doctors; God was good, and contagion was simply incompatible with His very being.

A few theologians broke with this general perspective and took a less benevolent view of the Black Death. They believed that the plague was a punishment visited on man by God because they had strayed from the straight and narrow path of true belief. This theory was taken from Old Testament exegesis, drawing heavily on examples such as God's punishment of the pharoahs. Most Islamic clerics told their followers that God was merciful toward the true believer, and that, like death in battle, plague was a mercy in its own right, insuring that the victim would gain salvation.

> The martyrs and those who died in their beds argue with Our Lord about those who were killed by plague. The martyrs say, our brothers died as we died. The deceased, on their beds, say, our brothers died on their beds as we died. Our Lord said: "Consider their wounds, which resemble the wounds of the slaughtered, and they are among us." And behold, their wounds had been similar, so they joined the martyrs.[9]

For many of the Islamic faithful, such injunctions must have been all the comfort necessary. But, for others, they were not. The Islamic medical community offered extensive advice, despite condemnation and ridicule by the mullahs and, judging from the popularity of medical works, many Muslims must not have been content with a fatalistic acceptance of God's judgment. Perhaps even more significant as a barometer of popular dissatisfaction with the Islamic clergy—after all, only a small, literate elite was able to afford and read medical treatises—was the spread among the lower classes of a kind of magic designed to ward off plague, or cure those who had already contracted it. The magic consisted mostly of special prayers using numbers or incantations, and talismans and amulets, particularly those made from gold or silver. Hex signs were popular, too, especially when carved in sapphires or ivory. All were considered to be prophylaxes and, as such, were uniformly condemned by the clergy, who claimed that such symbols were an insult to God. But their popularity persisted, another affront and challenge to the authority of the mullahs.

The damage inflicted on the Christian clergy was far more substantial.[10] In part, this was because the Christian institutional, hierarchical bureaucracy was more extensive than that of Islam; in part, it was because the institutional Christian Church had begun to decline at least two generations before the Black Death, at the time of the pontificate of Boniface VIII (1294–1303). The papacy became increasingly secular, preoccupied with fiscal gain and political advantages, and pretentious in its claims to universal power. It lost a series of battles with secular heads of state. In 1309, the seat of the papacy was moved from Rome to Avignon—a city under the legal auspices of the German emperor, but geographically and culturally French. Prior to this move, the bishop of Rome had been pope precisely because he was heir to St. Peter and the keys to the kingdom. In Avignon he had no such ties and was perceived by many Christians, figures of authority and common folk alike, as a creature of the king of France. In general, the papacy had grown ever more temporal from the early thirteenth century. It was increasingly concerned with fiscal gain and secular political advantages, and, at the very least, it gave the appearance of neglect in spiritual things. This aspect of papal decline predated the Black Death and was largely extraneous to the effects of depopulation. Further, most historians believe that, as a group, the Avignonese popes were of high caliber. Clement VI, for example, acted coolly and responsibly during the Black Death, waiting himself until the last minute to flee from the plague, and then doing so only on the advice of his doctor. However, when the Black Death brought the crisis of the imperial Christian Church to a head and provided it with as stiff a challenge as it had had since its earliest days, both its spiritual and educational offices were found wanting. Christians did not abandon their faith, but many of them sought alternative paths to spiritual peace and salvation.

The principal failure of the Christian Church was in not providing the necessary solace or support during the crisis. This failure took two forms. First, except for parts of northern Italy, the church supervised the education and licensing of physicians, almost all of whom were clerics. There were surgeons, apothecaries, and nonprofessional practitioners whose training and practice lay outside church jurisdiction, but they had little to do with the theories and tractates about infectious disease that flooded Europe after 1347. In the long run, virtually all medical advice proved to be useless. As the church would have taken credit had its physicians been able to assuage the pain of plague, so it was to shoulder much of the blame when they failed.

Second and more important, the church did not provide adequate spiritual comfort. Many parish priests fled, leaving no one to offer services, deliver last rites, and comfort the sick. Flight might have been intellectually explicable, but it was morally inexcusable. In the English dioceses of York and Lincoln, close to 20% of the parish priests in certain deaneries fled the Black Death.[11] Two popular north country verses expressed this discontent:

> You pope-holy priests, full of presumption
> With your wide furred hoods void of discretion
> Unto your own preaching of contrary condition
> Which causes the people to have less devotion.[12]
>
> [He] who reserves a benefice for richness and ease
> Should have his living in sickness
> Rather than serve God as he pleases
> He serves it or misses.[13]

In *Piers Ploughman,* William Langland wrote:

> So we need an antidote strong enough to reform these prelates who should pray for peace but are hindered by their possessions. Then take their land from them, you nobles, and let them live on their tithes! For surely, if property is a deadly poison that corrupts them, it would be good for Holy Church's sake to relieve them of it, and purge them of this poison before it grows more dangerous. . . .
>
> Every bishop who carries a crozier is thereby bound to travel through his diocese and show himself to his people. And he must teach them to believe in the Three Persons of the Godhead, and feed them with spiritual food and provide for the poor. For it is men like you bishops that

Isiah and Hosea are referring when they say that no one should be ruler unless he has both bodily and spiritual food to give to the needy: "In my house is neither bread nor clothing; make me not a ruler of the people."[14]

Given all these circumstances, it is not surprising that many Christians continued to follow their own path to salvation even after the plague had subsided and their priests had returned.

One direction the faithful took was a strong reinforcement of the traditional idea that works, as well as faith, would help in attaining salvation. To gain relief from the suffering of plague and to attain salvation were like climbing a ladder; the good Christian moved from rung to rung. It was a painful process that was fraught with temptation, and the seeker was always in danger of slipping. But the faithful could be boosted up as well, aided by various acts of benevolence. One of the most popular of these good works was pious charity, which blossomed after the Black Death and remained popular until the early sixteenth century.[15] In England, about a quarter of all testators' estates, land and movables, went to good works. Hospitals benefited. In France, donations to existing institutions rose about 50% from 1300 to 1350; in England, 70 new foundations were laid between 1350 and 1390. Family chapels were another favorite bequest and, in the fourteenth and fifteenth centuries, there was a marked rise in the number of private masses and chantry priests. This, in turn, was a reflection of the increased popularity of the concept of purgatory, that halfway house where those who would eventually be saved were made to serve time in hell-like conditions in order to purge themselves of sin before they were permitted to enter heaven. Time in purgatory could be shortened by private masses or any number of good works.[16] This charity system of private worship played a large role in late medieval religion and represented a considerable blow to monopoly over church services held by the traditional Christian hierarchy.

Charity was important for another reason. In the dislocation that followed the Black Death, many ecclesiastical institutions could not make ends meet. In a 1360 letter to the pope, an English bishop described the acute cash shortage in many houses and estates in the wake of the plague:

> Many of the houses, barns, and buildings erected by the earl have been in great measure ruined by the frequent overflowing of the Thames and by storms; that on account of diverse pestilence in times past they have suffered from a lack of tenants and cultivators and a murrain among

their cattle, sheep and horses; that on account of the numerous bequests [from] both rich and poor, the priory being held by the highways and near [a castle] and of other causes beyond their control, their revenues are greatly reduced.[17]

In some case, pious charity was the only income religious houses had for years after the Black Death. Because of the reduction of population by a third or more, the total sums received might well have been down, and there were some projects—the cathedrals at Siena and Winchester, for example—that could not be finished even with new infusions of charitable bequests. However, the tangible display of good works exerted a strong pull and, at least in England and Italy, per capita bequests were much higher in the 1350s than they had been earlier in the fourteenth century. In London, before 1348 about 5% of all testators registering their wills in the Hustings Court provided funds for hospitals. Between 1350 and 1360, this tripled, and the amount of the average bequest increased by almost 40%. Charity, especially to hospitals, was an opportunity for a twofold response to the Black Death. It provided for an institution that helped plague victims and it was the kind of good work that counted toward salvation, but could be done directly, without clerical involvement.

Another popular "good work" was pilgrimage to a religious shrine.[18] Here, too, the faithful were performing a religious act directly, using a saint rather than a priest to intercede in their behalf. Pilgrimage could be undertaken to a place of the first rank, such as Rome, Jerusalem, or St. James Compostela in Galicia, or to one of innumerable local shrines that contained relics or anything else of religious importance. All sorts of people—"base-born men and nobles alike"—went, some singly and others in groups that often were sponsored by another late medieval religious phenomenon, the confraternities. These were religious groups dedicated to good works, among other things. Pilgrimage was not an easy undertaking. Given the deplorable condition of late medieval roads and the threat of brigands and pirates, it was a very dangerous task. As such, it was considered one of the most important good works and counted a great deal toward salvation. Wills from England and Italy showed a marked upsurge in the number of bequests for pilgrims and pilgrimages. In the 1350s and 1360s, there was a glut of travel guidebooks—some sober and earnest, others fabricated and sensational—which describe the process of pilgrimage and tell the pilgrim where to stop to eat and spend the night, and even the proper way to venerate particular saints. Sir John Mandeville's *Travels*, written in 1357, was the most popular of these guides. Over 300 manuscript copies made between 1357 and 1500 have survived to the present day. By 1500, it had been translated from the original French into Latin, English, High and Low German, Danish, Czech, Italian, Spanish, and Irish Gaelic.[19] By the late fourteenth century, many municipalities were making official arrangements and accommodations for tourists. There was even something offered by authorities in Venice which might well be called a "package tour," complete with safe conduct passes and arranged housing. In many ways, pilgrimage represents all the changes, good and bad, which the Black Death brought to religion—the passion to do good deeds, the strong conviction that this would help to attain salvation, and the decision to take part of one's fate in one's own hands, combined with the frivolity and lightheartedness so evident in Chaucer's brightest pilgrim, the Wife of Bath.

Plague also brought more sudden changes to late medieval Christianity. A cult of new saints arose.[20] They were generally poor men recognized by the church hierarchy with great reluctance. The best example is St. Roch. Before the Black Death, the patron saint to call upon in case of plague was St. Sebastian. Shot to death in the third century by order of Emperor Diocletian, Sebastian was first connected with the disease when the arrows that riddled his body were alleged to be analogous to "darts of plague." In the sixth century, during the first plague pandemic, Sebastian acquired a prominent position in Christianity's pantheon of saints. Roch was a resident of Montpellier. During the successive epidemics of the late fourteenth century, he devoted his life to nursing poor victims. Humble and poor himself, seen by many as working outside the auspices of the hierarchical church, Roch was beatified and then invoked with Sebastian in times of plague.

The idealized selfless image of the Christian clergy suffered during and after the Black Death.[21] Many people believed, often unjustly, that the clergy were greedy, self-centered, and filled with a sense of their own importance. It must be stressed, however, that while confidence in the institutional church waned, faith in Christianity itself did not; rather, the imminence of death, brought closer than ever by plague, made the need for salvation more pressing. One consequence was the spread of mysticism and lay piety. Mystics, the most famous of whom were Meister Eckhart, John Ruysbroek, John Tauler, and Henry Suso, believed that God lived in every individual and that His presence was felt in proportion to one's ability to suppress intrinsic material and sensual inclinations and subject one's will to that of God. Obedience, self-denial, and prayer were crucial. Lay piety expressed itself in organizations such as the Brethren of Common Life, formed in the Netherlands in the late fourteenth century. Aside from their profound sincerity, the most striking characteristic of mysticism and lay piety was the lack of need for a formal clergy to lead the way to paradise. Many postplague Christians felt they could communicate directly with God.

It is tempting to tie the decline of the institutional church to the Protestant Reformation of the sixteenth century, as many historians of the nineteenth and twentieth centuries have done.[22] Such a direct connection, spanning close to 200 years, is a bit presumptuous. The Christian Church had many problems before the advent of the second plague pandemic. It was a huge, unwieldy, and vastly complicated institution, and, even at its nadir, there was much about it that was good. But the Black Death made an issue of the proper function of the clergy. It made people ever more conscious of the omnipotence of God and the inevitability of Judgment Day. A poorly behaved clergy made many people wonder about alternative means of salvation. Perhaps the best link between the Black Death, the decline of Holy Mother Church, and the Protestant Reformation of the sixteenth century was the growing role of indulgences in the fourteenth and fifteenth centuries. Attuned to the anxieties of their flock, churchmen redoubled the emphasis on good works. From the 1350s, apparently on papal orders, new stress was put on indulgences, or grants of time off from purgatory bestowed by the church, which drew on what it termed a "treasury of merits," or good deeds accumulated from Christ, the patristic fathers, and saints. Indulgences were not given freely, but usually in anticipation of a gift of money; always mindful of turning a profit, church leaders began to sell them in increasing numbers to a richer public. While indulgences were not the only thing that spurred Martin Luther, their use and sale inspired him to nail up his 95 Theses.

There were other changes in attitude brought by the Black Death. As stressed earlier, life took on more violent and emotional overtones.[23] Death was closer and life seemed even more tenuous than it had before the plague. As a result, virtually all of life's experiences, good and bad, were felt with more intensity and passion. Emotion, quick reaction, and spontaneity played key roles. A case in point was a homicide in the Benedictine Abbey of St. Edmunds, in England, in the 1360s.[24] Three monks, John de Norton, John de Grafton, and William Blundeston, quarreled among themselves. That night, as most of the monks slept, Grafton crept through the abbey dormitory and stabbed Norton to death. When the other monks awakened and discovered the body, they panicked. Instead of informing civil or even church authorities, they decided to bury the corpse without calling in the coroner, a violation of the law. But the body was poorly hidden in a shallow grave in the church cemetery, and Abbot John de Brinkeley soon discovered it. Fearing an adverse reaction from local townspeople, with whom the monks were involved in a series of disputes, Brinkeley began his own investigation of the incident. Both Grafton and Blundeston were discovered and imprisoned, the latter having acted as an accessory in the crime. But the imprisonment proved to be a sham. Within a year, both men were pardoned by King Edward III without ever having been brought to trial, based on the royal assumption that the crime was committed in "hot blood," and was thus explicable. The implication of the pardon is that such violence occurred with some regularity.

Much of the cruelty and violence, as well as the piety and joy, of the late fourteenth and fifteenth centuries can be understood only by keeping in mind the new omnipresence of plague and the possibility of sudden, painful death. In the High Middle Ages, an era of expansion and fruition, literature and art expressed a buoyant optimism. After the Black Death, this was replaced by a pervasive pessimism. In addition to the carefree tone of some of the works of Boccaccio, Chaucer, and Villon, a sense of melancholy entered the literature. A good example is the poetry of Eustace Deschamps:

> Happy is he who has no children, for babies mean nothing but crying and stench; they give only trouble and anxiety; they have to be clothed, shod and fed; they are always in danger of falling and hurting themselves; they contract some illness and die. When they grow up, they may go bad and be put in prison. Nothing but cares and sorrows; no happiness compensates us for our anxiety, for the trouble and expense of their education. The poet has no word.[25]

People were fascinated by death.[26] Preachers advised people to go to sleep every night as if it were their last and as if their beds were their tombs. The frailty of human life and the brevity of earthly glory were stressed. Ascetic mediation was best because everyone ended up as dust and worms. Putrefaction was evidence of sin; only saints' bodies did not decompose. In the Early and High Middle Ages, people accepted the inevitability of death and prepared for it, but they were rarely preoccupied with it. Burials were often in common graves, and elaborate tombs were rather rare. The Black Death changed all this. Funerals became festivals, the greatest event of a lifetime. Whenever possible, individual graves were dug so that "each body could have an eternal resting place." Funerary monuments were comparatively scarce before the Black Death, even among the nobility. In England, when they were used, funereal brasses usually showed a lord and his lady bedecked in all their finery. After the plague, funerary monuments and death masks became common, and their themes changed.[27] Many brasses showed shrouded, macabre corpses or skeletons with snakes and serpents surrounding and protruding from their bones; on their faces were grisly, toothy smiles. Tombs in the Netherlands showed hideous images of naked corpses with tightly clenched hands, rigid feet, gaping mouths, and bowels filled with worms. In Germany, woodcuts called "The Art of Dying" appeared. They were linked panels showing the drama of death. Death was painful—in contrast to the peaceful slumber of years past—and people were to tremble at its coming. All this marked the appearance of the *ars moriendi*, the cadaver and death as a major motif in art and literature.

Perhaps the best examples of this preoccupation with the motifs of death and despair were in the fine arts.[28] Tuscany was Europe's financial center. Its old ruling bourgeoisie had been imbued with a sense of independent inquiry in the arts, a natural outgrowth of the competitive economic system it had mastered. The members of this class were self-confident, wealthy, and, in some cases, keen patrons. The art they wanted was "new" (e.g., that of Giotto and Cimabue), uplifting, optimistic, and, above all, individualistic. This bourgeois elite believed that it could enjoy temporal life without endangering its chances for salvation.

The Black Death changed this. Tuscany was devastated, losing half its population. Further, there was considerable redistribution of the population that remained. Peasants fled from the countryside, which was beset by a drop in food prices, a temporary breakdown of local authority, and omnipresent criminal bands and mercenaries, for the economic opportunity and comparative stability of large urban centers such as Florence and Siena. Many of the new urban dwellers made their fortunes and, following the examples of the old elite, became patrons of the arts. But, even for them and the better-established patrons, the old optimism had been shaken, and it was diminished further with each new epidemic. Tastes were changing. The new patrons were more conservative and had doubts about their materialism, their goals, and sometimes even their success, in view of the new preoccupation with salvation. They were becoming increasingly guilty and introspective.

There were changes in the artists as well as the patrons.[29] The Black Death killed many individual artists and, in some cases, entire schools or guilds of painters, sculptors, and masons who had been inspired by similar themes and hence worked together. This not only eliminated some of Europe's greatest masters, but it made it very difficult to train and develop new talent. A good example comes from England, where thirteenth-century guilds of artists produced superb miniatures. The Black Death killed off such a great number of these artists that no new masters appeared, and the English could not maintain their standards in this special art form.

The effects of new patrons and artists were visible immediately. Preplague Tuscan art was warm and sympathetic. It stressed personal relationships and, when it dealt with religious themes, emphasized the humility of Jesus, the Virgin Mary, and the saints. Postplague art, like postplague thought and funerary monuments, was obsessed with the most gruesome aspects of pain, and with the image of death. This new image can be seen in many forms, one of the best examples being Francesco Triani's great fresco, "The Triumph of Death," in the Camposanto in Pisa, painted around 1350. Death is shown, not as an airy skeleton, as was usually the case before the Black Death, but rather, as a horrible old woman cloaked in black, with wild, snakelike hair, bulging eyes, clawed feet with talons, and a scythe to collect her victims, whom she feeds to snakes and toads. Death was like a bird of prey, sweeping down on its victims. A similar scene by Orcagni at St. Croce, Florence, shows several corpses plus a few miserable creatures, half alive, vainly imploring Death to take them and end their suffering.

Portraiture also reflected the loss of optimism. Contemporary artists claimed that "art has grown and continues to grow worse day by day." While many people in most ages bemoan contemporary art, even the masters of the postplague period agreed with the lament. It was not a decline in skills or execution, however, but the evolution of a new style. The rendering of religious themes, the principal form of artistic exposition in the fourteenth century both before and after the Black Death, shows this. Perhaps the most impressive Florentine painting of the postplague era is Orcagni's altarpiece in the Strozzi Chapel, Santa Maria Novella, done from 1354 to 1357. Parts of it show the Virgin Mary and baby Jesus. Their majesty and authority are emphasized, as in preplague paintings, but there is also distance and sternness between mother and child. In some scenes, the Madonna is depicted as a corpse consumed by snakes and toads, a motif unprecedented in Tuscan art history. Christ is swaddled and bound, and the characters seem repressed and unsympathetic, quite unlike the New Testament portrayals so common before the plague.

Another change was the place of prominence given to the Trinity. There were comparatively few Trinity scenes painted in the thirteenth and fourteenth centuries, and those which were done were usually placed against lavish, highly individualistic backgrounds, varying with the artist or patron. After the Black Death, such artistic distinctions were replaced by impersonal, uniform figures, the divine counterparts of the betrodden *Ciompi* workers who would rise in revolt against the oligarchs of Florence in 1378. There was a new emphasis on the supernatural, a change also evident in paintings of the Resurrection. Artists seemed to be motivated by the desire to endow Christ with more decisive, hierarchical superiority, and they stressed His miraculous and supernatural character.

In essence, the gay, light, individualistic themes begun in the thirteenth century by Giotto and his followers were replaced by the new conservatism and moralizing tone brought about by the Black Death. People worried about how material gains would affect their chances for salvation. In his "St. John the Evangelist," Del Biondo shows John trampling Avarice, Pride, and Vainglory, a message straightforward and obvious in its meaning. Plague and death were the new, popular themes for bourgeois, and even some aristocratic, patrons of art.

There were also changes in Northern art. The disasters of the fourteenth century did not cause a lessening of creativity, but rather, a change in direction. The old patrons of the preplague era were generally great churchmen, especially bishops and abbots. The new patrons, mostly members of the bourgeoisie, were less learned and sophisticated, and had more somber tastes. The art they sponsored no longer showed the harmony between man, reason, and nature—the forms of God placed in their proper, natural hierarchy and popularized in the twelfth and thirteenth centuries. Rather, the new art was narrative: it told stories, sometimes of God, but more frequently of secular things. Themes of earthly escapism were common. For better or worse, as bourgeois patrons became more important, artists were no longer auxiliaries of priests.

As in the fine arts, the Black Death brought changes in literary styles and ideas, most of which were somber.[30] A good example is the later works of Boccaccio. *The Decameron*, his literary masterpiece, was written in the vernacular and was enormously popular. Its cynicism reflected a common perception during and immediately after the Black Death. But his attitudes soon changed. While *The Decameron* is guilt-free, Boccaccio's later works show a more sober side. *The Corbaccio*, written in 1354–55, is gloomy, pessimistic, truculent, and ascetic, attitudes that hardened even more as Boccaccio grew older and began to think about his own salvation. In a 1373 letter, he condemned his earlier masterpiece:

> I am certainly not pleased that you have allowed the illustrious women in your house to read my trifles; indeed, I beg you to give me your word that you will not permit it. You know how much in them is less than decent and opposed to modesty, how much stimulation to wanton lust, how many things that drive to lust even those most fortified against it. . . . My feminine readers will judge me a filthy pimp and an incestuous old man, shameless, foul-mouthed and malignant, eager to spread tales of the dissolution of others.[31]

Boccaccio turned against love, passion, and even women; indeed, he became something of a misogynist. Perhaps he was affected by his idol and master, Petrarch. Petrarch lost his beloved Laura and four other intimates to the plague, resigned himself to religion, and turned to introspection. In a letter to Boccaccio, probably from 1363, Petrarch wrote: "Of all my friends, only you remain."

Plague brought similar changes to the literature of northern Europe. The brevity of life, the folly of exuberance, and the painful horror of death by plague were emphasized along with the more hedonistic themes of Chaucer. The purveyors of gloom and doom stressed that death did have at least one thing to recommend it—it brought equality to all the social orders. Exegesis became popular, but commentators offered little solace from the Bible. The Old Testament was drawn on more heavily than before, and it was stressed that God afflicted his chosen people as well as his enemies with plague. The most heavily quoted book from the New Testament was Revelations, where plague was described as God's punishment for the sins of man; in all, man no longer seemed to be God's favorite creature. Generally, the works of Chaucer and Villon notwithstanding, themes of youth, exuberance, happiness, and joy were played down. The dance of death became a common literary motif. Mystery plays with religious themes also became common, and they usually told of human decay and the torments of hell. There was much written about the ages of life, mostly in the form of calendars, with analogies drawn to the seasons of the year. In the thirteenth and early fourteenth centuries, the calendars emphasized spring and summer; in the late fourteenth and fifteenth centuries, they turned to themes of autumn and winter.

There were similar changes in the conceptions and realities of social order.[32] The trifunctional system of the eleventh and twelfth centuries began to come apart around 1250, but it was the Black Death, with its massive depopulation, that finally brought the old order down. The plight of the clergy has already been described. In their role as intermediaries with God, they failed to provide solace to plague victims, and the medical education system, built around them, failed to provide physical comfort. In a world in which performance of an appointed role was very important, many clerics no longer seemed to be doing their jobs.

The Black Death brought crisis to the nobility.[33] The loss of between a quarter and a half of the West's population ended Europe's subsistence crisis. Depopulation meant widespread mobility and fluidity for those not tied to the land. The value of agricultural products began to fall, and it stayed low relative to that of industrial goods until the sixteenth century; at the same time, depopulation made agricultural workers scarce and, thus, much more valuable. Wages rose rapidly. The English chronicler Henry Knighton observed the new relationship: "There were small prices for virtually everything. A man could have a horse, which was worth 40 shillings, for 6 shillings, 8 pence, a cow for 12 pence. . . . Sheep and cattle went wandering over fields and through crops, and there was no one to drive or gather them together."[34]

At Cuxham Manor in England, a ploughman who was paid 2 shillings a week in 1347 received 7 shillings in 1349, and 10 shillings, 6 pence, by 1350.[35] The result was a dramatic rise in standards of living for those in the lower part of the third order. William Langland noted in *Piers Ploughman* that hunger was no longer the peasants' master, that many beggars now refused as handouts that old standby, bread made from beans, and insisted on white bread and milk.[36] Day laborers not only received higher wages, but asked for and got lunches of meat pies and golden ale. The economic and social ramifications of this new relationship between wages and prices were far-reaching. But the social consequences were great, too, and were felt immediately after the Black Death. For the peasants who farmed the land, depopulation, providing they survived the plague, was a great boon. Yet for those who held the land as lords—the aristocracy and the clergy—it was disastrous.

At first, the landed classes tried to reinstate the trifunctional order through legislation issued by the representative bodies that they controlled. Authorities all across Europe promptly began to enact sumptuary laws. In France, a 1349 Statute of Labor attempted to limit wages to pre-1348 levels. This failed, and two years later a new law was enacted which allowed for a 33% rise. In 1349, the King's Council in England passed an Ordinance of Labour, that froze wages. This was followed in 1351 by a Parliamentary Statute of Labourers that tried to do the same thing. Parliament, it should be remembered, consisted almost entirely of men from the first two orders, with a few great merchants from the third, most of whom owned property in their own right. In 1350, the archbishop of Canterbury, very much a member of the landholding elite, issued a document called *Effrenata cupiditas*, or unbridled cupidity. It was a general critique of greed, with particular barbs aimed at clerics who worked only for cash or charged extra fees for ordinary services. All of these efforts were for naught, and landlords discovered that the only way to keep laborers was to pay the going rate.

Sumptuary laws were passed to regulate fashions, particularly those of the third order.[37] Rising standards of living and Epicurean attitudes had produced new tastes in fashion, particularly in clothing. The increasingly colorful and extravagant dress was a curious contrast to the somber tones of literature, but much in keeping with the general contradictions of the Later Middle Ages. Men took to tight pantaloons and long, pointed shoes, and women wore hairpieces and dresses with plunging necklines, some almost to the point of baring their breasts. Furs, which always had been popular, were now affordable for more people than at any time in centuries. They were big business in the Late Middle Ages, and provided Northern furriers and skinners with fine livings. Medieval authorities believed that furs ought to bear some relationship to the social status of the men and women who wore them and, in the fourteenth century, legislation was passed to ensure that this would remain the case.

In 1337, at the nadir of the subsistence crisis, the English Parliament had declared that only aristocrats and clerics with incomes of £1000 or more could wear furs; no one else was deemed worthy. Another law, from 1363, well illustrates the changes brought by the new standards of living. All people except the humblest manual workers were permitted to wear furs and were given a schedule of what they were allowed. Knights and ladies with incomes over £266 could wear optimum white and gray full furs from northern muscalids. Less prosperous knights were allowed the facings of ermine and weasel, but only on their hoods and cloaks. Gentlemen worth £200 a year and merchants valued at £1000 a year could wear white muscalid furs on their hoods. Gentlemen worth less than £200, and clerks, other merchants, and craftsmen valued at £500 a year wore lambskin, while all others valued at more than 40 shillings could affect sheep, rabbit, cat, or fox. This legislation failed, of course; if it had any effect at all, it was as a spur to the socially ambitious. Everyone wore whatever they could manage, social rank to the contrary. Such high standards—workmen wearing furs—would end by the early sixteenth century. But, by that time, the old trifunctional system had undergone dramatic changes.

The position of the nobility was affected by the Black Death in other ways. Plague did not honor social class, and mortality among the nobility approximated that of the general population. Since inheritance was more important to them than it was to the peasants, the biological crisis was more severe. This made an already bad situation worse. Given the high infant and child mortality rates of the Middle Ages—combined, they probably killed three of four children before age ten—and maternal mortality of about 20%, it was hard in the best of circumstances to produce an heir. In England, 75% of all noble families failed to produce a male heir through two generations.[38] This meant continual flux among the aristocracy as old families died out and new ones replaced them.

One response to this tremendous fluidity was a renewed emphasis by the older families on the importance of knightly ritual. In the Early and, to a slightly lesser extent, the High Middle Ages, the aristocracy had been warriors. In the Late Middle Ages, while they were still soldiers, their military ascendancy was being challenged by infantry men using new weapons. Consequently, late medieval aristocrats became more conscious than ever of their role as heavy cavalry, turned with disdain upon the baseborn footmen who as often as not defeated them on the battlefield, and immersed themselves in elaborate rituals of chivalry. Armor became plated rather than chain-linked. Tournaments, formerly held for practice and profit and usually conducted with the actual weapons of war, became dress celebrations, with combatants using blunted swords and lances. Great knightly orders such as the Garter and the Golden Fleece were established by kings and magnates, and ritual battles such as the Combat of the Twenty, which occurred during the Hundred Years' War, were held.[39] However obsolete they might become, such events helped the old aristocracy preserve their identity. A similar, albeit somewhat gentler, retreat for the lords was to manners and courtesy. Dozens of books were compiled on nurture and grace, and how to dress, act, eat, and think like a gentleman. The nobility were developing a contempt for manual labor and laborers, and even for merchants and the most profitable commercial activities.

High mortality among the aristocracy, then, was more damaging than it was among the peasantry because of the importance to the lords of proper patterns of inheritance. At the same time, there was a new balance between prices and wages. Land was no longer as valuable as it had been, but laborers were worth much more than before. Society was changing from a labor-intensive base to a land-intensive one, and markets for foodstuffs collapsed as population decreased. As more tenants died, lords had to hire wage laborers to farm their lands, and these workers demanded better pay and conditions. On the manors of the Clare estates in England, for example, reaping wages per quarter averaged less than five pence per acre between 1340 and 1349.[40] In 1349, wages doubled. Estate auditors did their best to reduce their labor costs, sometimes by arbitrarily slicing them in half. But, generally, such efforts were ineffective. Drawing an example from England again, aristocratic incomes fell over 20% between 1347 and 1353.

One of the most important effects of the Black Death was its role in the provocation of popular rebellion.[41] Plague alone did not cause the many rebellions of the fourteenth century; rather, they had a long and complex history. But until the late thirteenth century, rebellions in Europe were comparatively few and generally of religious inspiration. Beginning with the Sicilian Vespers in 1282 and several revolts in the Netherlands and rural France, this changed. These later uprisings first took on political overtones and then, exacerbated by the depopulation of the Black Death, became increasingly socioeconomic in nature.

The revolts after the Black Death had several common characteristics. First, they took place during a general breakdown in law and order.[42] Both the court and police systems in most of fourteenth century Europe were operated by local landholders. King and church might claim a superior jurisdiction, but, with the exception of parts of England and Italy, law enforcement was a local prerogative. As the economic and military power and social prestige of the landholders declined, their ability to uphold the law also diminished. Coupled with the increasing tendency toward violence, this resulted in an enormous upswing in crime. In England, where royal power was probably more extensive than elsewhere in Europe, the incidence of homicide from 1349 to 1369 was about twice that of the period 1320 to 1340, despite the general drop in population. As the fabric and structure of society deteriorated, people resorted increasingly to violence to settle their differences.

A second plague-related reason for the spate of revolts was a heightened sense of class of identity. This was especially so among the peasantry, on whose labor and produce the other classes depended. It was not so much that postplague peasants had, in Marxian terms, a positive sense of their economic value. Rather, they believed that their interests conflicted with those of the first two orders, the clergy and the nobility. This sense, perhaps first evident in the early fourteenth century as the effects of successive famines began to cripple the manorial system, was made even more apparent after the Black Death when the lords refused to recognize the peasants' changed situation.

The new relationship between wages and prices was a third reason. Boccaccio claimed that prices shot up during the Black Death. He was right, but by 1351 things had changed. Prices for industrial goods remained high, a reflection of increased demand and a shortage of skilled laborers to make special products. But population was reduced so much that, as soon as seeds were sown and crops harvested, the great subsistence crisis ended. It took another year or two for distribution systems to return to normal; then food prices began to fall. Because of the population decline, wages went up, and so did standards of living. The Late Middle Ages has with good reason been called the "Golden Age of Laborers," and many scholars believe that real wages were higher in the fifteenth century than at any time in history until the twentieth century. As discussed, members of the first two orders chafed at the rising wage level and tried to reverse this trend through legislation. To members of the third order, this was the cruelest blow of all. Having at last attained some economic security in a market economy, they were now being asked to live within new, artificial restraints.

Three major revolts resulted from postplague social and economic tensions. Two—the *Jacquerie* in France and the Peasants' Revolt in England—were peasant uprisings, and the other—that of the *Ciompi* in Florence—was an urban-industrial rebellion. The *Jacquerie* took place in 1358. It was the result of a number of things besides the Black Death. The king of France, Jean II (1350–64), had been taken prisoner by the English at the Battle of Poitiers in 1356. France was leaderless, and no one was quite sure how to fill the gap. Many members of the third order believed that the clerics and aristocrats who competed with the king for power were not making a serious effort to secure Jean's return. A curious phenomenon of the postplague revolts was the enthusiasm the rebels displayed for their king, no matter how inept he might be. The rebels believed that evil influence, rather than a malevolent monarch, was responsible for bad government. There were also the depredations of the *routiers*, or Free Companies, groups of mercenaries who, between battles of the Hundred Years' War, lived off the produce of the peasantry. And there was an *agent provocateur* of sorts, Charles of Navarre, who wished to be king of France himself and played the French off against the English, as it was in his interest to perpetuate the chaos of the postplague period.

The class tensions exacerbated by the Black Death were also crucial to the outbreak of the *Jacquerie*. The soldiers of the uprising were mainly peasants, but many of the leaders, including the spokesman, Etienne Marcel, were bourgeois. The bourgeoisie wanted political power commensurate with their economic gains. The landed classes, who were so besieged socially and economically that a contemporary claimed that "knights and brigands had become interchangeable," were reluctant to relinquish their political privileges. Members of the first two orders, particularly the *bellatores*, held members of the third order, particularly the peasants, in utter contempt. The very term "*Jacques*," from which the expression *Jacquerie* was taken, was a derisive reference to the leather jerkins peasants wore in battle in place of armor, which they could not afford. A noble proverb went: "Smite a villein and he will bless you; bless a villein and he will smite you." From *Le Despit au Villain* comes an extraordinary passage:

Tell me Lord, if you please, by what right or title does a villein eat beef? . . . And this troubles God. God suffers from it and I too. For they are a sorry lot, those villeins who eat fat goose! Should they eat fish? Rather, let them eat thistles and briars, thorns and straws and hay on Sundays and pea pods on weekdays. They should keep watch without sleep and have trouble always; that is how villeins should live. Yet each day they are full and drunk on the best wines, and in fine clothes. The great expenditures of villeins come at a high cost, for it is this that destroys and ruins the world. It is they who spoil the common welfare. From the villein comes all unhappiness. Should they eat meat? Rather, they should chew grass on the heath with the horned cattle and go naked on all fours.[43]

Such attitudes, embedded in aristocratic literature since the twelfth century, became even more emphatic as plague brought new economic conditions.

The peasants returned the feeling and, during the *Jacquerie,* put their feelings into action. The revolt lasted only a few weeks, but it was one of the bitterest and bloodiest in French history. Most of the action centered around the great estates of the Loire and Seine Valleys, the heart of the kingdom. The chronicler Froissart, supported by, and a supporter of, the aristocracy, wrote of the fury of the peasantry. He claimed that the *Jacquerie* began when

certain people of the common villages without any head or ruler, assembled together in the Beauvoison. In the beginning, they passed not a hundred. . . . They gathered together without any council, and without armor, saving with staves and knives, and so went to the house of a knight dwelling thereby, and broke up his house and slew the knight and the lady and all his children, great and small, and burned the house. And then they went to another castle, and took the knight thereof and tied him fast to a stake, and raped his wife and his daughter before his face, and then killed the lady and his daughter and all his other children, and then slew the knight by great torment, and burnt and tore down the castle. And so they did to diverse other castles and good houses; and they multiplied until they were a thousand. . . . These mischievous people thus assembled without captain or armor, robbed, burnt and slew all the gentlemen that they could lay hands on, and forced and ravished ladies and damsels and did such shameful deeds that no human creature ought to think on such, and he that did the most mischief was most praised with them and the greatest master: I dare not write the horrible deeds that they did to ladies and damsels; among others, they slew a knight and [then] put him on a spit and roasted him at the fire in sight of the lady, his wife and children, and after that the lady was forced and raped by ten or twelve of them, and then they made her eat of her husband, and after made her die an evil death with all her children.[44]

The peasants' successes were short-lived. Etienne Marcel, the Parisian draper who led the revolt, lost control of, and was killed by, a mob of rebels. Perforce, those Parisian merchants who had supported the peasants became afraid and abandoned the revolt. Charles of Navarre, always looking for personal advantages, raised troops to fight the peasants. The aristocrats regained their lost courage and set upon the peasants, who were put down with much savagery and carnage; thus ended the *Jacquerie*. But the resentment and the social tensions lingered on.

The *Ciompi* were workers in the Florentine textile industries. Prices for finished goods, especially deluxe textiles such as those made by the Florentines, remained high in the generation after the Black Death and, though wages were up, the industrialists made a great deal of money. But all was not well. The same political and social tensions that characterized the relations between lords and peasants in France, and that were dramatically exacerbated by the Black Death, held between employers and workers in Florence. Florentine writers proclaimed that their city was a democracy, with power divided among 21 guilds. But, in fact, the division was unequal, with the principal power resting in seven guilds that were controlled by an elite of bankers and long-distance traders. Further, the *Ciompi* workers had genuine financial complaints. While the great merchants generally dealt in florins, one of Europe's most stable currencies, the workers were paid their salaries in pennies. The value of the florin was kept steady by the ruling elite, but when the textile industry slumped briefly in the early 1370s, the penny was debased. In 1349, 240 pennies made 1 florin; by 1378, a florin was worth over 1000 pennies. The lords never suffered during the crisis, but the workers saw their standards of living crumbling. Florence was not unique.[45] Workers in other north and central Italian cities suffered from similar debasements and all had before them the example of the revolt of the lowborn in Rome, from 1347 to 1351, led by Cola di Rienzi. But it was in Florence that the mass violence and urban disorder so characteristic of the second half of the fourteenth century erupted.

The *Ciompi* revolt began in summer 1378, when many workers were laid off. During the most violent spell, in late July, the palaces and townhouses of the rich were looted, gutted, and burned. For almost five years, the workers were able to share in the government of the city. They demanded the right to form guilds of their own, tax reform, the abolition of financial privileges, and a moratorium on debts. By 1383, the textile crisis was over and much of the value of the pennies had been restored; the merchant elite managed to regain power, and the *Ciompi* were disenfranchised once again. But, unlike the *Jacques* of France, at least in economic terms, their lot had improved, and their wages would remain relatively stable into the fifteenth century.

The English Peasants' Revolt of 1381 is the best known of the postplague uprisings. The immediate cause of the revolt was a series of poll, or head, taxes assessed three times between 1377 and 1381. As with the *Jacquerie* and the *Ciompi*, most of the conditions that set off the English revolt had been festering before 1347, but plague accelerated the changes and general social tensions. The peasants wanted to preserve the high wages and new mobility brought by depopulation, and the lords, threatened on all fronts, wished to maintain the status quo despite the new economic conditions.

The revolt erupted in eastern England, the richest part of the kingdom, rather than in the depressed northern and western counties. It began when a number of peasants in Essex refused to pay the head tax and drove the collectors from their village. Spontaneously, peasants and townsmen rose against what they perceived to be injustices. The thrust of the rebellion, which was led by a wealthy peasant named Wat Tyler and an unemployed priest named John Ball, was antinoble, anticlerical, and antiauthoritarian. Tyler, leading a peasant army on London, exhorted his followers to "kill all lawyers and servants of the king." According to Froissart, Ball claimed: "Ah, ye good people, the matter goes not well to pass in England, nor shall not do so till everything be common, and that we may be all united together and that the lords be no greater masters than we be. What have we deserved or why should we be thus kept in serfdom; we be all come from one father and one mother, Adam and Eve."[46] From this came the famous jingle:

When Adam delved and Eve spanned
Who was then a gentleman?

The English Peasants' Revolt followed the patterns of the *Jacquerie*, the *Ciompi*, and other postplague revolts. After an early period of success, bloody revenge on their tormentors, and random violence—among other things, the archbishop of Canterbury was beheaded and most of the brothels in greater London were destroyed—the aristocracy and gentry regained their dominance and, as in France, brutally put down the rebels. But, in England, as on the Continent, the rebels came away with substantial gains. Poll taxes were eliminated and there were no more effective ordinances fixing wages or limiting mobility. The peasants benefited from high wages and, by 1400, the old bonds of villeinage had loosened or crumbled. There were no more peasant revolts in England in the Late Middle Ages because the peasants had no reason to revolt.

Both the urban and the rural disorders reflected the sharp class conflicts that developed after the Black Death. A general social discontent arose, not so much over conditions in postplague Europe as over the ruling classes' attempts to deny the lower order the better fortune depopulation brought. The breakdown of the old trifunctional system and the increasing violence made revolt easier and more palatable. The revolts were spontaneous and poorly organized and, in time, were easily put down. Perhaps their most telling legacy was the end of the traditional hierarchical social structure, which was replaced by interclass bitterness and tension. How might the changes affecting the generation which survived the Black Death be characterized? First, immediate depopulation of at least a third ended, in a single blow, Europe's subsistence crisis. By the early 1340s, most Europeans were getting poorer. They held and farmed less land, produced and, hence, consumed less food, and had a smaller say in determining their future than at any time since the Dark Ages. By contrast, the landlord class was becoming increasingly powerful. Europe was evolving, as were parts of Asia and Africa, into an impoverished "agrocentric" society. By 1350, this process was dramatically reversed. High wages and low prices were ruining the lords, while members of the third order were embarking on 150 years of comparative prosperity. But in the short term, for those who survived the first plague, the psychological effects of the Black Death were far more important. People were traumatized. They lost faith in their own abilities, in the old values, and if not in God then in the traditional ways in which He had been propitiated. Europe was plunged into a moral crisis. The old order was collapsing and the new one was not yet in place.

# CHAPTER 6
# The Stirrings of
# Modern Medicine

ONE OF THE MOST important legacies of the Black Death was the destruction of the existing medical system and the beginning of its modern successor.[1] In 1347, the members of Europe's medical community were rigid and generally inept. Medical practice was based primarily on the ideas of Hippocrates, Galen, and several Arabic commentators, especially the Persian Avicenna. All these physicians had written about infectious disease, but none had had firsthand experience with plague. Structurally, the medical community was composed of five distinct divisions: physicians, surgeons, barber-surgeons, apothecaries, and unlicensed or nonprofessional practitioners. These divisions were inspired to some degree by the Greek system, but were intensified and rigidified by medieval thinkers. The system worked well enough during the High Middle Ages, an epoch devoid of most of the great deadly epidemics, but proved inadequate in dealing with plague and the other newly recognized infections of the fourteenth and fifteenth centuries. The response of doctors to the new medical problems resulted in a series of changes that led to the evolution of modern clinical medicine in the seventeenth century.

In order to understand the first stages in this evolution it is necessary to look at the old system.[2] The structural division of medical professionals fitted well with the medieval conception of trifunctionalism. At the top were physicians. They were the elite, highly trained in current theories of medicine, small in number, and very exclusive; they were accorded a degree of respect and prestige in keeping with their role as the paramount authorities. They were the heirs to Hippocrates and Galen. Physicians were always men and, in northern Europe, usually members of the clergy. This religious connection was important, part of an association of medicine and religion extending to the Biblical world and, no doubt, beyond, in which the power to heal was associated with first magic, then the supernatural, and finally, special religious gifts. As a result, medieval medical education was generally connected with and supervised by the church. It was this university-based education more than anything else that distinguished physicians from other medical professionals.[3] By the fourteenth century, a student interested in medicine would have started his education in a grammar school at about age 9, concentrating on the Seven Liberal Arts—grammar, rhetoric, dialectic, arithmetic, geometry, music, and astronomy. If he could raise the money—higher education then, as now, was expensive—the promising scholar would enter a university between age 15 and 18 and spend another 4 to 7 years studying the Liberal Arts, usually specializing in one of the seven. Upon completing his studies and passing a series of examinations, he would earn a baccalaureate degree. It was at this point that his formal medical education began.

Most of the medical corpus was of classical origin or inspiration, but the format in which it was studied was medieval, modeled after the scholastic method popularized around 1100 by Peter Abelard, a teacher at the cathedral schools in Paris.[4] In his *Sic et Non*, Abelard emphasized the pedagogical importance of dialectic. He advocated arguing both sides of a point, examining the argument, and thereby producing a new, presumably correct, position drawn from the best aspects of both sides. Hence, a debate on anatomy might take Galen's position on a point and a second position of one of his commentators, perhaps Avicenna, present details from each, and yield a new result. Abelardian technique was useful, but it was an advance in style rather than substance. The medical corpus itself, with its classical basis, was predicated not on clinical research but on the close analysis of earlier texts. New propositions were usually rehashings of old ideas, and medical students did no research, observed very little, and hence were unable to respond to new diseases with effective treatment.

The basis of preplague medicine was the theory of humors.[5] The human body had four humors—blood, phlegm, yellow bile, and black bile—which, in turn, were associated with particular organs. Blood came from the heart, phlegm from the brain, yellow bile from the liver, and black bile from the spleen. Galen and Avicenna attributed certain elemental qualities to each humor. Blood was hot and moist, like air; phlegm was cold and moist, like water; yellow bile was hot and dry, like fire; and black bile was cold and dry, like earth. In effect, the human body was a microcosm of the larger world.

When one's bodily humors were in equilibrium, one was in good health; this was called *Eukrasia*. When one's humors were not in balance, one was sick, a condition called *Dyskrasia*, and it was the physician's job to find the means to restore the proper balance. Rest was usually the first prescription, but if the body's innate curative powers proved to be insufficient, the doctor went to work. First, the patient's diet was altered. For example, if he were too hot, various foods were prescribed to make him cooler or, in some cases, hotter still, to purge the infection. If this failed, the physician might recommend bloodletting, phlebotomy, cautery, or cupping. The belief that the object of medicine was to restore *Eukrasia* helps to explain the reaction of physicians to the Black Death. By modern standards, medieval plague remedies often seem ludicrous, but, given the state of medicine in the mid-fourteenth century, they were rational and well-advised. The Greeks and their Islamic commentators were fine theoreticians and, by their own standard, competent physiologists, but they based their ideas on theory rather than direct, clinical observation and experience. Medieval physicians stressed argument, especially syllogism. Consequently, they were poor anatomists, pathologists, and epidemiologists, and were able to do little to fight the plague.

By the fourteenth century, Europe had six principal medical schools, located in Salerno, Montpellier, Bologna, Paris, Padua, and Oxford.[6] The school in Salerno was the first to reach prominence, in the late eleventh century, and it benefited from contacts with nearby Arabic and Byzantine doctors. As a result of these contacts, its faculty stressed the teaching of anatomy. Unfortunately, the anatomy was based on the dissection of pigs. By the thirteenth century, the medical school in Salerno had grown moribund and lost its ascendant position to the school in Montpellier, which prided itself on its connection with leading Jewish physicians from Spain and North Africa. Jews were barred from other medical schools, and Montpellier was their only alternative. Further, officials of Montpellier paid their professors very highly and allowed them, rather than church or civic officials, to grant the licenses necessary for the practice of medicine. The standards for student admission were rigorous, for students could not matriculate until they had a bachelor's degree in medicine. These requirements combined to make Montpellier one of Europe's best medical schools; among its distinguished alumni and faculty members were the leading doctors in Europe, including Bernard Gordon, Henri de Mondeville, Arnold of Villanova, and Guy de Chauliac.

The medical schools at Bologna and Paris came into prominence in the thirteenth century. Bologna was unique among medieval universities in that it specialized in higher, or graduate, degrees rather than undergraduate ones. Its law school was probably the finest in Europe, but the medical school was justly famous as well, with a particular reputation for being innovative. The best known of its professors was the surgeon William of Saliceto, a pioneer in the methods of cautery, who stressed the importance of surgical classes.[7] Indeed, Bologna's most innovative feature was the prominence it gave to surgery, a subject not even on the curriculum of most of the other European schools. Dissection of human cadavers was begun in the 1260s and popularized in the early fourteenth century, when a Bolognese professor, Mondino de'Liuzzi, published his *Anatomia*, a fairly accurate text based on human dissection. It remained the standard text in Europe for almost a hundred years. Mondino described anatomy in clear and simple language: "After the muscle, the bones. Now the bones of the chest are many and are not continuous in order that they may be expanded and contracted, since it [the chest] has to be ever in motion."[8]

By the time of the Black Death, the medical school at the University of Paris was generally considered to be the most prestigious in Europe. It was, at the very least, the biggest and richest medical school, part of the biggest and richest university, primarily because of the lavish patronage of the king of France, the bourgeoisie of Paris, and the French church. Peter Abelard had made his reputation there (though the schools there were not officially designated a university until 1200), and his scholastic method was closely connected with it. The medical school in Paris was not as innovative as the one in Bologna, but because it was so well-supported and paid its faculty good salaries, it had the most famous and influential, if not necessarily the best, professors. It was to the faculty of the medical school of Paris that the pope would go for advice on the Black Death.

If university-trained physicians were at the top of the medical profession, surgeons stood second.[9] They had a professional standing of sorts, were incorporated into the university program in southern Euorpean medical schools, and were granted some recognition in the schools of the North. Before the Black Death, surgeons were clearly second-class medical citizens, regarded primarily as skilled craftsmen best-suited to bleeding and closing wounds. Many of them were literate and had some textbook training, but most of their knowledge was based on experience. Unlike physicians, who often never touched their patients, surgeons performed operations, including trephining (a kind of medieval brain surgery), phlebotomy, and cautery, and did much of the bone setting that is basic to medicine. While university-trained physicians were accounted the social equal of wealthy merchants (though not the equal of great bankers and long-distance traders) and lawyers, surgeons were rated at a lower level, with notaries and goldsmiths.[10]

Barber-surgeons were distinct from surgeons proper and made no pretense of being an elite.[11] Most were illiterate, none went to a university, and their training came entirely from practice during apprenticeship. They did some of the same things as surgeons, including phlebotomy and cautery, often directed by a physician or surgeon. More commonly, they performed rather menial tasks such as cupping, setting simple fractures, and applying poultices. They had less knowledge of infection and sanitary practices than did physicians and surgeons, and the traditional barbers' pole of red and white probably comes from the time when barber-surgeons hung out their bloody surgical rags to dry. Virtually all barber-surgeons were part-time doctors, shaving and cutting hair to augment their medical fees, and were sometimes joined in their casual practice by the butcher-surgeon. Barber-surgeons were generally organized in craft guilds, but their medical activities were usually regulated by local physicians or surgeons, who otherwise kept their distance. They had no knowledge of pathology, physiology, or epidemiology, and their principal attraction was the comparatively low fees that they charged.

Apothecaries were more difficult to classify.[12] They were, above all, pharmacists, which gave them an important place in the medical hierarchy, since pharmacy was a major part of the physician's cure. But apothecaries did more than just fill prescriptions and therein lies the problem of trying to place them in late medieval Europe's medical hierarchy. Many apothecaries prescribed drugs, and hence treatment, which made it difficult to distinguish their public role from that of the physician, who rarely touched the patient. Apothecaries' training, if they had any, was as herbalists, and they doled out their prescriptions as if following cookbooks, with little understanding of the human body or infectious disease. Their organization was also something of a mystery. In some cases, physicians and even surgeons regulated their medical and pharmaceutical practice, but because the apothecaries' drugs were usually made from valuable spices, many apothecaries doubled as merchants. Indeed, until the mid-thirteenth century, it was difficult to distinguish apothecaries from grocers and spicers. Apothecaries' incomes were often greater than those of physicians. Concomitantly, they sometimes occupied a higher social position than even the most distinguished, university-trained doctors.

Finally, there was a group of unlicensed or nonprofessional medical practitioners, people with no formal training, organization, or regulation.[13] The role of the nonprofessionals, like that of the apothecaries, is difficult to assess, but this is not because of ambiguity about their roles. Rather, little evidence of their activities survives. The nonprofessionals probably did a bit of everything, or at least attempted to, for without formal training they learned whatever they knew through trial and error. The appeal of the nonprofessionals lay in their fee schedules; they stood at the bottom of the doctors' social scale and charged the lowest rates. The nonprofessionals were not very common in cities or large towns, but were found primarily in rural areas, where professionals did not venture. Generally speaking, there was a correlation between the size of a settlement and the amount of education its doctor had. There was another important feature of the nonprofessional practitioners. A fairly high proportion of them, perhaps 15% to 20% judging from English sources, were women[14] and a lot of these were older women. Barred from the other areas of practice, women with medical inclinations were forced to work outside the formal hierarchy.

This, then, was Europe's medical community in the fourteenth century. It was slowly becoming more professional. Medical schools and municipal guilds provided strict regulation, and it seems that most doctors took their jobs seriously. But preplague medicine was firmly rooted in the Greek theoretical-philosophical past. Despite some limited gains, its corpus of knowledge was based on texts hundreds of years old and was completely inadequate in the face of the new diseases that came to Europe in the fourteenth century. Most physicians had little formal training in anatomy and pathology, and most surgeons had no theoretical background. Epidemiology was based on Galen's *Book of Fevers*, which was a thousand years old by 1347. It is little wonder that in 1348, when King Philip VI of France asked the medical faculty of the University of Paris for an opinion on plague, its advice was virtually useless.

The tractate produced by the Parisian doctors was one of a vast number of works written about plague.[15] The number of individual treatises is noteworthy in its own right, as is the survival of thousands of copies of the original treatises, since the laborious and expensive copying of manuscripts was reserved for the most important works. The treatises were written under great stress and in an atmosphere of terror, and give not only medical information but insight into the life and psychology of Europe's intellectual elite. Most of all, the tractates show clearly how the Black Death brought about a crisis in medieval medicine which stimulated professionalism, the rise of surgery, new laws of public health and sanitation, and the development of hospitals designed not just to isolate society's sick but to try to cure them.

It is not surprising that none of the medical treatises correctly described the cause of plague. Its precise etiology was not completely understood until the early twentieth century. But it is surprising that virtually all of the medical observers failed to make the connection between plague and the plethora of dead rodents that preceded an epidemic. A few commentators, including Avicenna, did claim that one of the portents of pestilence's coming was "when mice and animals living under the earth fled to the surface and were disturbed, as if they were drunk." Further, the Swedish bishop Bengt Knuttson, author of a popular fifteenth-century treatise, claimed that filth, "fleys," and vermin brought plague.[16] But these comments and others like them were made only in a general sense, without a true understanding of the connection of insects, rodents, and *Y. pestis*.

Most of the treatises were divided into three sections.[17] The first considered the causes of plague, the second dealt with preventive measures, and the third proposed cures. A number of causes were suggested; the most popular ones derived from astronomy and astrology. For example, the doctors at the University of Paris, who took their theory from Avicenna, claimed that on 20 March 1345, at 1:00 P.M., a conjunction of three higher planets—Saturn, Jupiter, and Mars—in the sign of Aquarius caused a corruption of the surrounding air. This portent of famine, pestilence, and high mortality was explicable in terms of the accepted humoral theory. Jupiter was believed to be a warm and humid planet, dominated by earth and water. Mars, being excessively hot and dry, set those elements aflame. No one was quite sure what Saturn had or did, but most experts felt that its combination with anything was bad. The differing geographic effects of the Black Death were due to regional variations in the intensity of rays from the planets.

This astral theory was also advocated by many Italian doctors. Gentile of Foligno, son of a Bolognese physician, was a lecturer in medicine at the University of Padua.[18] He claimed that the conjunction of the planets brought

> poisonous material which is generated about the heart and the lungs. Its impression is not from the excess in degree of primary qualities, but through properties of poisonous vapors having been communicated by means of air breathed in and out, great extension and transition of this plague takes place, not only from man to man but from country to country. And, as has been intimated before, it is no great matter in these causes whether it is a constellation or an earthly or antiquarian figure, if only we may know how to resist it, and that a stand be made against it lest it destroys us.[19]

A second popular explanation was environmental. Its chief proponents were Spaniards, especially Alfonso of Cordova. In some cases, the environmental theory was linked with the astral one by connecting the causes of natural phenomena, such as earthquakes, to the planetary conjunctions. Eurasia did suffer a series of earthquakes from 1345 to 1347, and many doctors believed that this released noxious fumes from the earth's core; some even claimed that the devil was behind it all. Neither Galen nor Avicenna spoke of earthquakes, and the theory seems to have originated in the fourteenth century.

A second environmental theory stressed changes in the earth's temperature. Its advocates claimed that climatic changes brought warmer, damper weather and severe southerly winds that carried plague. These scholars predicted plague by the colors of the evening sky, heavy rains, persistent mists, violent winds, cloud formations, and less probable phenomena such as raining multitudes of reptiles, frogs, and toads. Certain kinds of weather conditions are known to influence rodent and insect life cycles and could be considered as factors in the spread and frequency of pandemic plague, a relationship suggested by Avicenna, who believed that most epidemic diseases were brought by winds from the equator. Appropriately enough, two of the principal proponents of climatic causes for plague were the Spanish Muslims Ibn Khātimah and Ibn al-Khatib.[20]

Some theorists, basing their arguments primarily on Galen, claimed that whether the cause of plague be astral or environmental, its transmission between men could be explained by miasma-contagion, or corruption of the air. Galen had claimed that miasma was a disease substance that invaded an organism from the outside, while contagion was the disease substance actually generated within that organism and carried about by the corrupted air. Corruption was either partial or total. Partial corruption was the deterioration, but not the complete destruction, of the element air; in total corruption, the basic component was so contaminated that air was no longer recognizable in its elemental form. In the late fourteenth century, many doctors claimed that foul odors were another source of air corruption. Such odors could come from decaying matter, manure, corpses on a battlefield, or just about any spoilage of humans or animals. Since bad smells were common in the Late Middle Ages, this theory would account for plague's omnipresence.

Among the fourteenth century doctors who stressed the role of corrupt air were Ibn Khātimah, Gentile of Foligno, the German physician John Hakr, and the medical faculty of the University of Montpellier, who hastily threw together a tractate lest their Parisian counterparts be accepted as the sole authority.[21] The Montpellierians believed that the deadly vapors came from the South, and they advised that doors and windows on houses be given Northern exposures. It was believed that air was deadliest in the summer and early autumn—in fact, the peak time for flea-borne, and not air-borne, plague in most of northern Europe—because the hot weather opened the pores of the body, making individuals more susceptible to attack. This theory about open pores explains the general medical opposition to bathing and vigorous exercise during epidemics, and the varying vulnerability of individuals. The Montpellier physicians claimed

> sometimes the brain expels the windy and poisonous material through the concave optic nerves to the eyes, and then the sick person is in agony, holding his eyes as if they could not be moved from place to place, and there the ventosity receives a marvelous property, in that, thus standing and permanent, its toxic spirit is continually being made, and seeks a dwelling in some nature in which it can enter and lie quiet. And if any well person looks upon that visible spirit, he receives the attack of pestilential disease, and the person is poisoned more quickly than by inhaling

the air of the sick man, because the diaphanous poison penetrates more quickly than the heavy air.[22]

As the passage suggests, some authorities believed that corrupted air made plague transferable from person to person. It was thought that the breath, clothing, bedding, or even stare of an infected individual, could pass on the deadly plague.

A few medical authorities added further causes, ranging from "lust with old women" to overeating, but, in dealing with the origins of plague, most finished the opening parts of their tractates by addressing susceptibility and immunity.[23] Why did some people get it while others did not? Most doctors claimed that the answer rested in the theory of the four humors. Persons of hot, moist temperament were most likely to succumb. If those unfortunate types were also young and slightly corpulent and, even worse, passionate, sensual, *and* female, they were particularly vulnerable. So, too, were big eaters and drinkers, athletes, and the younger, more active members of society in general. The predominance of humors that gave them their youthful, active personalities also made them vulnerable to plague.

The second section of most plague treatises was devoted to prevention and resistance. On a strictly practical note, preventive steps were always urged, since doctors realized the inadequacies of their curative abilities. The best preventive measure was prayer, and both Christian and Muslim writers suggested the wearing of religious charms.[24] Christians wore crosses, while Muslims favored little gold lions, an astrological protector symbolizing a favorable period of the year. Christian and Muslim writers disagreed on the role of flight in preventing plague. Christian writers thought it was the second best prophylaxis. Flight was urged from any place with plague, and from places with low elevation, marshes, stagnant waters, southern exposures, or coastal areas to cool, dry, and/or mountainous environs. If flight were not possible, the conditions of the "safe" areas (e.g., mountains) were to be emulated as closely as possible. People were advised to stay in during the day, glaze or cover over any brightly lighted windows, and try above all to stay cool.

Islamic writers disdained flight for religious reasons. Like their Christian counterparts, most Muslim authorities believed that the ultimate cause of the Black Death was the wrath of God. But, to the Muslims, Allah's will was inevitable, and flight was useless and unnecessary. For the true believer, death from plague was actually a mercy, a gift from God, a release from the travails of life, and a ticket to paradise. It was only the infidel who needed to flee for, to him, death from plague meant damnation.

On the other aspects of preventive medicine, Christians and Muslims generally agreed.[25] Pleasant smells were important, for they drove away noxious plague fumes. Those threatened by plague were urged to burn aromatic softwoods such as juniper and ash. Oak, pine, rosemary, aloe, amber and musk were other good smells. Hands and feet were to be washed regularly and lightly sprinkled with rose water and vinegar, but bathing was to be curtailed because it opened the pores and thus made the body more vulnerable to attack. Exercise was not advised for the same reason, and also because fatigue made one more susceptible to the plague.

There was a school which advocated preventive pharmacy. Figs, filberts, and rue, all before breakfast on an empty stomach, were recommended. The best spices to ward off plague were myrrh, saffron, and pepper, all to be consumed later in the day, along with the best vegetables—onions, leeks, and garlic. These remedies were not to be used in excess since they might make the humors too hot and thus make one more vulnerable to plague. Readers were urged to keep gardens so that they would have a ready supply of the crucial herbs and spices close at hand.

There were additional ways in which the body could be readied to fight plague. Among the steps recommended was purgation through laxatives, diuretics, phlebotomy, and cautery. In the context of late medieval physiology, phlebotomy was quite rational and "scientific." Particular veins were linked with astral signs and the humors in order to change the flow of heat and fluids in the body. The proper humoral balance, maintained through bleeding, was essential to ward off plague.

Diet was important, too.[26] Here, medieval doctors followed Aristotle's advocacy of moderation in all phases of life, saying that a balanced diet helped to maintain the humors at peak efficiency. It was recommended that meals be light and be eaten very slowly with each bite well-chewed, so that one always would rise from one's meal still hungry. Meat, dairy products, and fish, all of which could spoil fairly quickly and hence begin to smell bad, were to be avoided. Bread, eggs, fruit, and vegetables were best, the latter two because they aided digestion. Desserts were forbidden, except for nuts, since it was believed that they also helped in digestion. Wine and clean water were the only safe drinks.

Too much sleep was bad, especially right after eating or during the middle of the day. Further, one was advised never to sleep on one's back, since this allowed potentially pestilential air to run down the nostrils and into the lungs. Rather, the experts advised sleeping on one's side and shifting back and forth, as this aided digestion and excretion, both crucial to a healthy balance of the humors and optimum strength for avoiding the plague. Much of this preventive lore was summed up in the early fifteenth century in the popular poem "Dietary and Doctrine for the Pestilence" by the English monk John Lydgate:

> Who will be whole and keep him from sickness
> And resist the stroke of pestilence
> Let him be glad and void of all heaviness
> Flee wicked aire, eschew the violence
> Drink good wine and wholesome meats take
> Walk in clean air, eschew mists black.[27]

The third section of most plague treatises dealt with treatments and cures. This was invariably the briefest section, since doctors were rarely able to offer positive help. Some authorities wrote of general cures to be used against all fevers, but most recognized the unique nature of plague and the necessity for trying to deal with it in a novel way. Islamic doctors, drawing on Avicenna, stressed bloodletting. Ibn Khātimah claimed: "After people learned this [phlebotomy], and saw its effects they began to have bloodletting done for themselves, without medical prescription, several times a month, without consideration or fear, without feeling harm or weakness, and without contracting sickness in consequence."[28] Islamic doctors also suggested lancing the buboes and then applying an ointment made from Armenian Clay, an iron-rich oxide whose healing properties were much praised by Galen. Other poultices, especially those made from violets, were recommended. These were to be rubbed into the lanced buboes while the patient drank fruit juices.

Some Christian doctors were often more scientific when discussing cures. Some of them believed that plague was carried through the body by the veins, or even by wormlike organisms, so they based their treatments on the bleeding of veins. Before discussing the cure, they described plague's symptoms: coughing, pains in the chest, shortness of breath, fever, buboes, and the vomiting of blood. The physiology of treatment usually followed the position of the University of Paris faculty. The Parisians claimed that the body needed natural heat to maintain itself. Under normal circumstances, air circulating through the lungs was thought to do this. But when plague attacked the pulmonary system, the body juices broke down, air stopped circulating, and eventually the victim died. The heart occupied the crucial position because the body's juices flowed from it. Accordingly, one effective way to treat plague was to bleed veins close to the heart. If the buboes appeared near other major organs such as the liver or the spleen, the veins leading to them were bled. In general, Christian doctors believed that pain and the appearance of buboes revealed where the body was being attacked and they began treatment at that point.

Beyond purgatives, bleeding, and the latter's allied treatments, cautery and cupping, there was little advice. Pharmaceuticals were occasionally prescribed for cures, but most authorities believed that they were more effective as a preventive measure. The following was one of the most popular:

A medicine for the pestilence. Take five cups of rue if it be a man, and if it be a woman leave out the rue, for rue is restorative to a man and wasting to a woman; and then take thereto five crops of tansey and five little blades of columbine, and a great quantity of marigold flowers full of the small chives from the crops that are like saffron chives. And if you may not get the flowers, take the leaves, and then you must have of the marigolds more than the others. Then take an egg that is newly laid, and make a hole in either end, and blow out all that is within. And lay it to the fire and let it roast till it may be ground to powder, but do not burn it. Then take a quantity of good treacle, and bray all these herbs therein with good ale, but do not strain them. And then make the sick drink it for three evenings and three mornings. If they [the sick] hold it, they shall have life.[29]

The fourth day after infection was believed to be the crucial one. Consequently, most medicines were designed to carry the patient until that day, when it was hoped the person's "natural restorative powers" would take over.

There were a few other cures, including proper nursing, bed rest, the drinking of a lot of fluid, and the application of herbal salves and ointments. Some physicians, adhering to the theory of the crucial fourth day, advised a wait-and-see attitude. But virtually all authorities believed that there was no sure cure, and this understanding, which served in part to change medical practice, was one of the most important legacies of the Black Death. The medical profession had been charged with maintaining the health of society. Its failure was widely noted, discussed, and criticized. Organized medicine, particularly the university-trained physicians, suffered a blow to its prestige and confidence. Medieval science, rooted as it was in a false Galenic base, was unable to change and respond successfully to its greatest challenge. Medical education, based on textual analysis rather than on clinical investigation and hypothesis, had ceased to progress by the thirteenth century and could not respond to the crisis of the fourteenth century. The result was collapse, rethinking, and reorganization.

In the generation after the Black Death, under the pressure of the second plague pandemic, medicine finally began to change. By 1500, modern medical philosophies and institutions had begun to evolve, and medicine had become professional. There were a number of steps in this process. First, many of the leading thinkers, theoreticians and practitioners of the medical establishment perished.[30] The Black Death killed some of the greatest medical writers, as well, including Gentile of Foligno and John Hakr, along with the chief physicians at the courts of the German emperor, the king of France, and the duke of Burgundy. Pope Clement VI (1342–52) was served during his pontificate by nine physicians and three surgeons; three of the physicians and two of the surgeons were killed by plague. It is hard to discern mortality from university records, since vacant professorships may show flight rather than mortality from plague. But at the University of Padua, which has the best records of any fourteenth-century medical school, there were vacancies in *all* the chairs of medicine and surgery in 1349. The effect of plague can be seen in another way, as well. In 1349, Padua had three professorships of medicine; by 1351 there were twelve. It is difficult to know exactly what these numbers mean. At the medical school of the University of Paris, the faculty shrank after the Black Death, from 46 in 1348, to 26 in 1362, to 20 by 1387. But in any case, many of the most prominent of the old guard were killed and, given the state of preplague medicine, this opened the discipline to new ideas.

A second postplague change was the rise of surgery and surgeons. As theoretical, university-based medicine failed, many people turned to more practical surgery. Even the universities recognized the need for new ideas, and northern European faculties began to recruit surgeons, who had long been accepted in Italian universities. At the University of Paris, anatomy and surgery became important parts of the medical program. At Bologna, where surgeons had been welcomed since the twelfth century, the surgical curriculum was intensified. Before the Black Death, dissection had been done at Bologna only in winter months, and each dissection had been completed in a day; after it, decomposition notwithstanding, dissection was done in all seasons, and more slowly, hence yielding fewer mistakes. The results were soon apparent; by the 1380s, anatomy texts were comparatively accurate. At Padua, the increasingly important role of anatomy and surgery had another effect. It changed the emphasis in the medical school from philosophy to practical physical science. Along with this shift went the rise throughout the University of Padua of what has been called scientific method.[31] Based on Aristotelian logic and Abelardian style, this approach consisted of postulation of a theory, testing of that theory based on selective and rigorous observation and analysis, reflection on the results, and an hypothesis confirming the theory or denying it and suggesting an alternative. Many scholars believe that the development of the scientific method, which drew inspiration at least in part from practical surgery and anatomy courses given at the university, led both to professionalism in medicine and to modern experimental science in the seventeenth century.

Surgical advances were not limited to the universities. They came at more practical levels as well. In the years after the Black Death, surgeons made a sharp break with barber-surgeons and based more and more of their training on written sources. This was not a regression to the ivory-tower learning of the physician, but rather, a new emphasis on practical surgical manuals written by practicing surgeons. Indeed, the two most famous medical practitioners of the late fourteenth century were surgeons Guy de Chauliac and John Arderne.[32] Chauliac was surgeon to the king of France and the pope, while Arderne served the king of England; their masterworks, Chauliac's *Surgery* and Arderne's *Practica*, were among the most widely read of all postplague medical books. Each was utilitarian, was based on years of experience, and dealt primarily with treatment and care, in contrast to physicians' books, which usually dealt with theories of causation.

All across Europe, surgeons took their place beside physicians as municipal doctors.[33] In June 1348, the rulers of Florence allowed surgeons to do postmortems on plague victims. Montpellier, Venice, and a host of other towns soon followed suit and, by September 1349, Nicholas of Ferrara, a surgeon, was praised by Venice's rulers as one of their city's finest doctors. Just a year earlier they had fined the surgeon Andreas of Padua for "acting as a physician," even though he had cured over 100 plague victims. This pattern of municipal acclaim continued apace throughout the fourteenth and fifteenth centuries.

In 1348, authorities in Oxford allowed local surgeons to form a guild distinct from, and with power over, the barber-surgeons; a few years later, surgeons were even allowed to lecture in the university's medical program. Between 1352 and 1362, surgeons were incorporated in London, and boards of surgeons were established to regulate surgical practice throughout the city. In 1356, Parisian surgeons were allowed to award the university degrees of Bachelor and Master of Surgery. They were even granted the privilege of wearing the long robes formerly reserved for physicians. In 1390, the medical faculty at Paris recognized their newly won distinction and invited them into the university. By 1400, surgeons all across Europe were recognized as distinct from barber-surgeons and as members, with physicians, of the elite of the medical profession. Surgeons were literate, certified, and, now, socially acceptable. They were perceived to be men of action who got results where physicians failed.

Another change, one closely related to the rise of surgery, was the growth of vernacular medical texts.[34] Until the 1340s, virtually all medical books were written in Latin. This was because Latin was the universal language of the university-educated physicians, and its exclusivity perpetuated the elite. By 1400, this had changed. All over Europe many medical texts were being written in, or at least translated into, vernacular languages. There were many reasons for this. First, it was a reflection of the decay in the quality of teaching in Latin, itself a legacy of the Black Death, and one which will be discussed in Chapter 7. Second, it was connected with the rise and spread in surgery. While, by 1400, most surgeons had some university training and knew at least a bit of Latin, they were not rooted in the classical tradition of the physician. Surgeons preferred to write in their native tongue, a phenomenon noted by several observers, including the famous teacher John Trevisa in his translation from Latin to English of Ranulf Higden's *Polychronicon*.

A third reason for the increase in vernacular medical writing was greater demand from the lay public. Educated laymen were disillusioned with physicians' responses to plague and, in the same spirit that had caused them to take their salvation in their own hands, many wished to get their medical knowledge firsthand. Dozens of practical guides were written, covering the spectrum of medical treatments and procedures—phlebotomy, pharmacy, health regimens, diagnosis, etc.—and telling the patient how to apply them. Some other vernacular treatises were translations of popular versions of earlier professional works. A good example is Henry Daniel's 1377 version of *The*

*Domes of Urine.*[35] It was a popularization of the seminal work on urology, an important medieval tool for diagnosis, by Issac Judaeus. *Domes* was filled with colored illustrations of urine flasks, and advised the reader to match his own sample with the illustrations in the text. This was the sort of home diagnosis that anyone could do. Another popular type of guide was the recipe, or leechbook, a list of pharmaceutical prescriptions, usually said to be a king's, queen's, or other famous personage's favorite cure for a host of ailments. For example, the following was the recipe of Queen Phillipa, wife of Edward III of England (1327–77), for easing the delivery of a stillborn child: "Take leek blades and scale them and bind them to the womb about the navel; and it shall cast out the dead child; and when she is delivered, take away the blades or she shall cast out all that is in her."[36]

Because they were written in the vernacular, these popular "how-to" texts were accessible to anyone who could read—apothecaries, barber-surgeons, nonprofessional practitioners, as well as the lay public. They were a symptom of the widespread interest in disease and personal health after the Black Death. And, in a sense, the glut of popular medical works is another example of the failure of the traditional, university-based, theoretical, text-bound physician to provide adequate professional care. In some ways, the proliferation of such home remedies ran counter to the growing professionalism of organized medicine, but it also facilitated the latter. Professional medicine is based on clinical experiment, and expertise based on the results of such experiments. Preplague medicine, with its texts of theses and antitheses, could be mastered in time by anyone who could read. Once the literate lay public gained access to it, it was demystified, and its weaknesses were made known to a fairly wide audience. It became clear to an ever-growing public that changes were necessary if plague were to be controlled.

Still another major medical development was the new role of hospitals.[37] Before the Black Death, hospitals were institutions designed primarily to isolate, rather than cure, the sick—to remove them from the mainstream of society so that they would not infect or offend the healthy. When a sick person entered a hospital, he was treated as if he were dead. His property was disposed of and, in many regions, a quasi-requiem mass was said for his soul; certainly, no one expected to see the poor wretch again. Further, many hospitals doubled as almshouses and pensionaries, while others took in widows, orphans, and even boarders. They offered little help to the victims of infectious diseases. After the Black Death, this began to change. Some hospitals remained isolation wards and pensionaries, but a substantial number began to try to cure their sick patients. Their methods were often crude, the cure rate very low by modern standards, with, in many instances, the cure probably worse than the disease. Nevertheless, the Black Death forever altered the goals of most hospitals, and began the process whereby they became permanently committed to the cure rather than isolation.

Among the many facets of this change were new techniques in management and organization. Most postplague hospitals were divided into wards—some for those with broken bones, others for different types of degenerative diseases, and still others for those with infectious diseases. Each ward had between 50 and 100 beds; like wards in twentieth century hospitals, those in the Late Middle Ages had beds lining the side walls, placed at right angles under windows, with space in the center for service. This had the disadvantage of extreme cold in winter, but the advantages of light and air in summer, and easier access for treatment and cleaning in all seasons. Beds were often shared, but the sheets were cleaned regularly, and most hospitals had running water, along with drains and pipes to carry away waste.

The best information about hospital management and organization comes from the Hotel Dieu in Paris.[38] When patients entered, they usually gave a dowrylike donation. Running a hospital was costly and patients who could afford it were expected to shoulder some of the operating costs. Patients' clothing was taken, their valuables were stored—a hopeful sign of possible departure—and hospital gowns and beds were provided. It appears to have been a very clean hospital. The walls were washed with lime biannually and, in one year, over 1300 brooms were purchased. Obviously, there were problems. When it was crowded, the Hotel Dieu often placed three or four patients in a single bed. The beds themselves could be problematic; they had straw mattresses tied to four wooden posts. Pillows were made from feathers and, although the bed sheets were linen, the coverlets were made from animal skins. Even with the weekly changings, the bedding got extremely dirty, and once a year furriers and coverlet weavers had to come in to eliminate the vermin and repair the damage. But looking again at the fourteenth-century improvements, the Hotel Dieu had a laundry staff of 15, and the number of patients was usually kept below 200. Most hospitals had landed estates from which to draw income and supplies, and the food was comparatively abundant and fresh. Meat was served four or five times a week, which was more than most people could afford even in the Late Middle Ages. The Hotel Dieu also insisted on high standards of personal hygiene. Each ward had several bathtubs, and there were weekly shampoos and visits from barbers.

The most important changes in postplague hospitals were medical. Many began or added to existing medical libraries. Several developed associations with doctors. In some Italian hospitals and the Hotel Dieu, such associations had begun before the Black Death, but in most places they were a legacy of the plague. In Bury St. Edmunds, for example, one of the town's five major hospitals developed a relationship with nearby Cambridge University wherein young medical students would serve a sort of internship at the hospital.[39] By 1450, the town's other hospitals had a similar arrangement with local physicians, a pattern which would become increasingly common all across Europe.

Another step in the evolution of modern medicine came in advances in public health and sanitation. The deplorable state of sanitation in preplague Europe has been discussed in Chapter 4, as have some of the new laws enacted by a few towns, such as Nuremberg.[40] But most important were the public health laws which developed in postplague Italy, and the rise of municipal boards of health. From Italy, they would spread to northern and central Europe until, by the sixteenth century, public health was a common phenomenon in most of Europe's urban centers. The idea of a municipal surgeons was an old one in Italy; it dated from the twelfth century and was based on the notion of free medical care for the poor. But the concept of a single, centrally controlled board of public health was born of the Black Death. At first, the boards' sole concern was plague prevention. But, by 1400, they had added supervision and, in some cases, actual control over virtually every aspect of health and sanitation.

The development of the boards can best be understood by looking at those in Venice, Florence, and Milan.[41] In March 1348, with the Black Death raging throughout the city, the Venetian Great Council appointed a Committee of Three, whose task it was "to consider diligently all possible ways to preserve public health and avoid corruption of the environment." The board was provisional and was terminated in 1351 when the Black Death came to an end. But it was revived in 1361 during the successive epidemics of the second plague pandemic. Eventually, it became clear that the establishment of a permanent board of public health was necessary, if only to serve as a beacon to warn of impending plague outbreaks, and, early in the fifteenth century, this was done. The Great Council appointed three noblemen as Commissioners of the Public Health, appointments which they could not refuse on pain of fine and imprisonment. They, in turn, supervised the city's doctors and appointed full-time subordinate health officials to watch over each district of Venice. The subordinates were assigned to keep an eye on medical practitioners in their neighborhoods, observe local sanitary conditions, and notify the central board of any cases of plague.

The board of public health in Florence was created in 1347 in circumstances similar to those in Venice.[42] Like the board in Venice, that in Florence was originally conceived as provisional and was made permanent only when the recurrent nature of the plague pandemic became apparent. By the mid-fifteenth century, the Florentine board's duties were clearly outlined: "to give full authority . . . for a period of three months to make provisions and issue ordinances, preserve public health, keep off the plague, and avoid an epidemic." Under Florentine inspiration—and sometimes auspices—similar boards were created in other Tuscan towns in the fifteenth century, including Livorno, Lucca, Orvieto, Pisa, Pistoia, and Pontremoli.

The most effective board of health was that of Milan. Milan suffered less from the Black Death than did any other large Italian town, and one reason may have been the decisive and prompt action of the Milanese authorities. On hearing of the approach of the Black Death, the Visconti rulers of the city, who were more powerful than the leaders of Venice or Florence, appointed a magistracy, or board, for public health and gave it sweeping powers. Its leaders were all noblemen, many of them members of the Visconti family, and its head reported directly to the duke. Milan's board was at least partly staffed by medical professionals, including physicians, surgeons, and apothecaries, some of whom were very distinguished doctors. In the mid-fifteenth century, for example, Ferrari de Grado, a professor of medicine from the University of Padua and personal physician to the city's ruling duke, served as the board's adviser. During his tenure, the board was constituted as follows: the health commissioner, always a lay noble; one university-trained physician; one surgeon; one notary; one barber-surgeon; two horsemen, used primarily as messengers and, to a lesser extent, along with three footmen, as police; one officer in charge of the bills of mortality; one carter, presumably to take away dead bodies in normal times, who would have additional helpers during epidemics; and two gravediggers, who also would be supplemented during times of crisis. The physician and surgeon were of higher rank and received more pay than the others, but, like the carter and gravediggers, were considered employees of the municipality. At all times, final control of the board was vested in lay hands.

The first job of all the public health boards was to report an epidemic; the next job was to try to isolate it. The latter was usually done by quarantine, which was rarely successful with plague. Medieval quarantines were designed to isolate people, not insects or rodents, and they followed the traditional theory of transmission by miasma-contagion. Infected persons and their goods and property were isolated from the healthy, and their movement was restricted. The infected area was then placed under a "ban." Movement in and out of the banned areas was possible only with a special pass issued by the board of public health. The pass identified the holder's name, place of origin, and business, and certified his good health; anyone who traveled into a banned zone risked his health. The rules of the ban were applied to denizens as well as aliens, and locals had to carry passes in times of epidemic in order to move about their own town.

After establishing the quarantine, the health boards collected certain information on bills of mortality. An appointed official, usually a notary, recorded the names, ages, and causes of death of the victims. The purpose of the bills was to identify the disease causing an epidemic so that it might be isolated more quickly. By the late fifteenth century, the boards of health had become so successful that they were granted powers similar to those of today's public health officials. These included the inspection for quality and marketing of foodstuffs and, in Milan and Venice, control over sanitation, hospitals, burials, hostelries, and the manufacture and sale of drugs. As their powers grew, the boards became increasingly unpopular. Many townspeople resented the restrictions imposed upon them, the interference with their movements, and the confiscation of their goods and property. Such resentment, especially when expressed by the most influential people in town, might explain why the officers of the boards were usually noblemen; as such, they were better able to resist attacks. Generally, such attacks consisted of grumbling and verbal abuse, but sometimes they got worse. A Milanese board member wrote:

> [We] were execrated by the ignorant populace, which listened to a few physicians, who, caring little for the public health, kept saying that there was no question of plague. . . . Fed and imbued with such delu-

sion, the populace began to slander [the public health officials] and when by accident [we] moved through narrow streets of the popular quarters [we] were vilified with foul and unseemly words, and were even pelted with stones.[43]

One response to this periodic violence was to give to health officers the authority to fine, arrest, and even torture offenders. Such powers were first written into law in Venice in 1504, and became general throughout Italy by the mid-sixteenth century. The effect of the board's police powers varied with the station of the offender. In 1490, for example, John the Devil, a well-known Venetian pimp, slandered the town's public health board, objecting to certain quarantine restrictions that limited prostitution and thus cut down on his profits. Health board officials had him arrested, publicly whipped, marched in chains throughout Venice, and then banished. By contrast, the boards were less successful in dealing with influential folk. For example, when the Florentine board banned all public church services, they ran afoul of the clergy and had to relent. When the movement of goods was stopped or goods were confiscated, the boards offended merchants; if the merchants were powerful enough, they could usually win exemptions. In essence, then, the effectiveness of the boards depended on governmental support in a late medieval context. As discussed, quarantines did little to restrict outbreaks of plague epidemics, but they did improve the sanitary conditions in towns, control the spread of many waterborne and pulmonary infections, and—perhaps most important of all—regulate the activities of medical professionals.

In addition to, and often as part of, the rise of the boards of health came another phenomenon of the postplague era—the plague doctor. In the more sophisticated parts of the West, beginning in Italy and then spreading to France, England, the Netherlands, and Germany, town councils or health boards hired municipal physicians and surgeons to treat plague victims. It was a difficult, dangerous, and unpleasant job and, to make matters worse, after the plague doctor had treated the victims, he had to endure a long quarantine of his own. Who, then, were these doctors, and why would anyone want the job? Very few were established doctors. Usually, the job was filled by second-raters who had difficulty establishing practices of their own, or by young physicians and surgeons, generally from rural areas, who were just starting out.

The professional life of one young plague doctor can be seen from a 1479 contract describing the "conditions agreed upon between the magnificent Community of Pavia and the doctor of medicine, Giovanni de Ventura, in order to treat the patients suffering from plague.''[44] Ventura was a fully certified physician with a university degree. He was paid 30 florins per month, provided with an "adequate house in an adequate location," and given various supplemental living costs, a cash advance, and two months' payment after he left his job. In return, Ventura was obligated to treat all plague victims, an agreement later expanded to include victims of all infectious diseases. It was a good, if not spectacular, contract. A skilled worker, provided he could find work, made about 60 florins a year; by comparison, the annual salary of Pavia's mayor was about 540 florins, that of a lecturer at the university was 200 florins, and that of a famous professor was 1000 florins. The greatest incentive for Ventura was probably not financial, but rather, the offer of citizenship and the possibility of setting up a more lucrative practice in the city after his term as plague doctor had ended.

To sum up, the idea of a municipal physician was an old one, extending back to the High Middle Ages. It began with the concept of free treatment for the poor, but was given impetus to expand by the Black Death and the second plague pandemic. The Black Death also stimulated the establishment of boards of public health. They were originally provisional, but, after recurring epidemics, were made permanent and vested with sweeping powers. By the end of the fifteenth century, these boards were common even in small towns and some villages throughout northern and central Italy, and had begun to spread to northern and parts of central Europe. Nuremberg's sanitary system has already been extolled; as was true of Milan, its comparatively low rates of disease morbidity throughout the later Middle Ages show the effectiveness of the best of the public health boards.

Another postplague medical phenomenon, which began in the late fourteenth century, was the evolution of professional deontology, or ethics. Distinct ethical codes, set internally by associations of medical practitioners, told the doctor how a professional acted.[45] Guy de Chauliac advised that

> the doctor should be well mannered, bold in many ways, fearful of dangers, that he should abhore the false cures or practices. He should be affable to the sick, kindhearted to his colleagues, wise in his prognostications. He should be chaste, sober, compassionate, and merciful; he should not be covetous, [or] grasping in money matters, and then he will receive a salary commensurate with his labors, the financial ability of his patients, the success of the treatment, and his own dignity.[46]

John of Arderne agreed. In his *Treatises of Fistula*, he extended
Chauliac's ideas to high standards of dress and deportment:

In clothes and other apparel he should be honest and not liken himself
in apparel and bearing to ministrels, but in clothing and bearing he
should show the manner of clerks. For why? It seems that any discreet
man clad in clerk's garb may occupy the boards of gentlemen. And be
he courteous at the lord's table, and be he not displeasing in words or
deeds to the guests sitting nearby, hear he many things but let him speak
but few. . . . And when he shall speak, let the words be short, and as far
as possible, fair and reasonable and without swearing. Beware that there
never be found double words in his mouth, for if he be found true in his
words few or none shall doubt his deeds.[47]

Still another prominent surgeon, the Fleming Jan Yperman, continued this theme, with special emphasis on conduct with female patients. A doctor must be morally upright and should not "broach
any other subject than that which concerns the treatment; neither
may he chat with the mistress of the house, the daughter, or the maid-
servant, nor look at them with leering eyes. For people are soon suspi-
cious, and by such things he is apt to incure enmity while the doctor
had better keep on friendly terms with them."[48]

Bedside manner was advised by Henri de Mondeville in his *Surgery:*

if the patient has a bold and hardy spirit or he may temper and soften
the warnings, or keep silent altogether if the patient is faint hearted or
good natured. . . . The surgeon should also promise that if the patient
can endure his illness and will obey . . . he will soon be cured and will
escape all of the dangers which have been pointed out to him; thus the
cure can be brought about more easily and quickly.[49]

Arderne discussed professional courtesy:

it is better if he has good excuses that he may refuse their [other physicians'] demands. . . . He may feign an injury, or illness, or some other
likely excuse. But if he accepts their demands, let him make a covenant
for his work and make it beforehand. . . . After he has visited the sick
person and if he thinks that the latter will recover, nevertheless he
should warn patients of the peril to come if treatment is not carried out
as he himself ordered.[50]

Two additional elements were needed to make medical practitioners truly professional. The first was outside support, be it from king,
local aristocrat, church, or municipal council. Approval by authorities meant more strength for medical boards and doctors. The second

was personal gain: prestige, a sense of power over the craft and science, self-esteem, and a good income. Late medieval medical practitioners, at least the physicians, surgeons, and apothecaries, became a financial elite after the Black Death, ranking with lawyers and wealthy merchants. The physician in Chaucer's *Canterbury Tales* shows this well:

> And yet he was right chary of expense
> He kept the gold he kept from pestilence
> For gold in physic is a fine cordial
> And therefore loved he gold exceedingly all.[51]

This attitude toward making a good living is also well-represented by Chaucer's contemporary, Arderne, who recommended that: "after inquiring about the state of [the patient's] health [the doctor should] ask boldly for more or less [in fees] but be he ever wary of scarce asking, for over scarce asking sets at naught both the market and the thing [the practice of medicine]."[52] Arderne also believed that

the physician should give . . . advice to only five classes of people: (1) to those who are really poor, for love of God; . . . (2) to his friends, from whom he does not wish to receive a fixed revenue or a definite sum of money; . . . (3) to those whom he knows to be grateful after a complete recovery; . . . (4) to those who repay poorly, such as our seigneurs and their relatives, chamberlains, justices and bailiffs, advocates, and all of those to whom he does not dare refuse council; . . . (5) to those who pay completely in advance.[53]

These developments—the rise of surgery, the transformation of the role of hospitals, the rise in standards of public health, and the development of deontology—were all part of the professionalization of medicine and crucial to all was the recurrence of plague. By the early sixteenth century, medicine had become a detailed, complex corpus of knowledge and skills which at its most arcane and successful levels could be understood only after long, intensive and specialized studies. Modern medicine had not yet evolved completely. A major step remained—the triumph of physical science in medical research. This process, which began in the sixteenth century with Paracelsus and Vesalius, was part and parcel of the scientific revolution and the rise of chemistry and physics in the seventeenth century, and was not completed until the eighteenth century. But its foundations were laid in the 150 years after the Black Death.

# CHAPTER 7
# Disease and the Transformation of Medieval Europe

IF THE BLACK DEATH had been the only plague epidemic of the later Middle Ages, its historical importance would be diminished. It would be remembered as a severe and catastrophic blow, but an isolated one. Human population is very resilient and responds to any single check, even one as severe as the Black Death. By 1360, population levels all across Europe were beginning to creep back toward their preplague levels. Had the high marriage and birth rates and low mortality rates of the 1350s continued unabated, the demographic damage of the Black Death would have been undone by the 1380s, and parts of Europe would once again have been in the throes of a subsistence crisis. By 1361, it appears that many people had forgotten the Black Death, and some aspects of daily life resumed. The changes in psyche and, consequently, in styles and modes of art probably would have remained, and the trifunctional system would still have been profoundly shaken. But many of the other social and most of the economic changes were just beginning and might have been nipped in the bud. This was not to happen.

In the spring of 1361 the *pestis secunda*, the second epidemic of the second plague pandemic, broke out in Europe. Plague was the only agent that could assure continuing high mortality. In Malthusian terms, it was the most severe "positive check" possible, and the only one which could keep mortality high enough to avert a renewal of the subsistence crisis that had impoverished Europe from the middle of the thirteenth century. Plague would recur every few years for the rest of the fourteenth and all of the fifteenth century, and initiate an era of depopulation that would last until the sixteenth century. From such depopulation would come changes even more profound than those brought by the Black Death.[1]

The *pestis secunda*, also called the *pestis puerorum* in reference to the large number of young people it killed, lasted through the winter and into the spring of 1362.[2] Given the etiology of *Y. pestis* and the ecology of its insect and rodent hosts, this is not surprising. Once plague is established in an area, it will recur in response to a combination of climatic and natural factors. But medieval people did not know this, and the return of plague was a nightmare reborn. While primarily an attack of bubonic plague and not as severe as the Black Death, the *pestis secunda* was still one of the most lethal epidemics in history. Many observers, including Guy de Chauliac, believed it was especially deadly for select groups, including the young—those born after the Black Death—and the landed upper classes. One Polish chronicler, exaggerating no doubt but relaying a valid impression, claimed that only aristocrats and children perished. Such narrative reports are reflected in administrative records. In England, for example, certificates of death among the landed classes, the *Inquisitiones Post Mortem*, indicate that mortality among the gentry was over 25%, about as high as it had been during the Black Death.[3] Perhaps mortality was highest among the landed elite and children, but it was also severe among the other strata of society. In Normandy, general rural mortality was around 20%; in urban Pisa and Pistoia, it was the same. Boccaccio claimed that 100,000 people were killed in Florence, and Petrarch believed that only 10,000 Florentines were left alive.[4] While they, too, exaggerated, about 20% of Florence's population probably did perish, an enormous death rate by any standards other than those of the Black Death.

It is not possible to give a definitive figure for mortality during the *pestis secunda*. As with the Black Death, the best records exist in England and, consequently, the most extensive research has been done there. In addition to the quarter of the gentry who died, about

20% of the magnates, or great lords, perished. In Bury St. Edmunds, the death rate in 1361–62 was nearly ten times higher than in any other year during the second half of the fourteenth century.[5] And in the archdiocese of York, close to 20% of the beneficed clergy were killed.[6] Mortality varied from region to region, but a national estimate of 20% for England seems reasonable; in Europe, the *pestis secunda* must have killed between 10% and 20% of the total population.

The shock of the return of the plague was enormous, the reactions of Boccaccio and Petrarch being good examples. But the worst was still to come. The occurrence of *pestis secunda* confirmed a plague cycle, as explained in Chapter 1, in which the dreaded disease recurred in intervals for the next four hundred years. A third epidemic came in 1369, convincing many observers that plague had become part of their environment. Chroniclers began noting plague's presence in matter-of-fact terms, and the *pestis tertia,* as the epidemic of 1369 was called, received little more than a mention in many records.[7] It was less severe than either of its predecessors, but it still took a considerable toll. In England, mortality among both the gentry and the clergy was about 13%, and it must have killed between 10% and 15% of the population all across Europe. William Langland's Piers Ploughman might have been sounding a warning for future generations when he claimed that "the rain that rains where we rest should be sickness and the sorrows that we suffer often."[8]

After 1369, the most important feature to the second plague pandemic was not the death rate in any given epidemic, but rather, the frequency with which those epidemics occurred. From 1369 to 1479, no epidemic would kill more than 10% to 15% of the people in any large region, and some took barely 5%.[9] But plague entered a cycle in which it recurred from five or six to ten or twelve years, depending on local insect and rodent ecological and climatic conditions. To use England as an example once again, there was a national outbreak of plague in 1375, followed by one in the North in 1379, one in the Midlands in 1381–82, one in East Anglia, Essex, and Kent in 1383 and 1387, and two severe national epidemics with mortality of more than 10% each in 1390 and 1399–1400. There was another national epidemic in 1405–06, making for three major blows in a 15-year period. There was a plague in western England and Wales in 1410–11, followed by yet another national epidemic in 1411–12. Two years later, all the British Isles were afflicted, followed by a plague in East Anglia in 1420, a national epidemic in 1423, a London visitation in 1426, and a national epidemic in 1428–29. Things may have been worst in England, but other areas in Western Europe show broadly similar trends of frequency and virulence. The effect of two, three, or even more epidemics in successive generations ensured a continuous check on population, whatever levels marriage and birth rates may have reached.

As bad as things were from 1369 to 1430, they proved to be even worse in the half century that followed. Again, England provides a good example. In the 1430s, plague entered a shorter frequency cycle. In 1431, all of eastern England from Kent north to Lincolnshire and west to Hampshire was stricken. This was passed in scope and virulence by a national epidemic that lasted from 1433 to 1435; this epidemic was facilitated by a dramatic drop in temperature in late November 1434, which apparently allowed bubonic plague to become pneumonic. There were local plague epidemics in 1437 in London, Canterbury, St. Albans, Bristol, and Bury St. Edmunds, followed in 1438–39 by a national epidemic. Another cold autumn probably brought on the deadlier pneumonic strain, and overall mortality was exacerbated by one of the few crop failures in the fifteenth century. In East Anglia, mortality during 1438–39 reached about 12% of the population; while no national mortality data are available, crude figures indicate that death rates in two provincial towns rose from about 3% per year to over 30%.

Parts of England experienced plague epidemics in 11 of the 18 years between 1442 and 1459. London was particularly hard hit, suffering on at least six separate occasions. From 1463 to 1465, another severe epidemic hit the entire kingdom, followed by one more in 1467. But all this simply set the stage for the terrible 1470s. Perhaps England's increased trade with the Continent brought in new bacterial strains, or perhaps there was a change in the primary and secondary host populations. Whatever the cause, in 1471, all of England was overwhelmed. In East Anglia, adult mortality reached 20%. John Paston, a Norfolk gentleman then in London, wrote home to his family:

> I pray you send me word if any of our friends or well wishers be dead, for I fear that there is great death in Norwich and in other boroughs and towns in Norfolk, for I assure you that this is the most universal death that I ever witnessed in England. For, by my troth, I can hear from pilgrims who travel through the country that no man who rides or goes in any country or borough town in England is free from the sickness.[10]

The epidemic of 1471 was brief in duration, but extreme in its virulence, a classic example of bubonic plague at its most destructive. It began in late August, peaked through September and the first week in October, remained deadly throughout that month and disappeared with the first frosts in November. In its wake, 10% to 15% of England's population lay dead.

There were additional, localized plague epidemics in the mid-1470s, but all served as a prelude for the epidemic of 1479–80. From autumn to autumn, a combined epidemic of bubonic and pneumonic plague devastated all of Britain. Total mortality, where it can be measured accurately, ranged up to 20%, around the levels of the *pestis secunda* of 1361–62. The narrative sources raised their voices as one to lament its devastation; even records such as the stately *Great Chronicle* of London, which had not noted any plague epidemics in the previous century, drew attention to this one.[11] The meeting of Parliament was postponed, and the king's court was dismissed from Easter 1480 to midsummer. All activity in the London Guildhall ceased, and at least three members of the Paston clan were killed.

In most cases, the local evidence for the Continent is not as good or heavily researched as that for England, but what has been studied corroborates the English picture. In the Netherlands, there were epidemics in 1360–62, 1363–64, 1368–69, 1371–72, 1382–84, 1400–01, 1409, 1420–21, 1438–39, 1450–54, 1456–59, 1466–72, 1481–82, 1487–90, and 1492–94.[12] Normandy had plague cycles approximately as frequent as those in eastern England and the Netherlands, from every four to twelve years, with especially virulent cycles in the 1390s, 1440, 1450s, and 1470s.[13] In Cambrai, there was a similar frequency pattern, with the 1430s and 1450s being particularly bad decades.[14] Paris was struck eight times between 1414 and 1439, and Barcelona had eleven epidemics between 1396 and 1437.[15] The Iberian Peninsula was visited fourteen times from 1391 to 1457. In the Umbrian town of Perugia, plague was present for nineteen years in the fifteenth century, while the German towns of Hamburg, Nuremberg, and Cologne suffered through at least ten epidemics each. As in England, the Continental patterns suggest that plague came at least two or three times a generation and was sufficiently virulent to keep population levels low. The best estimate is that from 1349 to 1450 European population declined between 60% and 75%, with the bulk of the depopulation in rural areas.

The fourteenth and fifteenth centuries were unique not just because of the presence of plague, but for the ongoing presence of and, in some cases, introduction of other infectious diseases. Smallpox, *la petite verolé*, remained a major problem. It continued to be chronic among children, and in the 1440s and 1460s was epidemic in parts of western Europe.[16] The red plague, as smallpox was sometimes called, killed more people in northern France in the 1440s than even bubonic plague. Malaria, or the ague, was chronic in several areas, including central Italy, southern France, southern Spain and Portugal, the Low Countries, most of the Jutland peninsula, southern Sweden, and eastern and southern England. More important still were the enteric fevers. These waterborne diseases were associated with the poor sanitation still present in many urban areas, despite the post-Black Death public health reforms. The deadliest were infantile diarrhea, dehydration from which was a major cause of infant mortality, as high as 50% of all children, and intestinal dysentery, the "bloody flux."[17] Dysentery proved especially lethal to armies, and could flare up in a given area after a campaign. In 1411, a severe epidemic of dysentery swept through Savoy, France, and England. In 1473, another visited East Anglia and killed between 15% and 20% of the adult male population in a three-month period. When these diseases are figured in with the omnipresent plague epidemics, the general frequency of major infectious lethal diseases was as little as three to five years apart from 1370 to 1470.

In essence, then, the impact of the second plague pandemic must be seen in two ways. First, there was the immediate and stunning effect of the Black Death, with the loss of between one-third and one-half the population. Second, there were the relentless onslaught of subsequent epidemics and the resulting long-term depopulation. In many ways, because human population is so resilient in the wake of one epidemic, the combined effects of the later epidemics may well have been the more important of the two. One recent theory claims that the social and economic watershed of the later Middle Ages came, not in 1250 or 1348, but, rather, with the epidemic of 1374–75.[18] In any circumstance, it is worth reiterating that several attacks from plague in a single generation made demographic growth impossible for at least a century after the Black Death. Primarily because of pandemic plague, Europe's population in 1430 was 50% to 75% lower than it had been in 1290. In some places it began to rise in the 1450s, in others in the 1480s, and in others still not until early in the sixteenth century. Most observers agree that it was not until the mid-sixteenth century that Europe regained its thirteenth-century population levels. And in the late fourteenth and fifteenth centuries, dominated by depopulation and manpower shortages, came changes which profoundly influenced the course of western history.

The most basic of these changes were in Europe's economy.[19] The Black Death brought tremendous short-term dislocation, but it was continuing depopulation that was responsible for long-term economic change. First, and most important, since it affected about 80% of Europe's population, were changes in the way land was farmed and held. Depopulation ended the manorial system, at least in the West. Years ago, scholars believed that manorialism lasted into the fourteenth century and was destroyed by the Black Death. This was not quite the case. The system was in trouble by the late thirteenth century. But the Black Death, subsequent epidemics, and resulting depopulation assured its demise throughout much of western and central Europe by 1500.

Several things contributed to this demise. One of the most important was a condition called *Wüstungen*, the depopulation of rural areas. Although urban populations were diminished as much and perhaps more from plague than were those in the countryside, towns offered greater economic opportunity.[20] However much plague depleted urban populations, there were always country folk ready to replace them. This migration to towns combined with the effects of disease in rural regions to cause a pronounced shortage of agricultural workers. The best arable continued to be farmed, but more marginal fields, especially those assarted during the halcyon expansion years of the twelfth and thirteenth centuries, could no longer be cultivated. In many ways, this was good. Forest and pasture lands were restored and overcropping ended. But, along with the fallow fields, many villages were abandoned, or "lost."[21] In England, more than 1300 villages were deserted between 1350 and 1500, almost all in areas with marginal arable. A good example was the Brecklands, in the eastern part of the kingdom. This region was dry and sandy and, until 1100, was virtually deserted. But, between 1100 and 1349, population pressure forced its settlement and cultivation. By 1400, this process was reversed, and 28 villages, more than half those in the region, were completely abandoned. Contemporaries were aware of the situation. John Rous, an historian who traveled through western England in the 1470s, counted 58 villages that had been lost, and claimed that this was but the tip of the iceberg: "If such destruction as that in Warwickshire took place in other parts of the country, it would be a national danger. Yet not all my list is of Warwickshire villages; some, although a few, are in Gloucestershire and Worcestershire, but none of them more than a dozen miles from Warwick."[22]

*Wüstungen* extended to the Netherlands, France, Germany, and eastern Europe. In Thurungia, along the north German plain, there were 179 villages in 1300. By 1500, 146 had been abandoned. The area most effected was northeastern Europe. Part and parcel of the *Drang nach Osten*—the German conquest and colonization of Pomerania, Prussia, northern Poland, and Livonia—was the continued migration into the area of peasants from the Netherlands and western Germany. The peasants went east, at least in part, because they were offered better terms of tenure.[23] But, as will be discussed below, most Western peasants were freed from tenurial obligations after the Black Death. Hence, land was readily available to many farmers near their homes, and there were fewer of them to migrate in any case. This end of Germanic migration led to abandoned villages, on the one hand, and to a return to Slavic language and culture in some areas, on the other.

Perhaps most important, *Wüstungen* brought environmental changes. By 1200, virtually all of the Mediterranean Basin and most of the north German plain had been deforested and cultivated. Indigenous flora and fauna were replaced by domestic grasses and animals, and invaluable woodlands were lost. With depopulation, this process was reversed. Much of the primeval vegetation returned, and abandoned fields and pastures were reforested. Given the importance of wood as a building material and fuel, this alone guaranteed a rise in standards of living. Some of the old wildlife, such as the auroch and wisent, were extirpated from all but a few isolated places, but other species returned. A good barometer of the state of the wild is the presence of wolves. By 1300, they had been so heavily hunted that they remained only in the Far North, in mountain areas, and in Russia. In the fourteenth and fifteenth centuries, this situation changed. English and French chroniclers mention their presence even around towns and, in the 1420s, several were seen roaming through the suburbs of Paris.[24] Population density in preplague Europe was so high and the size of the arable was so extensive that it was in danger of undergoing the natural impoverishment that troubled parts of Africa and Asia. The Black Death reversed this; with a few exceptions, the forests of twentieth-century Europe date from the Late Middle Ages.

There were also profound changes in land tenure.[25] Depopulation virtually ended serfdom in western Europe. For the first time in centuries, peasants were mobile enough to pick up and move from one manor to the next if they were unhappy with the conditions under which they held their land. A peasant could leave in the middle of the night, go to the next manor, and expect to be welcomed, so short was the supply of labor. Any lord who hoped to keep his workers had to offer them better terms of tenure than they had had before the Black Death. By the 1360s, this had resulted in much lower rents in most of western Europe. This development was followed by the commutation of traditional labor and boon services, that is, the substitution of cash payments for old labor services. Then, in the course of the fifteenth century, most of the other labor services and many of the banalities were eliminated, replaced by money rates and long-term leases. In effect, while the lords still owned the land or held it of a higher lord, they did so with hired labor rather than unfree peasants holding on customary tenure. The peasant worked all the land he could and paid only rent. By about 1400 in Italy and England, 1450 in France and the Netherlands, and 1500 in much of central Europe, serfdom and custom holding had been replaced by a new form of tenure called copyhold. In copyhold, so named because both the peasant and the lord had a copy of the tenure agreement, a lord and peasant made their best business deal, whereby the peasant got use of the land and the lord got a fixed, annual payment.

Serfdom did not end everywhere. It lingered throughout parts of the West and, in much of eastern Europe, was actually introduced after the Black Death.[26] Poland, Prussia, and Hungary were among the best grain-growing areas in Eurasia; in the specialized agricultural system that developed after 1350, they became Europe's breadbasket, feeding the towns of the Netherlands and the Rhineland. Grain growing could be kept profitable only by using cheap, unfree laborers, and many Eastern lords used force to keep their peasants in place. Without kings to appeal to for aid, or towns to flee to as an alternative, eastern European peasants lacked the resources and mobility of their counterparts in the West. For them, depopulation was disastrous. Thus, the second plague pandemic changed the nature of land tenure all across Europe. In the West, it nurtured a prosperous, free peasantry, who would become the yeoman of Shakespeare's time; in the East, it led to the serfdom and misery of peasants, which persisted in some places until the nineteenth century.

For landlords in the West, the new tenurial conditions were potentially catastrophic.[27] Many lords were forced to abandon any form of direct cultivation and lease their entire estates, collecting cash as *ren-*

*tiers* and usually becoming absentee landlords. In an era of rising prices, this could be disastrous, especially when the tenants held the land with long-term copyhold leases. But for enterprising lords, disaster need not come, for there was a solution to the new land-intensive economy. High labor costs and low prices for foodstuffs meant an end to wheat farming, except on a large scale and in the places with the best arable, such as southern and Midlands England, central France, Prussia, and Poland. But there were still ways in which farmers could make money. For a lord with a very large tract of land, animal husbandry was a profitable alternative to grain farming. There were several reasons for this. First, the increase in living standards meant a greater demand for meat. Sheep were particularly popular. They were easy to keep, required the supervision of only a shepherd and a few dogs, and could get along nicely on wild grass and shrubs rather than fodder. Further, mutton kept comparatively well, always an important consideration in the days before refrigeration. There is good evidence for this increased demand for mutton and other meats in the Middle East.[28] In the early fourteenth century, before the Black Death, an average individual in Syria had consumed a daily diet of about 1154 calories, including 45.6 grams of protein, 196 grams of carbohydrates, and 20 grams of fat. By the mid-fifteenth century, this had risen to 1930 calories, consisting of 82 grams of protein, 294 grams of carbohydrates, and over 45 grams of fat. Before the Black Death, a monthly mutton ration for a family of four had been about 12 kilograms; after the Black Death, it rose to 30 kg.

There was a second, even more profitable reason to go into husbandry; animals provided other sources of riches besides their meat. Cattle hides could be made into leather and sheep fleece into wool. Wool was in particular demand and could be collected every year, giving it a great advantage over cowhide. Throughout Europe enterprising lords stopped growing wheat and began to raise sheep—hence, the English proverb, "sheep's hooves turn sand into gold."

The raising of sheep and cattle on a grand scale was an option limited to large landholders, usually lords.[29] There were other forms of animal husbandry, however, which could be practiced by small landholders. Dairy farming was particularly popular in northwestern Europe. Another technique was practiced by peasants in the low-lying areas of the West, such as eastern England, the Netherlands, and Jutland. A field was flooded and filled with fish, usually carp. In a year or two, the pond was drained, the fish were collected, and the field, newly fertilized, was sown.

Another farming method popular with small landholders throughout Europe was the cultivation of specialized cash crops. In France, Italy, Spain, and those parts of Germany where climate permitted, viticulture was extended, greater demand for wines being still another aspect of rising standards of living. In parts of the Mediterranean Basin, sugar and fruits were raised. In the North, where cold weather restricted the growth of most fruits, new apple and pear trees were added to old groves. Also popular in the North were special grain crops such as barley and oats. Barley was used for ale and the newly popular beer, while oats were used as fodder for the growing livestock population. Specialized agriculture included a number of industrial crops, most of them connected with textiles, Europe's principal industry. In Italy and parts of Spain, silkworms were raised. In northern Europe, particularly Germany, hemp, flax, and the dyestuffs woad, madder, and kermes were collected or grown. Industrial crops often required as much labor as did wheat, but, unlike wheat, they continued to fetch high market prices.

These tenurial and economic agricultural changes had enormous social effects.[30] For the wealthiest artistocrats—those holding hundreds of manors and tens of thousands of acres—economic changes brought some fall in income, but posed less of a threat to their privileges than did the decay of trifunctionalism and the changes in military techniques. Most of them simply settled into the life of *rentiers* and absentee landlords, and many moved to towns or country estates that did not have working farms. For the lesser lords—the gentry who held just a few manors and hundreds of acres—the new conditions were potentially catastrophic. Many, perhaps most, gentlemen did not have enough land to survive in an age of low long-term leases, high commodity prices, and reduced rents. They were forced either to cultivate their estates directly, or to find some supplemental income—usually through service in the military or the clergy, or marriage with a wealthy merchant. Those gentlemen who refused to adjust to the new agrarian conditions risked impoverishment and, ultimately, the loss of their armigerous status.

Gentlemen on their way down might be passed by upwardly mobile peasants.[31] The postplague period was the era of the rich and prosperous peasant, the yeoman or kulak. The size of the average peasant land holding increased considerably in most places. On Redgrave Manor in England, for example, the average size of a peasant's holding in 1300 was about 12 acres.[32] By 1400, it was 20 acres and, by 1450, it was over 30 acres. In France, Germany, Spain, and Poland, the patterns were similar. Added to this was the fact that, because of depopulation, only the best arable was planted and fields were again allowed to lie fallow. Thus, by the early fifteenth century, if not sooner, the soil exhaustion of the early fourteenth century came to an end, and seed yields began to rise. On the estates of the bishop of Winchester in southern England, seed yields for wheat were 4.2 to 1 in 1300.[33] By 1350 they were 4.4 to 1 and, by 1400, about 5 to 1. From 1300 to 1400, yields in barley rose from 3.8 to 4.3, and those of oats from 2.4 to 3.8. Obviously, not all peasants increased their holdings, and there were food shortages and a few famines in the postplague era. But malnutrition and hardship were rare, and wages were so high that even cottars and *famuli*, or migrant workers, could usually keep body and soul together, as they never had been able to do between 1250 and 1347.

It was easy for ambitious peasants to increase their arable and grow special crops for the new diversified markets. It is worth reiterating that virtually any peasant who was unhappy with his status and land allotment on one manor could pick up, go to another, and almost surely be welcomed. One of the best barometers of the new prosperity among the peasantry was the change in inheritance patterns.[34] Before the Black Death, in the midst of Europe's subsistence crisis, only sons, and then usually only the eldest son, had a chance to inherit the father's property. By the fifteenth century, this had changed. Most male progeny were given some property and, by 1450, it was not uncommon for daughters to get a piece of the estate.

Like the agricultural changes, the industrial changes in the postplague period reflected the effects of depopulation.[35] Total industrial production in Europe was lower in 1450 than it had been in 1300. Manpower was the basis of late medieval output and, even with the growth of specialized markets after the Black Death, depopulation led to a smaller work force and lower production. In some of Europe's traditional industrial regions, especially parts of the Netherlands and northern and central Italy, production fell so much that the results can best be described as a depression.[36] Many scholars have used this decline, particularly in the Flemish textile industry, as evidence of a general economic downturn in the fourteenth and fifteenth centuries. But this interpretation requires modification. Postplague Flemish industry was typical of preplague European industry, in that it produced simple, fashionless, inexpensive woolen cloth for a mass market. Its large-scale operations employed more than half the workers in several towns; they had to "punch in" and "out" on medieval versions of twentieth century timeclocks.

Depopulation helped to ruin this industry. It depleted the mass market, and the survivors, anxious to spend their money, were attracted by more sophisticated clothing. Other factors contributed to the ruin of the Flemish economy. The Hundred Years' War disrupted trade routes, and there were labor problems and social tensions between workers and management. Perhaps most important, Flemish woolworkers failed to obtain reliable alternative sources of wool when the supply from England, the traditional source, began to dry up around 1400. In effect, Flemish industry was analogous to those farmers who continued to grow wheat and failed to keep step with the new economic conditions.

But new industries came of age in the late Middle Ages.[37] In other parts of the Netherlands, notably Brabant and Holland, diversified textile production was developed which took advantage of the more sophisticated tastes that evolved after the Black Death. There was continuing demand for fine brocaded cloth and linen, the latter popular for use as undergarments, which had come into fashion. In southern Germany, linen and fustians were produced. One of the best examples of postplague industrial adaptation came in Tuscany. Before the plague, Tuscan woolen cloth production ranked next to that of Flanders; after it, Tuscan producers were faced with the same problems of changing markets, the failure of traditional suppliers, and labor troubles. But, at least to some degree, Italian industry changed, and if the number of pieces made in 1450 was not as great as it had been in 1300, the decline was far more gradual than that in Flanders. Enterprising Tuscan merchants went to Castile and North Africa to get wool when it was no longer available from England. Alternatively, they bought rough, unfinished English or even Flemish cloth and then refined, refurbished, brocaded, and otherwise improved it. Some Tuscan towns developed a silk industry, and exported the product throughout Europe and the Middle East. Flexibility and quick reaction to changing tastes were the keys to success in the age of depopulation.

Depopulation was also directly responsible for advances in industrial technology.[38] The period from 1250 to 1500 was one of the most innovative in history. Some of the changes predated the Black Death, and others which came after 1347 had little to do with the plague. This was the case with the perfection of eyeglasses and, to some extent, gunpowder, and clocks. But the continued development of guns and clocks was accelerated by the postplague lack of manpower and the new perception of time. A number of other important technological breakthroughs, most notably printing, came at Europe's population nadir. There was a direct relationship between technology and depopulation. For example, in England, the Netherlands, and France, the value of windmills and watermills more than doubled after the Black Death. Furthermore, all over Europe and the Middle East, plague caused a shortage of skilled workers, especially among masons and carpenters, whose training was long and arduous. Wages reflected the shortages. In France, adjusting for inflation, masters and journeymen in both crafts were earning more than twice as much in 1500 as they were in 1300. This created hardship and, in some places, led to industrial decline.

But shortage was the mother of medieval invention. Depopulation put a premium on new techniques that could save work time. A good example is the fishing industry.[39] Fishing was big business in the Late Middle Ages, as fish was an important source of protein in most people's diets, especially during Lent. Before the Black Death, fishermen had to come ashore to salt (i.e., preserve) their catch. But, around 1380, Dutch fishermen perfected a method of salting, drying, and storing their catch aboard ship. This allowed them to stay at sea longer, sail farther from shore, and bring home more fish. There were also advances in mining technology. Most experts agree that there was a general expansion in mining and metallurgy after the Black Death, stimulated in large part by increasing demand for bullion and metals for guns. The number of miners, never large before the plague, suffered from the same extent of depletion as did the ranks of masons and carpenters. In essence, the mining industry faced disaster at a time of optimum demand. But, in the fifteenth century, there were new developments in water pumps, which allowed mines to be dug deeper, and new techniques in shaft shoring, which enabled miners to go into deeper holes and do so more safely than ever before.

The economic changes brought by depopulation can also be seen in trade patterns.[40] Before the plagues, Western commercial routes were dominated by Italians and, to a lesser extent, by the Hanseatic League in northern Germany. In 1300, Europe's long-distance trade routes converged around the towns of the Netherlands, where the Italians controlled most of the transactions by using superior business skills and the stable, gold-based currencies of Venice and Florence as their mediums of exchange. By 1500, this had begun to change, with Northerners playing a larger role, and a trade imbalance draining the resources of the South. Many of the reasons for the transformation were only tangentially related to the plague pandemic; among these were the spread of literacy in the North and the mastery by Northern merchants, after a period of about 300 years, of the sophisticated business and banking techniques developed in Italy.

The decline of the Italians had political overtones as well. For hundreds of years, they had been the middlemen in the valuable spice and luxury trades between the West and southern Asia. They had set up trading colonies in the Levant and along the coast of the Black Sea, and had exacted commercial privileges from local Muslim rulers. But, in the fourteenth century, the Ottoman Turks, a new, militantly Islamic people, took control over much of the Middle East and began to limit, and then to eliminate, the Italian middlemen. However, despite all the travails, it would be incorrect to draw too rigid an image of Southern decline and Northern prosperity by 1500. Venice remained the richest, most prosperous and populous city in Europe, and many parts of the North, including most of the Hanseatic towns and the county of Flanders, were in the midst of economic contraction. Indeed, so general was this contraction that many scholars are inclined to label the Late Middle Ages as a commercial, as well as an industrial, depression.

Depression, however, does not accurately describe Europe's economic state. A distinguished economic historian has summed up the situation rather nicely: "The historian contemplating the economic evolution of this period had the impression that he is witnessing a relay race, with the torch being taken over in turn by one town after another."[41] In the late fifteenth century, the Hanse towns lost their monopoly in the Baltic hinterlands to Dutch and English merchants.[42] In the Netherlands, Flemish industrialists and workers and Italian merchants and bankers played a diminished role, and there were fewer goods to trade. Bruges, in Flanders, Europe's greatest entrepôt in the thirteenth and early fourteenth centuries, declined, but its place was taken by Antwerp, in nearby Brabant. An increasing share of the trans-Alpine trade was carried by southern Germans from Nuremberg, Augsberg, and other towns. So aggressive were these Germans that by the late fifteenth century they had established *fondaci*, or trading centers, in cities as prominent as Venice. And while they would not carry as great a volume of goods as the Italians until the mid-sixteenth century, increasing numbers of fifteenth-century Dutch and English merchants such as John Free and Robert Sturmy began to venture into the Mediterranean.[43] By 1500, Europe's economic center was shifting to the Northwest.

General environmental conditions played a major role in this economic transformation. Some changes were brought by the weather.[44]

One of the reasons for the commercial decline of Bruges, Pisa, and Florence, for example, was the silting up of the rivers through which most of their trade was carried. Another "natural" change concerned the deposit of raw materials. The North was the richest part of the Western world; it had the best farmlands and raw materials (e.g., wood, iron, wool, and foodstuffs). These supplies had been tapped, but not exhausted, during the expansion of the High Middle Ages; in the case of renewable sources such as high-quality arable and woodlands, depopulation actually proved to be a boon.

By contrast, the Mediterranean Basin was poor in raw materials and natural resources, and generally lacking in proper distribution of rainfall. As a result, the expansion of the twelfth and thirteenth centuries proved to be too much of a drain, even with depopulation. Topsoil was washed away and woodlands were completely depleted. Southern merchants had lived off their wits and the domination of special commercial and financial skills. When Northern merchants picked up these techniques, the Southerners had one less resource to fall back on.

Plague also played a direct role in the economic changes. Depopulation meant that the days of continually expanding markets, at least in Europe proper, were over. No northeastern or Iberian frontiers remained to be opened. Furthermore, the psychological changes brought by recurrent plague created new types of markets. People had more money, wanted to spend it, and wanted to spend it on finer and more luxurious goods.[45] The breakdown of the trifunctional system meant that material things brought more status than they had before the Black Death. Postplague markets were there for the enterprising, flexible merchant. A good example of these new entrepreneurs was the Merchant Adventurers of England. Formed in the fifteenth century, mostly by mercers from London and York, the Adventurers sold cloth and anything else they could get, loading goods into their boats and taking them across the Continent, in some cases as far east as Prussia. The Adventurers replaced the more sedentary Merchants of the Staple, a fourteenth-century group given a monopoly on trading wool, who were rooted into one, specified area (or staple, hence the name) and just one commodity. It was this entrepreneurial spirit which propelled Iberian, English, and Dutch merchants to look for new markets, and open trade from Europe to the rest of the world from 1400 to 1600. The economy of Europe in the postplague period cannot be characterized entirely as being in decline, at least not throughout the continent. Rather, it was a period of transition, in which northern Europe played an increasingly important commercial role, and in which the center of economic activity was shifting from the Mediterranean to the northwest.

Depopulation contributed to constitutional changes and the rise of bureaucratic government. Herein, the Black Death and the second plague pandemic accelerated changes which had begun in the twelfth and thirteenth centuries, and which might best be approached by looking at what has been described as the laicization of society.[46] By 1200, there were three types of government in Europe: baronial, royal, and imperial/Christian. Before 1200, the baronial and imperial/Christian types had generally been dominant, but royal government also had had a significant role. In the course of the thirteenth century, as the trifunctional society began to break down, so did the tripartite layers of authority. A principal reason for this breakdown was the proliferation of lay officials, who cut into the hegemony of the clerical bureaucrats who had dominated government since the end of the classical world. Further, as secular schools developed and more of their graduates went to work in the expanding governments of the thirteenth century, many bright young men who might have entered the clergy became lay officials instead. Lay officials rarely had extensive personal landed wealth before they took office. Most were paid by, and thus dependent on, the governments for which they worked. They supported them and acted as propagandists. This process was predicated on steady income from taxes, which royal governments seemed to collect more effectively than either baronial or imperial/Christian governments. All indications were that the secularization would have continued even without the intervention of plague.

Depopulation accelerated the laicization of society. In the first place, the Black Death killed indiscriminately, and probably afflicted as many lay as ecclesiastical bureaucrats. It took a long time to train new officials, and growth at all levels of government was slowed for at least a generation. But the number of lay officials seems to have grown more quickly, perhaps because secular governments were better able to marshal their resources and begin the training process anew. Secular schools also seem to have recovered more quickly than parochial ones. In the English town of Bury St. Edmunds, all three schools closed during the plague. But, while the burgesses who operated the grammar and song schools managed to open their institutions by 1351, church authorities did not begin teaching until 1355. By 1500, members of royal bureaucracies, generally trained at secular schools such as those in Bury, had become a self-perpetuating class.

The Mores in England were a good example; they were what observers of a later age would call an "aristocracy of the robe," to distinguish them from the "aristocracy of the sword," the traditional, privileged, landed classes. Just as the old nobility began to distinguish itself by its bloodlines, the new nobility—the bureaucrats—relied on service.

Many of these new bureaucrats were lawyers.[47] Like doctors, lawyers developed as a distinct and elite profession in the Late Middle Ages; in fact they probably were even more important than doctors. It was the lawyers, mostly in the late fourteenth and fifteenth centuries, who worked out the theory of the state, predicated primarily on royal authority and government. This new state had definite and fixed boundaries, rather than the spheres of influence common in preplague Europe. Within the limits of the boundaries, the sovereign was able to issue orders—in particular, to levy the taxes that supported the bureaucracy—and to dispense justice, the two most important prerogatives of a ruler. Within this framework, there was no higher authority than that of the sovereign. Insofar as control was possible in a medieval setting, with its limited means of communication and transportation, it was now vested in the secular state, which in England, France, and most of Iberia was dominated by kings, not barons or a universal ecclesiastical or imperial authority.

Second, the Black Death caused at least the temporary collapse of all forms of governmental authority.[48] This meant that any sovereignty that was quick to recover had the opportunity to extend its power into new areas. Quick recovery, in turn, was predicated on the resources a government had and could mobilize, particularly its tax base and means of collection. At first, the plagues and other calamities of the fourteenth century weakened royal power and allowed for resurgent local, usually baronial, power. But the new baronial power of the postplague period was not like that of the twelfth and early thirteenth centuries. The decay of the trifunctional system, especially the erosion of aristocratic economic and military power, limited the ability of the nobles to make good use of their new opportunities.

Furthermore, the nature of the bond between the nobles themselves had changed. It was not a "feudal" bond—one intertwined with oaths of personal service and loyalty, property holdings, military interdependence, and a clear sense of intraclass hierarchy, ranking, and order. Rather, at least in England and France, it had developed—some might say, degenerated—into a proprietary relationship called "bastard feudalism." In bastard feudalism, a noble gathered about him a series of retainers in a sort of clientage relationship in which lords and retainers were bound by annual cash payments, rather than the traditional endowment of property holdings. In this kind of relationship, the lord with the greatest and most readily available sources of cash would be the most powerful. Ultimately, whatever their short-term setbacks and however much tax collection had been disrupted by plague, kings had greater resources than even their most powerful barons.

Third, the Black Death contributed to the rise of central, royal government because, when it changed Europe's economy, it also altered its tax base. Taxes were harder to collect in a society in which most of the basic hierarchy of law and bureaucracy had broken down. Further, while per capita income rose in the late fourteenth century, there were fewer folks from whom taxes might be collected, and old, preplague rates could not easily be raised. When changes were made or vigorous efforts were undertaken to collect assessments, the response, as in England in 1381, was frequently rebellion. This meant that all fourteenth-century governments were challenged in the most fundamental way. Some succeeded, and others did not; those that did not usually collapsed and were replaced by new forms of government.

Three examples—the towns of Siena and Bury St. Edmunds, and the kingdom of France—illustrate the variety of responses.[49] Siena lost over half its people during the Black Death, and its bureaucracy suffered accordingly. Experienced workers were in such short supply in the town's two most important magistracies, the *Biccherna* and the *Gabelle*, that for the first time laymen, rather than clergy, were recruited—another example of the laicization of society. Hence, the initial priority of the Sienese, once order was restored, was to get the town's finances back into shape so that officials, soldiers, and other civic workers, whose salaries were now higher than ever, could be paid. The authorities acted quickly and performed well. First, they assessed residents of both the city proper and the *contado*, the surrounding countryside controlled by Siena, in order to get as many taxpayers as possible on the rolls. Next, they established a *gabelle*, a new, indirect tax on salt. Both efforts were successful and, by the 1360s, Siena seemed to be as stable as it had been before the Black Death.

But all was not well. While exhaustive taxation allowed Sienese officials to balance their budgets, it had portentous social and economic consequences. The town's high wages, promise of opportunity, and many diversions proved to be a powerful attraction for peasants from the *contado*. This migration to the town, coupled with continuing low food prices and a depressed agricultural economy, further depopulated the countryside. A Sienese chronicler claimed: "the workers of the land and those who customarily worked the land and the orchards, because of their great extortions and salaries that they received for their daily labors, totally destroyed the farms of the citizens and the inhabitants of the state of Siena, and deserted the farms and lands of the aforesaid citizens."[50]

Officers of the commune, in effect, were taxing the suburbs to ruin. Officials tried other things to meet costs, but plague had depleted the tax base too much for them to deviate much from their original postplague patterns. They confiscated the estates of those who died intestate and attempted a number of indirect taxes in addition to the *gabelle*. When all this began to fall short in the late fourteenth century, Sienese officials began to seize the estates of widows and orphans on trumped-up technicalities.

The new economy and taxation system brought other social changes in Siena. There was an increase in violence and crime. Much was part of the general increase in crime which accompanied the decay of the trifunctional system, but in Siena there were special causes. Some of the crime was the result of people's being uprooted from the country to unfamiliar urban surroundings. In a few cases, these countryfolk were taken advantage of by more sophisticated city dwellers, and in other cases the immigrants simply lashed out in frustration at the strange urban environment. There were other reasons for the social tensions. Some very enterprising peasants made great fortunes and tried to enter Siena's ruling circles. In response, the old oligarchs passed four wage control and sumptuary laws between 1348 and 1350. These laws failed; many of the nouveaux riches gained political power. In the 1370s, they began to take revenge, for example, by enacting a law that ended the monopoly on banking held by the old guard. In all, Siena experienced great financial instability in the late fourteenth century and underwent a general decline in the Late Middle Ages. Plague disrupted government and depleted the tax base. Quick response by Siena's rulers and a series of new taxes made for a rapid, but temporary, recovery. In the long term, exhaustive taxation impoverished the countryside and destroyed the rural economy. For a small sovereign unit such as the town of Siena, the Black Death and the financial exigencies it brought proved fatal. By 1370, Siena's great era was over; by 1430, it was dominated by Florence.

The effects of plague, taxation, and the development of government on a much larger entity, the kingdom of France, were quite dif-

ferent. France had experienced fiscal problems before the Black
Death as a result of the general subsistence crisis that began in the
mid-thirteenth century and the Hundred Years' War with England. In
1346, the French suffered a crushing and humiliating defeat at Crecy.
In 1347, a meeting of the Estates General, France's representative assembly, was called to approve new taxes for an increased war effort.
In March 1348, it assessed one of the highest, most comprehensive
rates in French history. But by then the Black Death had spread
throughout the kingdom. France's plight has been described in Chap-
ters 3 and 4. As Perroy wrote, under pressure from plague, French
"taxable material melted like snow in the sun."[51] For at least the next
two generations, the tax base remained significantly diminished.

The towns and provinces of France show the connection between
depopulation, shrinking tax bases, and the evolution of government.
Perpignan was struck hard by the Black Death.[52] If municipal records
are accurate, the heaviest mortality was among middle-aged, well-to-
do males, the group that paid the largest share of the town's taxes.
Furthermore, this group included most of the scribes and notaries,
who assessed, collected, and recorded tax payments. In Perpignan, as
in most of France, the collection of taxes, the fuel of government bureaucracy, virtually came to an end. At the royal court, Perpignan's
problems were mirrored on a grander scale. About a third of the notaries died, making the accounting processes difficult even when revenues did come in. The provincial *parlements*, which collected the
taxes for local governments, were faced with similar dislocations. In
some places, including Normandy, Languedoc, Toulouse, and Ca-
hors, mortality was so high that the *parlements* were cancelled altogether.[53] Studies have also been made on the effects of plague on taxation in Montpellier and Marseille. In early 1348, the rulers of
Montpellier promised the king £6000 for men-at-arms. Then the
Black Death struck, the town was devastated, its tax base was depleted, and its collection and recording systems were eliminated. In
Marseille, it was the same. By January 1349, mortality was so high
that the crown made the townspeople quit of all their assessments.

In Siena, a small sovereign entity, the collapse of the tax base
proved calamitous, and contributed to the end of the town's independence. In France, a much larger sovereignty, the effect was somewhat
different. First, the development of both central and provincial corporations was severely retarded. Their major charge was financial,
and they grew throughout the early fourteenth century as revenue assessments and collections increased. Had such subsidies, particularly
those of 1347–48, continued to be successfully collected, the role of

the *parlement* and other local authorities would have continued to grow. Plague disrupted this trend. For the French crown, on the other hand, the effects were quite different. The Black Death also took its toll on the powers of royal government and proved fatal to the kingship of Philip VI. As John Henneman wrote, the Black Death was the "crowning misfortune of a far from happy reign."[54] But this proved to be only a short-term setback. The French kingship was well-established and had extensive resources; while plague was important in causing its fiscal woes, so was the war with England, and that war would soon turn in France's favor. It was far easier for the king of France to recover from the devastation of the plague than it was for the *parlements*, the other provincial corporations, or any of the barons. Thus, by the mid-fifteenth century, the king was more powerful in relation to local groups and individuals than ever before. In general, depopulation helped those in government with ready resources who were able to respond quickly to the new economic conditions.

A final European example is the growth of municipal power in Bury St. Edmunds.[55] In the early fourteenth century, Bury was dominated politically and economically by the Benedictine Abbey of St. Edmunds, one of the wealthiest monastic houses in Christendom. The town was a prosperous market center, but owed most of its successes to the abbey; its secular elite had very little constitutional autonomy. They chafed at this, and revolted several times, but on every occasion the abbey, supported by the king, was able to put down the rebels and retain all of its ancient prerogatives.

The Black Death changed this. It killed about half of Bury's population and temporarily disrupted the commercial system so crucial to the town's well-being. By the 1370s, Bury's commercial network was again intact, featuring woolen cloth, a popular commodity in the postplague West. Townsfolk became wealthier than ever and, by the early sixteenth century, some of them ranked among the wealthiest individuals in England. But the abbey's fate was different. Its wealth was rooted in its landed estates, farm products, and rents. Abbey management was rigid in its techniques and refused to turn to land-intensive or cash-crop farming; it insisted on producing wheat in the old fashion. In the new economy brought about by depopulation, this was disastrous. Hence, as the town grew richer, the abbey became poorer and, by the late fifteenth century, was forced to sell off parts of its endowment to stay solvent.

The townspeople continued their efforts to gain political power commensurate with their economic strength. In 1381, they rose in revolt as they had before the Black Death. Once again, the king supported the abbey and the rebels were put down. But, after 1381, the town elite switched tactics and began to flex their economic muscles. They took the abbey to court time and again, hiring batteries of London lawyers to represent them. At the same time, they went to the king, who was always in need of cash, and bought privileges and exemptions. These ploys worked. By the end of the fifteenth century, the town was virtually free of the abbey, which before the Black Death had controlled just about every aspect of its political and economic life.

The Black Death brought political and constitutional changes to the Islamic, as well as the Christian, world.[56] In Egypt, plague was most severe among the ruling elite, the Mamlūks. Compounding this was a problem concerning the nature of the Mamlūk community. They were the descendents of slaves, usually taken from Circassia, along the northeastern coast of the Black Sea, and new slaves were essential in keeping up their numbers. After depopulation, these Circassians, unique in the Muslim world because of their blue eyes and fair skin, were no longer available. This depletion, coupled with the continuing biological attrition of their ranks—a problem which seems to have been common among virtually every Eurasian political elite—caused Mamlūk ranks to dwindle. Eventually, they were fair game for a new wave of Turkic invaders, the Ottomans, who conquered Egypt early in the sixteenth century.[57] The Ottomans did not have as rigidly defined an elite as the Mamlūks, and were able to draw their leaders from a wider pool of achievers. Yet they, too, were affected by depopulation. Early in the fourteenth century, these Turks crossed Asia Minor into the Balkans and, taking advantage of the weakness of the Byzantine and Serbian states, conquered much of southeastern Europe. But plague depleted Ottoman ranks. They were able to conquer the Balkan peoples but were not populous enough to replace them as settlers. They became a Muslim aristocracy, ruling over a subordinate population of Christians. With the exception of the Albanians, few of the peoples of Ottoman-controlled Europe converted in large numbers to Islam. McNeill, one of the great authorities on plague and the peoples of the steppes, believes that this fact, in turn, allowed for the survival of Christianity in the Balkans and facilitated the region's ultimate reconquest.[58]

McNeill goes further in his estimate of the political damage caused by the plague. He believes, as do some other experts, that the second plague pandemic came from the steppes and was most virulent there. McNeill claims that it devastated the nomadic population of central Asia, and put an end to thousands of years of invasions and conquests in Europe, the Middle East, India, and China by the steppe nomads. By contrast, the settled populations at the fringe of the grasslands recovered more quickly from the Black Death and suffered somewhat less severely from the next few epidemics. These "settlement peoples" gradually reversed the process of conquests and began to encroach upon the grasslands. In McNeill's view, the Black Death led to nothing less than the "disembodiment of steppe society."[59]

By the thirteenth century, then, civic and royal government throughout much of Europe had become more powerful than baronial or imperial authority. In the fourteenth century, a succession of environmental disasters, most notably plague, produced a fiscal crisis. In some places, for a short time, there was a baronial resurgence. But the second pandemic changed Europe's economic balance. Land, the source of aristocratic economic power, lost much of its value. An increasingly larger portion of Europe's wealth, albeit still a minor share, came from trade and industry, and could be tapped for taxation by the crown. The growing trend toward secular education meant a continuous pool of laymen, especially lawyers and notaries, who were eager to make careers in government service. The new conditions of depopulation favored the formation of centralized bureaucracies, forerunners of the full-fledged governments that emerged in the modern period.

The second plague pandemic also affected the cultural and intellectual development of Europe. Its effect on the fine arts has been discussed; there were also important changes in philosophy and education, including the exacerbation of an earlier trend away from rational thought.[60] In 1277, after a half century of bitter controversy, the works of Aristotle, his Islamic commentators, and a number of European interpreters were eliminated from the curriculum of the University of Paris, Europe's most prestigous institution of higher education. The condemnation was extended to the works of virtually all scholars who stressed reason, or a combination of faith and reason, in the study of theology. Included were most of Europe's greatest thinkers, even Thomas Aquinas. The works of Aristotle were still studied in a few places, but in most universities all that remained were treatises by the intellectual "right-wing," essentially the writings of conservative Franciscans such as Bonaventura, who emphasized the importance of faith and revelation in philosophy, as well as theology. After 1277, most important thinkers turned to a kind of sterile skepticism, doubting the ability of man to understand any theology at all.[61] This was the path followed by the three greatest thinkers of the Late Middle Ages, John Duns Scotus, William Ockham, and Gabriel Biel. Hence, Europe's intellectual community was in decline before the plague, which served to accelerate this "flight from the intellect."

The flight from the intellect can be seen in many ways. One was the trend toward millenialism among some intellectuals[62]. Millenialism, which is discussed in Chapter 4, is the belief that the world is about to end and that the kingdom of heaven is forthcoming. Some of the medieval millenialism was connected with flagellism, but much of it was not. Rather, it was a conscious intellectual step away from reason by many scholars and churchmen. Many millenarians connected the second coming with the conservative intellectual movements that dominated university curricula after 1277, and with the need for faith, penance, and revelation. A good example is John of Rupecissa's *Liber secretum eventum*. Finished in November 1349, it presents millenarianism as a view of the future. In 1370, Christ would return and slay the anti-Christ, and a new, blessed world would emerge; in 2370, after another millenium, Judgment Day would occur and there would be heaven on earth. In effect, Rupecissa presented an optimistic view, but one that sought to explain metaphysics and, more important, epistemology without any rational basis.

The Black Death contributed in other ways to Europe's intellectual malaise.[63] Mortality among the clergy, still the most literate group in society despite the educational gains of the bourgeoisie, was as high as, and perhaps higher, than that of the laity. At least 28% of all cardinals died between May and August 1348, along with 25 archbishops and 207 bishops. These princes of the church were among the most generous patrons of the intellectual community; the death of so many of them brought a temporary halt to an important source of patronage. Further, the Black Death killed many of Europe's greatest scholars and thinkers, including the mathematicians Bernard Barleian and Thomas Bradwardine, the historian Giovanni Villani, and probably the philosopher and theologian William Ockham. Such losses, which included between a quarter and a third of Europe's university teachers, crippled the university system, which had been expanding rather steadily since the twelfth century. In 1349, Europe had 30 universities; 5 disappeared by 1360, and 15 others by 1400.[64] Depopulation reduced the number of actual and potential students, as well as faculty. By 1349, Cambridge had such a shortage of baccalaureates who would go on to become priests that the bishop of nearby Norwich began the process that eventually led to the foundation and endowment of Trinity Hall. Similar reasons led to the foundation of Gonville College in 1349, Corpus College in 1352, and New College Oxford in 1379.[65]

Problems existed outside of England as well. Things were so bad at the University of Avignon that, in 1361, students there petitioned Pope Innocent VI:

> Most Holy Father, at a time when the university body of your *studium* at Avignon is deprived of all lectures, since the whole number has been left desolate by the death of pestilence of doctors, licentiates [persons granted a papal license to practice a particular profession; in this case, probably teachers], bachelors and students, some also of the survivors of the same *studium*, who have spent many sleepless nights in the acquisitions of holy canonical knowledge, are unable because of the ravages of wars, as is also the case with some of them and of others because they are weighed down by contests over benefices due them and by the burden of poverty, to be of service to themselves and others, to recover their books, or to be promoted to the degrees which they deserve.[66]

All historians agree that the Black Death affected medieval higher education, but there is some dispute as to just what it did. One view popular among scholars working before World War II claimed that depopulation was an unmitigated disaster from which the universities did not recover until the sixteenth century. Among the results was the rise of nonuniversity-based cultures, particularly Italian humanism. Recent research has modified this perspective, and some historians now claim that mortality among academics was considerably lower than that of the rest of the populace.[67] The best work has been done at Oxford, where fairly comprehensive lists survive of the university's faculty and student communities. Data from the theology school show that morbidity was lower there than at Cambridge and most of the Continental universities. Between 5% and 10% of the faculty and about 30% of the students died, although these figures do not account for the many academics who fled before plague arrived. After the Black Death, the demand for places at Oxford was still strong; although enrollments were disrupted for a few years, they recovered by the mid-1350s and remained steady throughout the late fourteenth and much of the fifteenth centuries, despite the general diminution of England's population. In the 1360s, there was actually a temporary increase in the number of students at song and grammar schools, the secondary institutions that fed into the universities.

But comparatively low mortality and a quick recovery did not mean that Oxford and English higher education in general were left unscathed by the plague. At Oxford, some of the university's most distinguished dons, including Thomas Bradwardine, Richard Rolle, and John Baconthorp, perished.[68] At Merton College, the faculty had begun developing a program in experimental physical science; in their initial stages, the new theories of motion and impetus that they proposed were basically correct. But several key theorists died of plague, their replacements were not of the same high caliber, and the Merton program came to naught.

The shortage of skilled researchers, theoreticians, and teachers was disastrous to ecclesiastical education.[69] To fill faculty positions and keep school enrollments up, church authorities embarked on a concerted program to train new clerics. As a result, the most able priests were generally siphoned off to universities, often from primary and secondary schools where they had been teachers. This left less able, and sometimes poorly trained and even incompetent, teachers to take their places. The result was a marked decline in the quality of preuniversity education. By 1400, if not sooner, many students entered universities inadequately trained and unable to write and converse in Latin. This, in turn, helps to account for the sterility and ultimate failure of late medieval scholasticism.

There were other consequences of this siphoning process; one of the most important was the general growth in the use of vernacular languages.[70] In England, Latin and French had been the languages of culture and government since the eleventh century. After the Black Death, this changed. In 1353, English was proclaimed the official language in London's sheriffs' courts; in 1362, it was designated the language of all the high courts of law. A year later, the king's chancellor opened Parliament with a speech in English. In 1385, John Trevisa, the best-known schoolmaster of his time, proclaimed that "nowadays [English] boys know no more French than their left heel."

The Black Death and the second plague pandemic played as profound a role in educational and intellectual change as they did in economic and constitutional change. Many skilled, highly trained people perished and could not be replaced. For example, plague killed a large proportion of Europe's master masons, the men who executed the detailed work on cathedrals, castles, and town halls.[71] The survivors were too few to train enough new craftsmen, and too few even to do much of the skilled work so characteristic of preplague Gothic architecture. The result was a general decline in architectural standards which would not be rectified until the late fifteenth century.

Great care and caution must be taken in assessing the long-term effects of the second plague pandemic. There is the danger of making *a posteriori* arguments, that is, of determining the state and problems of Europe in the late fifteenth century and then working backwards, assuming that depopulation was at fault. The second plague pandemic was not responsible for all the important changes in the fourteenth and fifteenth centuries. Many, particularly those in government, probably would have occurred in other circumstances. But these changes would have developed in a different fashion and certainly would have been longer in taking form. Thus, the Black Death and the other plague epidemics of the later Middle Ages had the crucial effect of telescoping change.

The second plague pandemic reached an etiological turning point in the late fifteenth century, which began Europe's transition to a new disease era.[72] From 1478–1480, a plague epidemic struck across the Continent. It was one of the worst of the Late Middle Ages, and probably the most severe since the *pestis secunda* of 1361–62. In England, the Netherlands, and France, data suggest that at least 15% of the population died. But after this epidemic, the insect and rodent hosts crucial to the transfer of *Y. pestis* to people apparently underwent considerable change, with plague shifting to a longer span between outbreaks. Using the British Isles as an example, there were no major plague epidemics after 1480 for nearly twenty years. Plague had by no means disappeared. There were severe epidemics all across Britain in 1499, 1509–1510, 1516–17, and 1527–30.[73] Furthermore, these early-sixteenth-century epidemics ranked in virulence with the most severe plagues of the fifteenth century. But they differed in their frequency. Plague no longer came three, four, or even five times in a single generation, and this allowed for some recovery between epidemics. As a result, population began to rise slowly in the 1480s and then more quickly by the early 1500s. By 1530, the English population was about the same as it had been before the Black Death.

Available evidence from other parts of Europe suggests trends of plague cycles and population generally similar to those of the British Isles.[74] By 1500, the demographic crisis of the Late Middle Ages had come to an end. The second plague pandemic would last until the late seventeenth century, but it would not be as important a social determinant as it was in the fourteenth and fifteenth centuries.

There were other indications in the late fifteenth century that a new disease epoch was commencing.[75] As plague patterns changed, new diseases appeared and old ones grew in importance. The first continuous records of typhus, or jail fever, appear in the fifteenth century. Facilitated by filth, typhus is caused by the microorganism *Rickettsia*, which is carried by the human body louse. It is highly contagious and relatively lethal; in fact, by the sixteenth century some typhus epidemics were nearly as deadly as those of plague. Typhus originated on the Indian subcontinent, and its precise European beginnings are obscure. Since famine and malnutrition exacerbate it, the conditions of depopulation which followed the Black Death may have delayed its spread. But, by the fifteenth century, there were increasing indications of its possible presence in Europe—heavy spring mortality without mention of the "pockys" diseases, and smaller-than-usual harvests coinciding with extraordinary mortality. In Germany and France, typhus might have struck as early as the 1430s, and there are definite references to it in the 1450s and 1470s. England might have experienced it in the 1430s, but the first fairly certain reference to it was in 1444 in Newgate Prison, London. In the course of one week, 5 jailers and 64 prisoners died from what sounds like a textbook description of jail fever. Typhus's major depredations would come in the sixteenth and seventeenth centuries, but its European roots are clearly medieval.

Influenza was present throughout the West and the Middle East during the Middle Ages, but seems to have become more virulent with the colder and wetter weather that began in the thirteenth century.[76] Influenza is one of the most common infectious diseases. It presents itself in over 300,000 different strains, making specific immunity to more than a tiny fraction of these strains impossible. Further, since it is airborne and respiratory in its communication, influenza is a disease that virtually everyone experiences periodically in a lifetime. Generally, the disease produces a mild reaction, dangerous only to the very young, the very old, or the very sick. But, occasionally, a highly lethal strain appears and becomes a major killing disease. Such was the case in 1918–20, when the Spanish Flu killed more people than the battles and privations of World War I; such also was the case in the flu epidemic of 1426–27, which swept throughout Spain, France, the Netherlands, and the British Isles. In eastern England, where excellent data are available, about 5% of the population died. More infamous was the Sweating Sickness, or Picardy Sweat, which first appeared in 1485 in the lands abutting the English Channel, and returned at least six times until 1551. It came to England in autumn 1485 and killed three lord mayors of London in as many months. The Sweat would ultimately prove to be less deadly than plague epidemics, but in some cases it killed up to 10% of selected local populations.

Syphilis also appeared during the environmental watershed of the late fifteenth century.[77] Venereal diseases, especially gonorrhea, had been present in Europe since antiquity, and had proved to be a particular problem for soldiers. After his 1475 campaign in France, Edward IV of England commented on the frequency among his troops of the "French Pox," to which he "lost many a man that fell to the lust of women and were burned by them, and their penises rotted away and fell off and they died." But the medieval origins of syphilis, the most deadly of the venereal diseases in the modern era, are more mysterious. Two principal theories have been offered to explain its appearance in Europe at the very end of the Middle Ages. One, the Columbian theory, attributes its arrival to the discovery of the New World. Archaeological and paleological evidence suggest that syphilis was well-established among the Amerindian population of Meso-America, and was brought to Europe by Columbus, his sailors, and a few Indian captives. There are weaknesses in this theory, particularly concerning the rapidity of syphilis's spread from so few individuals. But new diseases often spread quickly in exposed populations and, even more important, contemporary medical and literary observers were convinced of the disease's American origins.

The second explanation, called the Unitarian theory, stresses the African origins of syphilis through the guise of yaws, a skin disease caused by the same treponema spirochetes that are responsible for syphilis. In the mid-fifteenth century, in their search for gold, slaves, and a direct sea route to India, Portuguese sailors began to establish trading posts along the west coast of Africa. Within a few years, they brought African slaves, some of whom may have had yaws, back to the Mediterranean Basin. For treponema to survive as a skin disease, the climate must be very hot and damp and, in the cooler North, it may have mutated. The Unitarian theorists claim that it retreated deep into the body, to the nervous system, and over a period of several decades became transmitted venereally, always protected in the warm, damp recesses of the human body. This argument has the strength of numbers—there were many more Africans in Europe by 1490 than there were Amerindians or Europeans who had had sexual contact with them—and fits in with the disease's long incubation period. Its weakness lies in the Columbian theory's strengths—the conviction of contemporaries and the 1490s' timing.

Whatever syphilis's actual cause, its impact was staggering. The army of the French king, Charles VIII, brought it north with them after a 1493–94 campaign in Spanish-held southern Italy. Made up of Frenchmen, Germans, Walloons, Swiss, Scots, and Irishmen, the army disbanded after the campaign, and the soldiers took the disease to their respective homelands. By summer 1495, it had spread across all of German-speaking central Europe. By winter 1496, it was in the Netherlands and the British Isles and, by the end of 1496, was as far east as Russia. Italians called it the "French Pox," which proved to be its most popular name, but French called it the "Italian Pox," English called it the "Spanish Pox," Poles called it the "German Pox," and Russians called it the "Polish Pox." The German humanist Ulrich von Hutton wrote a treatise describing his personal experiences with it, and among those alleged to have been infected were Christopher Columbus, Ferdinand I of Spain, Henry VIII of England and his minister Cardinal Wolsey, Charles VIII and Francis I of France, Pope Alexander VI , Ivan IV of Russia, and the humanist Erasmus. As with plague, syphilis entered the art and literature of everyday experience; one of the best examples is Albrecht Dürer's 1496 woodcut, *The Syphilitic*.

Syphilis is not an immediate killer. More commonly, it takes the form of a degenerative disease, and for this reason is less important historically than plague, smallpox, influenza, or typhus. But it has a terrible, debilitating effect on its victims, and leaves a mark on future generations, often rendering the victims or their offspring sterile. Further, the epidemic in the 1490s and 1500s was so virulent that it seems to have been communicable by nonvenereal means, and may have been immediately fatal to a few of its victims.

The arrival of syphilis in Europe ended the medieval era of infectious diseases. In biomedical terms, the Middle Ages was the most varied and most important period in the formation and establishment of Western infectious diseases. Successive migrations of peoples and animals from Africa and Asia to Europe, especially to the Mediterranean Basin, brought smallpox, measles, plague, leprosy, dysentery, influenza, typhus, and other infectious diseases. When Europeans began their global expansion and conquests around 1500, they spread these diseases to new areas. In demographic terms, infectious diseases were the most important element controlling mortality in the fourteenth and fifteenth centuries, and one of the most important in the entire period before the beginning of the Industrial Revolution in the eighteenth century. Further, during the Late Middle Ages, levels of fertility were extremely low despite optimum conditions and opportunities for land ownership and inheritance, the usual determinant in marriage and childbearing. Demographers have been at a loss to explain why this was the case, though many believe there were psychological causes, including a reluctance to bear children in an era of such crisis.[76] But one thing is clear. The period from about 1350 to 1500 was one of marked and general depopulation, with extraordinarily high mortality and surprisingly low fertility levels. In crude terms, when plague and other infectious diseases were rife, population contracted; when they were less frequent and virulent, population expanded.

# Epilogue: Europe's Environmental Crisis

F ROM THE MID-THIRTEENTH CENTURY to the end of the fifteenth century, Europe and much of the Middle East, North Africa, and Asia suffered the most severe environmental crisis in history. Biological and climatic determinants influenced virtually every aspect of human life, and did so to a greater degree than at any time since the beginning of civilization. The most horrific of these determinants was plague. Governed by cycles of insect and rodent ecology, plague epidemics recurred throughout the Late Middle Ages, touching man when conditions were right among fleas and rats for transfer of plague. Perhaps the key to understanding the fourteenth and fifteenth centuries, the watershed between medieval and modern civilizations, is man's helplessness before nature.

Some of the changes that the environmental crisis brought benefitted society. Most survivors became richer. Western European peasants were, for the most part, freed from their customary bonds, and Europeans in general were spared the relentless pauperization that unbridled population growth caused in other areas of the Old World. But the beneficial aspects of such disasters ought not to be over-

161

stated.[1] Many, indeed most, of these advantages are apparent only through hindsight, and were not evident to late medieval people. Survivors of a famine or an epidemic might benefit in the long run from a rise in *per capita* income or a few extra head of livestock. But they might also use up their new surpluses with a few extravagant purchases or lavish feasts. More important, an attack of plague or the onslaught of some other disaster was a shocking, horrifying, and painful experience. The day of judgment, a terrifying prospect even for the most faithful, loomed omnipresent. Disaster and depopulation brought no good to those whose lives ended prematurely, and no sense of comfort, security, or well-being to those who survived but lived in bereavement and fear of the next attack.

For these reasons and others, the environmental crisis brought to the people of the later Middle Ages a violent, anxious, and skewed perspective on life. It brought to a crescendo the moral crisis which began in the thirteenth century. A principal characteristic of medieval society was its sense of community. People, at least in theory, shared a spiritual and material life and worked together for a common good. Property was never owned, but held of a higher authority, ultimately God. Society, theorists have noted, was structured and hierarchic, clearly divided between haves and have-nots. But earthly life was considered ephemeral. What counted was the eternal life of the spirit, God's salvation, and the Kingdom of Heaven. This helps to explain the continuing popularity of monasticism. Life in the monastery approximated on earth the ideal community of heaven more closely than any other form of existence.

Naturally, such idyllic notions of community were never put entirely into practice, not even in monasteries. And beginning around 1100, many members of society—for example, merchants with profits on their minds or peasants with too little food in their bellies—found other ideals more to their liking than those of the community, either monastic or secular. But it took recurrent pestilence, severe famine, and protracted foul weather to shake profoundly the old corporate world of the High Middle Ages, and eventually to shatter its ideals. Many aspects of this medieval corporatism would linger through the nineteenth century. But its demise, beginning around 1300, was accompanied by a growing emphasis on individualism, one of the most important characteristics that scholars regard as typically modern. Plague, in general, and the Black Death, in particular, caused enormous upheaval—"the world turned upside down," as a popular poem put it.[2] It engendered a new society with new attitudes, layers and bonds of authority, sources of wealth, and, most important, new ideas. There are few historical epochs as fluid as the Late Middle Ages.

Lynn White has argued that Christian Europeans saw the world about them in terms different from those of their non-Christian neighbors.[3] Christians stood in awe of nature, but tried to understand and work with it. "Nature, the vicar of almighty lord," was to be mastered. Surely this idea was the motivation for Europe's great clockmakers and explorers. And it was the inspiration, too, of many of the doctors who practiced medicine after the Black Death. Older, ineffective methods and traditional authorities were cast away. New ideas, tools, and techniques were put into practice, and if they did not work, still newer ideas were tried. In the fourteenth and fifteenth centuries, the seeds of empirical, experimental science, perhaps the most distinctive characteristic of modern Western Civilization, were sown.

The impact of the Black Death, the greatest ecological upheaval, has been compared to that of the two world wars of the twentieth century.[4] To a degree this is true. But the Black Death, compounded as it was by subsequent epidemics of the second pandemic and unstable weather patterns, wrought even more essential change. Civilizations are the result of complex combinations of institutional, cultural, material, and environmental characteristics. When these underpinnings are removed, the civilizations collapse. The environmental crisis of the Late Middle Ages caused existing social and political systems to stagnate or to regress. Deeprooted moral, philosophical, and religious convictions were tested and found wanting. Generally, traditional standards seemed no longer to apply. The effects of this natural and human disaster changed Europe profoundly, perhaps more so than any other series of events. For this reason, alone, the Black Death should be ranked as the greatest biological-environmental event in history, and one of the major turning points of Western Civilization.

# Notes

## Introduction

1. Michael of Piazza, *Bibliotheca scriptorum qui res in Sicilia gestas retulere*, I, p. 562.
2. Agnolo di Tura del Grasso, *Cronaca senese*, in *The Black Death*, ed. William Bowsky (New York: Holt, Rhinehart & Winston, 1971), pp. 13–14.
3. Francesco Petrarch, *Epistolae Familiares*, VIII, p. 290.
4. F.A. Gasquet, *The Great Pestilence* (London: Marshall, Hamilton & Kent, 1893).
5. G.G. Coultan, *The Black Death* (New York: Cope & Smith, 1930).
6. J.W. Thompson, "The Aftermath of the Black Death and the Aftermath of the Great War," *The American Journal of Sociology*, 26: 1920–21.
7. Yves Renouard, "Conséquences et intérêt démographique de la Peste Noire de 1348," *Population*, 3 (1948).
8. E.A. Kosminsky, *Studies in the Agrarian History of England* (New York: Kelley & Millman, 1956).

9. M.M. Postan, *Medieval Agriculture and General Problems* (Cambridge: Cambridge University Press, 1973).

10. Raymond Delatouche, "La crise du XIVᵉ siècle en Europe occidentale," *Les Études Sociales,* n.s. 1959.

11. J.F.D. Shrewsbury, *A History of Bubonic Plague in the British Isles* (Cambridge: Cambridge University Press, 1970).

12. David Herlihy, *Medieval and Renaissance Pistoia* (New Haven, Conn.: Yale University Press, 1967); Élizabeth Carpentier, *Une Ville devant la Peste* (Paris: S.E.V.P.E.N., 1962).

13. Édouard Baratier, *La Démographie Provençale du XIII au XVI Siècle* (Paris: S.E.V.P.E.N., 1961); Guy Bois, *Crise du Feodalisme* (Paris: Presses de la Fondation Nationale des Sciences Politiques, 1976).

14. E. Jutikkala & M. Kauppinen, "The Structure of Mortality during Catastrophic Years in a Pre-Industrial Society," *Population Studies,* 25 (1971); J.D. Chambers, *Population, Economy, and Society in Pre-Industrial England* (Oxford: Oxford University Press, 1972); John Hatcher, *Plague, Population, and the English Economy, 1348-1530* (Macmillan: London, 1977); J-N. Biraben, *Les Hommes et la Peste,* 2 vols. (The Hague: Mouton, 1975); E. LeRoy Ladurie, "Un Concept: L' Unification Microbienne du Monde," *Schweizerische Zeitschrift Für Geschichte,* (1973).

15. William McNeill, *Plague and Peoples* (New York: Doubleday, 1976).

16. Philip Ziegler, *The Black Death* (New York: Harper & Row, 1969).

17. Stephan d'Irsay, "Notes on the Origin of the Expression *'Atra Mors',*" *Isis,* 8 (1926).

## Chapter 1

1. Fernand Braudel, in his classic, *The Mediterranean and the Mediterranean World in the Age of Philip II,* has shown how crucial a study of environmental conditions is for understanding premodern history. Also see: Georges Duby, *Rural Economy and Country Life in the Medieval West* (London: Edward Arnold, 1968); and B.H. Slicher van Bath, *The Agrarian History of Western Europe* (London: Edward Arnold, 1966). One of the best environmental studies is W.G. Hoskins, *The Making of the English Landscape* (London: Hodder & Stoughton, 1955).

2. The following books deal with the broad sociological effects of disease: Henry Sigerist, *Civilization and Disease* (Ithaca, N.Y.: Cornell University Press, 1943); MacFarlane Burnet & D.O. White, *Natural History of Infectious Disease,* 4th ed. (Cambridge: Cambridge University Press, 1972); William McNeill, *Plagues and Peoples* (New York: Doubleday, 1976).

3. Thomas Smith Hall, *A Source Book in Animal Biology* (New York: McGraw-Hill, 1951). Also see A.H. Gale, *Epidemic Diseases* (London: Penguin Books, 1951); Major Greenwood, *Epidemics and Crowd Diseases* (New York: Macmillan, 1935); Ronald Hare, *An Outline of Bacteriology and Immunity* (London: Longmans, 1956).

4. This position is taken by McNeill in *Plagues and Peoples* (New York: Doubleday, 1976) and *The Human Condition: An Ecological and Historical View* (Princeton: Princeton University Press, 1980).

5. McNeill, *Plagues and Peoples,* pp. 77–147.

6. August Hirsch, *Handbook of Geographical and Historical Pathology* (London: New Sydenham Society, 1886).

7. Galen, *On the Parts of Medicine,* ed. Malcolm Lyons (Berlin: Verlag Paul Parey, 1969).

8. St. Cyprian, *Treatises,* ed. Roy Deferrari (New York: Fathers of the Church, 1958), p. 210.

9. Arthur E.R. Boak, *Manpower Shortage and the Fall of the Roman Empire* (Ann Arbor: University of Michigan Press, 1955).

10. The definitive study of plague is J-N. Biraben, *Les Hommes et la Peste,* 2 vols. (The Hague: Mouton, 1975). A good supplement is "The Plague Reconsidered," *Local Population Studies,* (1977).

11. There are two studies of the first plague pandemic: J.C. Russell, "That Earlier Plague," *Demography,* 5 (1968); J-N. Biraben & J. LeGoff, "The Plague in the Early Middle Ages," in *Biology and Man in History,* ed. Robert Forster & Orest Ranum (Baltimore: Johns Hopkins University Press, 1975).

12. Procopius, *History of the Wars,* I, ed. H.B. Dewing (New York: Macmillan, 1914).

13. The data are from Russell, "That Earlier Plague."

14. Biraben and LeGoff, "The Plague in the Early Middle Ages," pp. 58–59.

15. Russell, "That Earlier Plague."

16. The best European record for the period is Georges Duby, *The Early Growth of the European Economy* (Ithaca, N.Y.: Cornell University Press, 1974). A good study of England is Charles Creighton, *A History of Epidemics in Britain* (Cambridge: Cambridge University Press, 1894).

17. Saul N. Brody, *The Disease of the Soul: Leprosy in Medieval Literature* (Ithaca, N.Y.: Cornell University Press, 1974).

18. There is a good discussion in McNeill, *Plagues and Peoples*, pp. 144–47.

19. A good example is *A Leechbook or Collection of Medical Recipes of the Fifteenth Century,* ed. W.R. Dawson (London: Macmillan, 1934).

20. McNeill, *Plagues and Peoples,* pp. 176–78.

21. Medievalists are usually reluctant to give population figures. One who is not is Carlo Cipolla, and the figures have been taken from his *Before the Industrial Revolution* (New York: Norton, 1980), pp. 150–57.

22. McNeill, *Plagues and Peoples,* pp. 134–47.

## Chapter 2

1. This point was first made by Lynn White, Jr., in *Medieval Technology and Social Change* (Oxford: Oxford University Press, 1962).

2. Rates of growth are discussed in: Georges Duby, *The Early Growth of the European Economy* (Ithaca, N.Y.: Cornell University Press, 1974); Carlo Cipolla, *Before the Industrial Revolution* (New York: Norton, 1980).

3. Wilhelm Abel, *Agarkrisen und Agarkonjunktur,* 3rd ed. (Hamburg & Berlin: Verlag Paul Parey, 1978).

4. Georges Duby, *The Three Orders: Feudal Society Imagined* (Chicago: University of Chicago Press, 1980).

5. The best descriptions of tenure are to be found in the works of R.H. Hilton, particularly his Ford Lectures in *The English Peasantry in the Later Middle Ages* (Oxford: Oxford University Press, 1975). A nice survey is J.Z. Titow, *English Rural Society* (London: George Allen & Unwin, 1969).

6. Seed yields and the productivity of the land are discussed in: Georges Duby, *Rural Economy and Country Life in the Medieval West* (London: Edward Arnold, 1966); B.H. Slicher van Bath, *The Agrarian History of Western Europe* (London: Edward Arnold, 1966); J.Z. Titow, *Winchester Yields: A Study in Medieval Agricultural Productivity* (Cambridge: Cambridge University Press, 1972).

7. There are many studies; see Cipolla, *Before the Industrial Revolution,* pp. 143–49; J.C. Russell, *Medieval Regions and Their Cities* (Bloomington, Ind.: Indiana University Press, 1972).

8. Joseph R. Strayer has described the state and development of medieval government. A good starting point is his *On the Medieval Origins of the Modern State* (Princeton: Princeton University Press, 1970).

9. The initial formulation of this approach was by Charles Homer Haskins, *The Renaissance of the Twelfth Century* (Cambridge, Mass.: Harvard University Press, 1927). The best recent approach is that of M-D. Chenu, *Nature, Man, and Society in the Twelfth Century* (Chicago: University of Chicago Press, 1980).

10. High medieval Christian expansion is discussed in many works. A good starting point is R.W. Southern, *The Making of the Middle Ages* (New Haven, Conn.: Yale University Press, 1953).

11. Two good summary accounts of historical studies of climate are: E. Le-Roy Ladurie, *Times of Feast, Times of Famine* (New York: Doubleday, 1971); Robert I. Rotberg & Theodore K. Rabb, eds., *Climate and History* (Princeton: Princeton University Press, 1981).

12. LeRoy Ladurie, *Times of Feast, Times of Famine,* p. 253.

13. These patterns are summarized in B.H. Slicher van Bath, *The Agrarian History of Western Europe;* J.Z. Titow, "Evidence of Weather in the Account Rolls of the Bishopric of Winchester, 1209–1350," *Economic History Review,* 2nd series (1960).

14. These problems are discussed in detail in M.M. Postan's *Medieval Agriculture and General Problems* and *Medieval Trade and Finance,* both (Cambridge: Cambridge University Press, 1973).

15. Duby, Postan, and Titow discuss this "pauperization." Also see Wilhelm Abel, *Massenarmut und Hungerkrisen in vorindustriellen Europa* (Hamburg & Berlin: Verlag Paul Parey, 1974).

16. Postan, in the works cited in note 14, has made this case. A good general discussion of Malthusian-subsistence crises is E.A. Wrigley, *Population and History* (New York: McGraw-Hill, 1969).

17. R.H. Hilton, *The Decline of Serfdom in Medieval England* (London: Macmillan, 1969); Georges Duby, *Rural Economy and Country Life in the Medieval West.*

18. The classic study is J. Hajnal, "European Marriage Patterns in Perspective," in *Population in History,* ed. D.V. Glass & D.E.C. Eversley (London: Edward Arnold, 1965). The most comprehensive treatments of medieval marriage are: Georges Duby, *Medieval Marriage* (Baltimore: Johns Hopkins University Press, 1978); F.R.H. DuBoulay, *An Age of Ambition* (New York: Viking, 1970); Zvi Razi, *Life, Marriage, and Death in a Medieval Parish* (Cambridge: Cambridge University Press, 1980).

19. Two general studies of famine are: Cornelius Walford, "The Famines in the World, Past and Present," *Journal of the Statistical Society,* 41 (1879); H.W.F. Curschmann, *Hungersnöte in Mittelalter* (Leipzig: B.G. Teubner, 1900). The best accounts of the fourteenth-century famines are: H.S. Lucas, "The Great European Famine of 1315, 1316, and 1317," *Speculum,* 5 (1930); Ian Kershaw, "The Great Famine and Agrarian Crisis in England," in *Peasants, Knights, and Heretics,* ed. R.H. Hilton (Cambridge: Cambridge University Press, 1976); E. Carpentier, "Famines et epidemies dans l'histoire du XIVe siècle," *Annales E.S.C.,* 6 (1962).

20. As quoted in Lucas, "The Great European Famine of 1315, 1316, and 1317," pp. 343–347.

21. There are many studies of this process. Two summary accounts are: Daniel Waley, *The Italian City-Republics* (New York: McGraw-Hill, 1969); Lauro Martines, *Power and Imagination: City-States in Renaissance Italy* (New York: Knopf, 1979).

22. Giovanni Villani, as quoted in Ferdinand Schevill, *History of Florence* (New York: Frederick Ungar, 1961), p. 237.

23. Behavior during the famine is described in *The Cambridge Economic History of Europe*, I, 2nd ed., pp. 672–74.

24. Kershaw, "The Great Famine and Agrarian Crisis in England." Also see John Bellamy, *Crime and Public Order in the Later Middle Ages* (London: R.K.P., 1973).

25. Kershaw, ibid.

26. The fundamental work on famine is Wilhelm Abel's *Agarkrisen und Agarkonjunktur.* Other important studies include: Helen Robbins, "A Comparison of the Effects of the Black Death on the Economic Organization of France and England," *Journal of Political Economy* (1928); M.J. Larenaude, "Les Famines in Languedoc aux XIVᵉ et XVᵉ Siècle," *Annales du Midi* (1952).

27. A brilliant discussion of late medieval social change is Jacques LeGoff, *Time, Work, and Culture in the Middle Ages* (Chicago: University of Chicago Press, 1980), especially the essays in Parts I and II. Other good studies are: Robert Boutruche, *La Crise d'une Societé: Seigneurs et Paysans du Bordelais pendant La Guerre de Cent Ans* (Paris: Belles Lettres, 1947); Robert Brenner, "Agrarian Class Structure and Economic Development in Pre-Industrial Europe," *Past and Present,* 70 (1976).

## Chapter 3

1. William McNeill, *Plagues and People* (New York: Doubleday, 1976), pp. 149–98.

2. J.D. Chambers, *Population, Plague, and Society in Pre-Industrial England* (Oxford: Oxford University Press, 1972), pp. 9–72.

3. In describing the course of plague in Asia, I have made extensive use of Michael Dols's *The Black Death in the Middle East* (Princeton: Princeton University Press, 1977).

4. Dols, *The Black Death in the Middle East,* pp. 38–43.

5. Robert S. Lopez, *The Commercial Revolution of the Middle Ages, 950–1350* (Englewood Cliffs, N.J.: Prentice-Hall, 1971), pp. 56–122.

6. Dols, *The Black Death in the Middle East,* p. 49.

7. As described in Dols, *The Black Death in the Middle East,* p. 62.

8. See V.J. Derbes, "De Mussis and the Great Plague of 1348," *The Journal of the American Medical Association* 196 (1966).

9. C.S. Bartsocas, trans., "Two Fourteenth Century Greek Descriptions of the Black Death," *Journal of the History of Medicine and Allied Sciences,* 21 (4) (1966).

10. Bartsocas, "Two Fourteenth Century Greek Descriptions of the Black Death," p. 395.

11. Angeliki E. Laiou-Thomadakis, *Peasant Society in the Late Byzantine Empire* (Princeton: Princeton University Press, 1977), pp. 223–98.

12. Dols, *The Black Death in the Middle East,* pp. 35–67.

13. Ibid., pp. 241–42.

14. Ibid., p. 61.

15. Ibid., p. 64.

16. Ibid., p. 67.

17. Bartsocas, "Two Fourteenth Century Greek Descriptions of the Black Death," p. 395.

18. Michael of Piazza, *Bibliotheca scriptorum qui res in Sicilia gestas retulere,* I, p. 562.

19. Ibid., pp. 562–63.

20. After England, the most detailed research has been done on Italy. For Genoa, see Jacques Heers, *Gênes au XVe Siècle* (Paris: S.E.V.P.E.N., 1961).

21. David Herlihy, *Pisa in the Early Renaissance* (New Haven, Conn.: Yale University Press, 1958).

22. Iris Origo, *The Merchant of Prato* (New York: Knopf, 1957); also see her article, "The Domestic Enemy: Eastern Slaves in Tuscany in the Fourteenth and Fifteenth Centuries," *Speculum,* 39 (1955).

23. David Herlihy, *Medieval and Renaissance Pistoia* (New Haven, Conn.: Yale University Press, 1967).

24. E. Carpentier, *Une Ville devant la Peste: Orvieto et la Peste de 1348* (Paris: S.E.V.P.E.N., 1962).

25. William Bowsky: "The Impact of the Black Death upon Sienese Government and Society," *Speculum,* 39 (1964); and *Finances of the Commune of Siena, 1287–1355* (Oxford: Oxford University Press, 1970).

26. Angolo di Tura, *Cronaca senese,* in *The Black Death,* ed. William Bowsky (New York: Holt, Rhinehart & Winston, 1971), pp. 13–14.

27. The two best books on plague in Florence are: Ferdinand Schevill, *History of Florence* (New York: Frederick Ungar, 1961); Gene A. Brucker, *Renaissance Florence* (New York: Wiley, 1969).

28. Giovanni Boccaccio, *The Decameron,* trans. Frances Winwar (New York: Modern Library, 1955), xxiii–xxiv.

29. Ibid., p. xxviii.

30. Frederic C. Lane, *Venice: A Maritime Republic* (Baltimore: Johns Hopkins University Press, 1973).

31. Carlo Cipolla, "Per la Storia delle Epidemie in Italia," *Rivista Storica Italiana,* 75 (1963).

32. There are three good accounts for southern France: E. LeRoy Ladurie, *The Peasants of Languedoc* (Urbana, Ill.: University of Illinois Press, 1974); John Bell Henneman, "The Black Death and Royal Taxation in France, 1347–1351," *Speculum,* 43 (1968); Richard Emery, "The Black Death of 1348 in Perpignan," *Speculum,* 42 (1967). Henneman's *Royal Taxation in Fourteenth Century France* (Princeton: Princeton University Press, 1971) is also useful.

33. Emery, "The Black Death of 1348 in Perpignan."

34. Yves Renouard, "La Peste Noire," *Revue de Paris* (1950).

35. LeRoy Ladurie, *The Peasants of Languedoc,* pp. 11–50.

36. This concept is attributed to Wilhelm Abel, *Wüstungen des ausgehenden Mittelalters* (Stuttgart: Fischer, 1955). Also important is Maurice Beresford, *Lost Villages of England* (London: Lutterworth, 1954).

37. Gabriel Jackson, *The Making of Medieval Spain* (New York: Harcourt, Brace, Jovanovich, 1972), 146–54.

38. In *The Making of Medieval Spain,* Jackson describes anti-Semitism in Europe.

39. Giovanni Villani, as quoted in Schevill, *History of Florence,* pp. 239–40.

## Chapter 4

1. L. Pouquet, *La Peste en Normandie* (Paris: Librairie Hachette, 1926), p. 77.

2. Guy Bois, *Crise du Feodalisme* (Paris: Presses de la Fondation Nationale des Sciences Politiques, 1976), pp. 239–70.

3. E. Carpentier, "Autour de la Peste Noire," *Annales E.S.C.* (1962), p. 1065.

4. Jean de Venette, *The Chronicle,* ed. Richard Newhall (New York: Columbia University Press, 1953), pp. 48–49.

5. Carpentier, "Autour de la Peste Noire."

6. Jean de Venette, *The Chronicle,* p. 49.

7. There are three fundamental works. Two are by H. van Werveke: *De Zwarte Dood in de Zuidelijke Nederlanden, 1349–1357* (Brussels: H.

Hayez, 1950); "La Famine del An 1316 en Flandre et dans les Régions Voisines," *Revue du Nord* (1959). The third is W.P. Blockmans, "Effects of Plague in the Low Countries," *Revue Belgie de Philologie et Histoire*, 58 (1980).

8. J. Schreiner, *Pest og Prisfall i Sen Middelalderen et Problem i Norsk Historie* (Olso: J. Dybwad, 1948). A good general source is Karl Helleiner, "The Population of Europe from the Black Death to the Eve of the Vital Revolution," in *The Cambridge Economic History of Europe*, IV, ed. E.E. Rich & C.H. Wilson (Cambridge: Cambridge University Press, 1967), pp. 5-20.

9. Gwyn Jones, *The Norse Atlantic Saga* (Oxford: Oxford University Press, 1964), pp. 72-74.

10. Three general studies are: Charles Creighton, *History of Epidemics in Britain*, I (Cambridge: Cambridge University Press, 1894); J.F.D. Shrewsbury, *A History of Bubonic Plague in the British Isles* (Cambridge: Cambridge University Press, 1971); John Hatcher, *Plague, Population, and the English Economy, 1348-1530* (London: Macmillan, 1977).

11. Henry Knighton, *Chronicon*, ed. J. Lumby (London: Rolls Series, 92), p. 61.

12. C.E. Boucher, "The Black Death in Bristol," *Transactions of the Bristol and Gloucestershire Archeological Society*, 60 (1938).

13. John Hatcher, *Rural Economy and Society in the Duchy of Cornwall, 1300-1500* (Cambridge: Cambridge University Press, 1970), pp. 102-21.

14. Hatcher expresses this opinion generally for England in *Plague, Population, and the English Economy, 1348-1530*.

15. P.D.A. Harvey, *A Medieval Oxfordshire Village: Cuxham, 1240-1400* (Oxford: Oxford University Press, 1965), pp. 49-154.

16. Zvi Razi, *Life, Marriage, and Death in a Medieval Parish* (Cambridge: Cambridge University Press, 1980), pp. 99-113.

17. Wilkins, *Concilia*, II, pp. 735-36.

18. F.A. Gasquet, *The Great Pestilence* (London: S. Marshall, Hamilton, Kent & Co., 1893), p. 96.

19. Thomas Courtenay, "The Effect of the Black Death on English Higher Education," *Speculum*, 55 (1980).

20. A. Hamilton Thompson: "The Pestilences of the Fourteenth Century in the Diocese of York," *Archeological Journal*, 71 (1914); and "Registers of John Gynewell, Bishop of Lincoln, for the Years 1347-50," *Archeological Journal*, 68 (1911).

21. G.G. Coultan, *The Black Death* (New York: Cope & Smith, 1930), p. 496.

22. S.L. Thrupp, *The Merchant Class of Medieval London* (Chicago: University of Chicago Press, 1948), pp. 41–52.

23. Robert S. Gottfried, *Epidemic Disease in Fifteenth Century England* (New Brunswick, N.J.: Rutgers University Press, 1978), pp. 142–50.

24. Barbara Green & Rachel M.R. Young, *Norwich: The Growth of a City* (Norwich: City Museum, 1972), pp. 16–18.

25. Robert S. Gottfried, *Bury St. Edmunds and the Urban Crisis, 1290–1539* (Princeton: Princeton University Press, 1982), pp. 46–72.

26. A. Hamilton Thompson, "Registers of John Gynewell."

27. John Fordun, *Chronicle*, ed. W.F. Skene (Edinburgh: Edmonston and Douglass, 1880), p. 225.

28. W. Rees, "The Black Death in Wales," in *Essays in Medieval History*, ed. Richard Southern (London: Macmillan, 1968).

29. Ibid., p. 186.

30. John Clyn, *Annalium Hibernae Chronicon*, ed. R. Butler (Dublin: Irish Archeological Society, 1849), p. 37.

31. The work of Wilhelm Abel is the best guide, especially *Agarkrisen und Agarkonjunktur*, 3rd ed. (Hamburg & Berlin: Verlag Paul Parey, 1978). Also see R-H. Bautier, *The Economic Development of Medieval Europe* (New York: Harcourt, Brace & Jovanovich, 1971), pp. 180–88.

32. Philippe Dollinger, *The German Hansa* (Stanford, Cal.: Stanford University Press, 1970), pp. 59–61.

33. Gerald Strauss, *Nuremberg in the Sixteenth Century* (New York: Wiley, 1966), pp. 190–93.

34. There are two good accounts of flagellism: Norman Cohn, *The Pursuit of the Millenium* (New York: Harper & Row, 1961), pp. 124–48; and Gordon Leff, *Heresy in the Later Middle Ages*, II (Manchester: Manchester University Press, 1967), Chapter 4.

35. Jean de Venette, *The Chronicle*, pp. 51–52.

36. Jean Froissart, *Chronicles*, ed. Geoffrey Brereton (Baltimore: Penguin Books, 1968), pp. 111–12.

37. Cohn, *The Pursuit of the Millenium*, p. 141.

38. Jean de Venette, *The Chronicle*, pp. 51–52.

39. This topic has not received the attention it deserves. See Cohn, *The Pursuit of the Millenium*, pp. 49–139; Cecil Roth & I.H. Levine, eds., *The World History of the Jewish People*, 2nd series (New Brunswick, N.J.: Rutgers University Press, 1966); Seraphine Guerchberg, "The Controversy Over the Alleged Sowers of the Black Death in the Contemporary Treatises on Plague," in *Change in Medieval Society*, ed. S.L. Thrupp (New York: Appleton-Century-Crofts, 1964), pp. 209–24.

40. Jean de Venette, *The Chronicle*, pp. 49–50.

41. A good survey is Geoffrey Barraclough, ed., *Eastern and Western Europe in the Middle Ages* (New York: Harcourt, Brace, & Jovanovich, 1970), especially Chapter 4 by M.M. Postan.
42. Jerome Blum, *Lord and Peasant in Russia* (Princeton: Princeton University Press, 1961), p. 60.

## Chapter 5

1. See Philip Ziegler, *The Black Death* (New York: Harper & Row, 1969), pp. 224–31; Jean Froissart, *Chronicles,* ed. Geoffrey Brereton (Baltimore: Penguin Books, 1968), p. 111.
2. Giovanni Boccaccio, *The Decameron,* trans. Frances Winwar (New York: Modern Library, 1955), pp. xxv–xxvi.
3. Geoffrey Chaucer, *The Canterbury Tales,* ed. Nevill Coghill (Baltimore: Penguin Books, 1951).
4. François Villon, *Poems, Including the Testament,* ed. Norman Cameron (New York: Harcourt, Brace and World, 1962).
5. Jacques LeGoff, *Time, Work, and Culture in the Middle Ages* (Chicago: University of Chicago Press, 1980), pp. 3–97.
6. Leon Battista Alberti, *The Family in Renaissance Florence,* trans. Renee Neu Watkins (Columbia, S.C.: University of South Carolina Press, 1969), p. 165.
7. LeGoff, *Time, Work, and Culture in the Middle Ages,* p. 40.
8. Michael Dols, *The Black Death in the Middle East* (Princeton: Princeton University Press, 1977), pp. 109–21.
9. Ibid., p. 113.
10. The bibliography of works about the late medieval church is vast. A starting point is Owen Chadwick, *The History of the Church: A Select Bibliography* (London: Historical Association, 1962). Three monographs of great use are: J.B. Morrall, *Gerson and the Great Schism* (Manchester: Manchester University Press, 1960); Brian Tierney, *The Foundations of the Conciliar Theory* (Cambridge: Cambridge University Press, 1955); Walter Ullman, *The Origins of the Great Schism* (Hamden, Conn.: Archon Books, 1967).
11. The data are in two articles by A. Hamilton Thompson: "The Pestilences of the Fourteenth Century in the Diocese of York," *Archeological Journal,* 71 (1914); "The Registers of John Gynewell, Bishop of Lincoln, 1347–50," *Archeological Journal,* 68 (1911).
12. Thomas Wright, *Political Poems and Songs* (London: Rolls Series, 14, 1859–61), p. 251.
13. British Library, British Museum, Digby MS. 102, f. 33.

14. William Langland, *Piers Ploughman,* ed. J.F. Goodridge (Baltimore: Penguin Books, 1959), pp. 194–95.

15. Joel Rosenthal, *The Purchase of Paradise: The Social Function of Aristocratic Benevolence, 1307–1485,* (London: R.K.P., 1972).

16. These ideas are dealt with in Geoffrey Barraclough, *The Medieval Papacy* (New York: Harcourt, Brace, & Jovanovich, 1968), pp. 118–96.

17. *Calendar of Papal Letters, 1362–1404* (London: H.M.S.O., 1906–55), p. 163.

18. Jonathan Sumptien, *Pilgrimage: An Image of Medieval Religion* (Totowa, N.J.: Rowman & Littlefield, 1975).

19. Margaret Aston, *The Fifteenth Century: The Prospects of Europe* (New York: Harcourt, Brace & Jovanovich, 1968), pp. 85–116.

20. Henry Sigerist, *Civilization and Disease* (Chicago: University of Chicago Press, 1943), pp. 131–47.

21. Aston, *The Fifteenth Century: The Prospects of Europe,* pp. 117–73.

22. An example is G.G. Coultan, *The Black Death* (New York: Cope & Smith, 1930).

23. J. Huizinga, *The Waning of the Middle Ages* (New York: Anchor, 1954).

24. Robert S. Gottfried, *Bury St. Edmunds and the Urban Crisis, 1290–1539* (Princeton: Princeton University Press, 1982), p. 217.

25. Eustace Deschamps, as quoted in Huizinga, *The Waning of the Middle Ages,* p. 65.

26. Three good books are: Philippe Ariès, *Western Attitudes Toward Death* (Baltimore: Johns Hopkins University Press, 1974); T.S.R. Boase, *Death in the Middle Ages* (New York: McGraw-Hill, 1972); Philippa Tristram, *Figures of Life and Death in Medieval English Literature* (New York: New York University Press, 1976).

27. Georges Duby, *The Age of Cathedrals: Art and Society, 980–1420* (Chicago: University of Chicago Press, 1980), pp. 191–274.

28. Described in Millard Meiss, *Painting in Florence and Siena after the Black Death* (Princeton: Princeton University Press, 1951), a fundamental text that I have used extensively.

29. The next few pages are based on the Duby and Meiss books cited in notes 27 and 28. Also used is Aston, *The Fifteenth Century: The Prospects of Europe* pp. 175–203.

30. Meiss, *Painting in Florence and Siena after the Black Death* pp. 105–65.

31. Giovanni Boccaccio, *The Corbaccio,* as quoted by Meiss, Ibid., p. 161.

32. LeGoff, *Time, Work, and Culture in the Middle Ages,* pp. 43–52.

33. K.B. McFarlane, *The Nobility of Later Medieval England* (Oxford: The Clarendon Press, 1973).

34. Henry Knighton, *Chronicon*, ed. J. Lumby, (London: Rolls Series, 92), pp. 61–62.

35. P.D.A. Harvey, *A Medieval Oxfordshire Village: Cuxham, 1240–1400* (Oxford: Oxford University Press, 1965), pp. 84–86.

36. William Langland, *Piers the Ploughman*, ed. J.F. Goodridge (Baltimore: Penguin Books, 1959), p. xiv. Also see Morton Bloomfield, *Piers Plowman as a Fourteenth Century Apocalypse* (New Brunswick, N.J.: Rutgers University Press, 1961).

37. Elspeth M. Veale, *The English Fur Trade in the Later Middle Ages* (Oxford: The Clarendon Press, 1966), pp. 133–55.

38. McFarlane, *The Nobility of Later Medieval England* pp. 142–76.

39. Huizinga, *The Waning of the Middle Ages*, pp. 85–107.

40. George Holmes, *The Estates of the Higher Nobility in Fourteenth Century England* (Cambridge: Cambridge University Press, 1957), pp. 90–91.

41. Edward P. Cheyney, *The Dawn of a New Era* (New York: Harper, 1936), pp. 110–41. Two excellent studies are: Michel Mollat & Philippe Wolff, *Popular Revolts in the Late Middle Ages* (London: Allen, Unwin, 1973); Rodney Hilton, *Bond Men Made Free* (London: Temple-Smith, 1973).

42. John Bellamy, *Crime and Public Order in England in the Later Middle Ages* (London: R.K.P., 1973). No one disputes the fact that crime increased, but opinions differ as to the degree of increase. See Richard Kaeuper, "Law and Order in Fourteenth Century England," *Speculum*, 54 (1979).

43. *Le Despit au Vilain*, as translated in Barbara Tuchman, *A Distant Mirror: The Calamitous Fourteenth Century* (New York: Knopf, 1978), p. 175.

44. Froissart, *Chronicles*, pp. 151–52.

45. Carlo Cipolla, *Money, Prices, and Civilization in the Mediterranean World* (Princeton: Princeton University Press, 1956), pp. 27–37.

46. Froissart, *Chronicles*, p. 212.

## Chapter 6

1. Three general works that I have used are: Thomas McKeown, *The Role of Medicine* (Princeton: Princeton University Press, 1979); Charles Talbot, *Medicine in Medieval England* (London: Oldbourne, 1967); Vern L. Bullough, *The Development of Medicine as a Profession* (New York: Hafner, 1966). The growth of medicine as a profession is outlined in three other works: A.M. Carr-Saunders & P.A. Wilson, *The Profes-

*sions* (Oxford: Clarendon Press, 1933); Carlo Cipolla, "The Profes-
sions," *The Journal of European Economic History* (1973); Thomas
McKeown, "A Sociological Approach to the History of Medicine,"
*Medical History* (1970).

2. The works described in note 1 are helpful. Also important are the fol-
lowing: Loren MacKinney, *Early Medieval Medicine* (Baltimore: Johns
Hopkins University Press, 1937); C.D. O'Malley, *The History of Medi-
cal Education* (Berkeley, Cal.: University of California Press, 1970);
George Gask, *Essays in the History of Medicine* (London: Butterworth
& Co., 1950); Charles H. Talbot, "Medicine," in *Science in the Middle
Ages,* ed. David Lindberg (Chicago: University of Chicago Press,
1978).

3. These books discuss university medical education in general terms:
Hastings Rashdall, *The Universities of Europe in the Middle Ages,* 3
vols., ed. F.M. Powicke & A.V. Emden (Oxford: Oxford University
Press, 1936); John W. Baldwin, *The Scholastic Culture of the Middle
Ages, 1000–1300* (New York: Heath, 1971); Gordon Leff, *Paris and Ox-
ford Universities in the Thirteenth and Fourteenth Centuries* (New
York: Wiley, 1968).

4. A fine interpretation of Peter Abelard's importance can be found in
Norman Cantor, *Medieval History* (New York: Macmillan, 1969), pp.
361–71.

5. Two good references for humoral theory are: Henry Sigerist, *Civilization and Disease* (Chicago: University of Chicago Press, 1943), pp.
150–156; E.D. Phillips, *Greek Medicine* (London: Thames & Hudson,
1973).

6. The following studies are helpful for particular universities: Stephan
d'Irsay, "Teachers and Textbooks of Medicine in the Medieval Univer-
sity of Paris," *Annals of Medical History,* 8 (1926); P.O. Kristeller,
"School at Salerno," *Bulletin of the History of Medicine* (1945); and
the following works of Vern L. Bullough—"Teaching of Surgery at the
University of Montpellier in the Thirteenth Century," *Journal of the
History of Medicine,* 15 (1960); "The Medieval Medical School at Cam-
bridge," *Medieval Studies,* 24 (1962); "Medieval Medical University at
Paris," *Bulletin of the History of Medicine* (1957); "Medical Study at
Medieval Oxford," *Speculum* (1961). Also see Pearl Kibre & Nancy Si-
raisi, "The Institutional Setting: Universities," in *Science in the Middle
Ages,* ed. David Lindberg.

7. Two books by Charles Singer are fundamental: *The Evolution of Anatomy* (London: Paul, Trench, 1925); *A Short History of Anatomy and
Physiology* (New York: Dover, 1957).

8. Mondino de'Liuzzi, *Anatomia,* ed. Charles Singer, *Monumenta Medica,* II (Florence: R. Lier, 1925), i, pp. 80–81.

9. Hedley Atkins, *The Surgeon's Craft* (Manchester: Manchester University Press, 1965). Bullough, *The Development of Medicine as a Profession,* is best on surgery.

10. One of the best preplague surgical manuals is Lanfrank of Milan, *Science of Surgery,* ed. Robert von Fleishhacken, *Early English Text Society,* 102 (1874).

11. Most of the work on barber-surgeons has been on local groups. See: G. Parker, *The Early History of Surgery in Great Britain* (London: Black, 1920); Sidney Young, *The Annals of the Barber-Surgeons of London* (London: Blades, East & Blades, 1890).

12. Leslie G. Matthews, *History of Pharmacy in Britain* (Edinburgh: E. & S. Livingston, 1962); G.E. Trease, *Pharmacy in History* (London: Bailliere, Tindall, 1964).

13. Margaret Pelling & Charles Webster, "Medical Practitioners," in *Health, Medicine and Mortality in the Sixteenth Century,* ed. Charles Webster (Cambridge: Cambridge University Press, 1979).

14. Eileen Power, "Some Women Practitioners of Medicine in the Middle Ages," *Proceedings of the Royal Society of Medicine,* 15 (1928).

15. An original copy of this tractate is in the British Library, The British Museum, Harl. MS. 3050. Substantial portions are analyzed and translated in: D.W. Singer, "Some Plague Tractates," *Proceedings of the Royal Society of Medicine,* 9 (2): 159; and Anna Montgomery Campbell, *The Black Death and Men of Learning* (New York: Columbia University Press, 1931).

16. Bengt Knuttson, *A Little Book for the Pestilence* (Manchester: John Rylands Library, 1911), p. 6.

17. Campbell, *The Black Death and Men of Learning.*

18. Ibid., pp. 9–13.

19. Gentile of Foligno, as quoted in Campbell, ibid., pp. 38–39.

20. Michael W. Dols, *The Black Death in the Middle East* (Princeton: Princeton University Press, 1977), pp. 84–109.

21. They are discussed in Campbell, *The Black Death and Men of Learning,* pp. 7–33.

22. The University of Montpellier, as quoted in Campbell, ibid., pp. 61–62.

23. Robert S. Gottfried, *Epidemic Disease in Fifteenth Century England* (New Brunswick, N.J.: Rutgers University Press, 1978), pp. 63–77.

24. Dols, *The Black Death in the Middle East,* pp. 121–42.

25. There are many medieval leechbooks. A good one is *A Leechbook or Collection of Medical Recipes of the Fifteenth Century,* ed. W.R. Dawson (London: Macmillan, 1934).

26. There are many dietary books. One is *Tacuinum Sanitatis (Medieval*

*Health Handbook),* ed. Luisa Cogliati Arano (New York: George Braziller, 1976).

27. John Lydgate, "Dietary and Doctrine for the Pestilence," in *Lydgate's Minor Poems, II,* ed. H.N. MacCracken, *Early English Text Society,* 192 (1933), p. 702.

28. Dols, *The Black Death in the Middle East,* p. 105.

29. "Recipe for Edward IV's Plague Medicine," *Notes and Queries,* 9:343 (1878).

30. See Campbell, *The Black Death and Men of Learning,* pp. 147–80; Bullough, *The Development of Medicine as a Profession,* pp. 74– 111.

31. John Herman Randall, *The School of Padua and the Emergence of Modern Science* (Padua: Editrice Antimore, 1961); Jerome Bylebyl, "The School of Padua," in *Health, Medicine, and Mortality in the Sixteenth Century,* ed. Charles Webster; Nancy G. Siraisi, *Taddeo Alderotti and His Pupils* (Princeton: Princeton University Press, 1981).

32. John of Arderne, *De Arte Phisicali et de Cirurgia,* ed. d'Arcy Power (Oxford: Oxford University Press, 1923); Guy de Chauliac, *Surgery,* ed. M.S.Ogdan (Oxford: Oxford University Press, 1971).

33. Carlo Cipolla, *Public Health and the Medical Profession in the Renaissance* (Cambridge: Cambridge University Press, 1976). This is a seminal study.

34. Talbot, *Medicine in Medieval England,* pp. 186–97.

35. Henry Daniel, *On the Nature of Urines.* To the best of my knowledge, it has not been printed. A manuscript reference is The British Library, The British Museum, Sloane MS. 433.

36. Dawson, *A Leechbook or Collection of Medical Recipes of the Fifteenth Century,* pp. 96–97.

37. R.M. Clay, *Medieval Hospitals of England* (London: Frank Cass Reprints, 1966); Cipolla, *Public Health and the Medical Profession in the Renaissance;* Talbot, *Medicine in Medieval England,* pp. 170–85.

38. Talbot, ibid., pp. 170–85.

39. Robert S. Gottfried, *Bury St. Edmunds and the Urban Crisis, 1290–1539* (Princeton: Princeton University Press, 1982), pp. 193–207.

40. Gerald Strauss, *Nuremberg in the 16th Century* (New York: Wiley, 1966), pp. 191–93.

41. Cipolla, *Public Health and the Medical Profession in the Renaissance,* pp. 11–66.

42. Carlo Cipolla, *Cristofano and the Plague* (London: Collins, 1973).

43. Cipolla, *Public Health and the Medical Profession in the Renaissance,* p. 37.

44. Carlo Cipolla, "A Plague Doctor," in Harry A. Miskimin, et al., *The Medieval City* (New Haven, Conn.: Yale University Press, 1977).

45. There are a few good studies of deontology. See: Darrel W. Amundsen, "Medical Deontology and Pestilential Disease in the Late Middle Ages," *Journal of the History of Medicine*, 23, (1977); M.C. Welborn, "The Long Tradition: A Study in Fourteenth Century Medical Deontology," in *Medieval and Historiographical Essays in Honor of James Westfall Thompson*, ed. J.L. Cate and E.N. Anderson (Chicago: University of Chicago Press, 1938).

46. Chauliac, *Surgery*, p. 19.

47. John of Arderne, *Treatise of Fistula in Ano*, ed. d'Arcy Power, *Early English Text Society*, 139 (1910), pp. 4-7.

48. Jan Yperman, *De Cyryrgie*, ed. E.C. van Leersum (Leiden: E.J. Brill, 1912), pp. i, iv.

49. Henri de Mondeville, *Chirurgie*, ed. E. Nicaise (Paris: Félix Alcan, 1893), p. 145.

50. Arderne, *Treatise of Fistula in Ano*, p. 5.

51. Geoffrey Chaucer, *The Canterbury Tales* (Baltimore: Penguin Books, 1952), Prologue.

52. Arderne, *Treatise of Fistula in Ano*, p. 5.

53. Arderne, *Treatise of Fistula in Ano*, p. 110.

# Chapter 7

1. Sylvia Thrupp, "The Problem of Replacement Rates in Late Medieval English Population," in *Society and History: Essays by Sylvia L. Thrupp*, ed. Raymond Grew & Nicholas Steneck (Ann Arbor, Mich: University of Michigan Press, 1977); on p. 186, Thrupp calls the Late Middle Ages "the golden age of bacteria." See: John Hatcher, *Plague, Population, and the English Economy* (London: Macmillan, 1977); Robert S. Gottfried, *Epidemic Disease in Fifteenth Century England* (New Brunswick, N.J.: Rutgers University Press, 1978); Édouard Baratier, *La Démographie Provençale du Xiie Siècle* (Paris: S.E.V.P.E.N., 1961).

2. Not much has been written on the *pestis secunda*. See: Hatcher, *Plague, Population, and the English Economy;* Guy Bois, *Crise du Feodalisme* (Paris: Presses de la Fondation Nationale des Sciences Politiques, 1976).

3. K.B. McFarlane, *The Nobility of Later Medieval England* (Oxford: Clarendon Press, 1973), pp. 168-71.

4. Bois, *Crise du Feodalisme*; David Herlihy, "Population, Plague, and Social Change in Rural Pistoia," *Economy History Review*, 18 (1965).

5. Robert S. Gottfried, *Bury St. Edmunds and the Urban Crisis, 1290–1539* (Princeton: Princeton University Press, 1982).

6. A. Hamilton Thompson, "The Pestilences of the Fourteenth Century in the Diocese of York," *Archeological Journal,* 71 (1914).

7. Hatcher, *Plague, Population, and the English Economy*; Charles Creighton, *History of Epidemics in Britain* (Cambridge: Cambridge University Press, 1894).

8. William Langland, *Piers the Ploughman,* ed. J.F. Goodridge (Baltimore: Penguin Books, 1959).

9. Robert S. Gottfried, "Plague, Population, and the Sweating Sickness: Demographic Movements in Late Fifteenth Century England," *Journal of British Studies* (Fall 1976).

10. *The Paston Letters,* III, ed. J. Gairdner (London: Chatto & Windus, 1904), pp. 74–75.

11. *The Great Chronicle of London,* ed. A.H. Thomas (London: G.W. Jones, 1938), p. 226.

12. W.P. Blockmans, "Effects of Plague in the Low Countries," *Revue Belgie de Philologie et Histoire,* 58 (1980).

13. Bois, *Crise du Feodalisme,* pp. 270–308.

14. H. Neveux, "La Mortalité des Pauvres à Cambrai, 1377–1473," *Annales Demographie Historique,* 1968.

15. Most of the subsequent epidemics are nicely summed up in R-H. Bautier, *The Economic Development of Medieval Europe* (New York: Brace, Harcourt, & Jovanovich, 1971), pp. 170–200.

16. *Journal d'Un Bourgeois de Paris sous Charles VI et Charles VII,* ed. André Mary (Paris: Henri Jonquières, 1929), p. 265.

17. Gottfried, *Epidemic Disease in Fifteenth Century England,* pp. 43–46.

18. A.R. Bridbury, "The Black Death," *Economic History Review,* 2nd series, 24 (1973).

19. A good general survey of late medieval Europe is: John Hale, Roger Highfield, Beryl Smalley, *Europe in the Late Middle Ages* (Evanston, Ill.: Northwestern University Press, 1975). I have followed the themes in: A.R. Bridbury, *Economic Growth,* 2nd ed. (New York: Barnes & Noble, 1975); Douglass C. North & Robert Paul Thomas, *The Rise of Western Europe: A New Economic History* (Cambridge: Cambridge University Press, 1973). Another viewpoint is expressed in *The Cambridge Economic History,* I–III (Cambridge: Cambridge University Press, 1941–66).

20. Wilhelm Abel, "Wüstungen und Preisfall in Spätmittelalterlichen Europe," *Jahrbuch für Nationalökonomie und Statistik,* 1953.

21. M.W. Beresford, *The Lost Villages of England* (London: Lutterworth, 1954).

22. John Rous, *Historia regni Angliae*, as quoted in Beresford, ibid., pp. 81–82.

23. Philippe Dollinger, *The German Hansa* (Stanford, Cal.: Stanford University Press, 1970); M.M. Postan, "Economic Relations Between Eastern and Western Europe," in *Eastern and Western Europe in the Middle Ages*, ed. Geoffrey Barraclough (London: Thames & Hudson, 1970).

24. Fernand Braudel, *Capitalism and Material Life* (New York: Harper Torchbooks, 1974), p. 34.

25. For English land tenure, see R.H. Hilton: "Freedom and Villeinage in England," in *Peasants, Knights, and Heretics*, ed. R.H. Hilton (Cambridge: Cambridge University Press, 1976); *The Decline of Serfdom in Medieval England* (London: Macmillan, 1969). For the Continent, see: Georges Duby, *Rural Economy and Country Life in the Medieval West* (London: Edward Arnold, 1968); Jerome Blum, *Lord and Peasant in Russia* (Princeton: Princeton University Press, 1965); E. Perroy, "Wage Labour in France in the Later Middle Ages," in *Change in Medieval Society*, ed. S.L. Thrupp (New York: Appleton-Century-Crofts, 1964).

26. F.L. Carsten, "Medieval Democracy in the Brandenburg Towns and its Defeat in the Fifteenth Century," in *Change in Medieval Society*. ed. S.L. Thrupp. Also see the books cited in note 23.

27. Among the many very good studies are: F.R.H. DuBoulay, *The Lordship of Canterbury* (London: Nelson, 1966); Edward Miller, *The Abbey and Bishopric of Ely* (Cambridge: Cambridge University Press, 1951); E. LeRoy Ladurie, *The Peasants of Languedoc* (Urbana, Ill.: University of Illinois Press, 1974).

28. Eli Ashtor, "An Essay on the Diet of the Various Classes in the Medieval Levant," in *Biology of Man in History*, ed. Robert Forster and Orest Ranum (Baltimore: Johns Hopkins University Press, 1975).

29. Bautier, *The Economic Development of Medieval Europe*, pp. 188–209; Harry Miskimin, *The Economy of Early Renaissance Europe* (Englewood Cliffs, N.J.: Prentice-Hall, 1969).

30. Margaret Aston, *The Fifteenth Century* (New York: Harcourt, Brace, & Jovanovich, 1968).

31. F.R.H. DuBoulay, *An Age of Ambition* (New York: Viking, 1970); F. Graus, "The Late Medieval Poor in Town and Countryside," in *Change in Medieval Society*, ed. S.L. Thrupp.

32. The Redgrave Records, University of Chicago. I have followed the guide outlined by Richard Smith; see *The Sir Nicholas Bacon Collection: Sources of English Society, 1250–1700* (Chicago: University of Chicago Library Publication, 1972), pp. 3, 14, 18, 24, 30, 34.

33. J.Z. Titow, *Winchester Yields* (Cambridge: Cambridge University Press, 1972).

34. Alan MacFarlane, *The Origins of English Individualism* (Cambridge: Cambridge University Press, 1978).

35. Bautier, *The Economic Development of Medieval Europe*, pp. 209–233; Miskimin, *The Economy of Early Renaissance Europe*, pp. 81–115.

36. R.S. Lopez & H.A. Miskimin, "Economic Depression of the Renaissance," *Economic History Review*, 2nd series, 15 (1962).

37. H. Van der Wee, *The Growth of the Antwerp Market and the European Economy* (The Hague: Mouton, 1963).

38. Carlo Cipolla, *Before the Industrial Revolution* (New York: Norton, 1976); Lynn White, "Cultural Climates and Technological Advances in the Middle Ages." *Viator*, 2 (1971).

39. A.R. Bridbury, *England and the Salt Trade in the Later Middle Ages* (Oxford: Clarendon Press, 1955).

40. Bautier, *The Economic Development of Medieval Europe*, pp. 233–46; Miskimin, *The Economy of the Early Renaissance Europe*, 116–63; Ralph Davis, *The Rise of the Atlantic Economies* (Ithaca, N.Y.: Cornell University Press, 1973), pp. 1–36; M. Malowist, "Poland, Russia, and Western Trade in the Fifteenth and Sixteenth Centuries," *Past and Present*, 13 (1958).

41. Bautier, ibid., p. 176.

42. Dollinger, *The German Hansa;* M.M. Postan, *Medieval Trade and Finance* (Cambridge: Cambridge University Press, 1973), pp. 232–304.

43. E.M. Carus-Wilson, *Medieval Merchant Venturers* (London: Methuen, 1954), pp. 1–97; R.J. Mitchell, *John Free: From Bristol to Rome in the Fifteenth Century* (New York: Longmans, 1955).

44. Fundamental works on environmental changes are: Wilhelm Abel, *Agarkrisen und Agarkonjonktur,* 2nd ed. (Hamberg & Berlin: Verlag Paul Parey, 1966); B.H. Slicher van Bath, *The Agrarian History of Western Europe* (London: Edward Arnold, 1966).

45. DuBoulay, *An Age of Ambition; The Secular Spirit: Life and Art at the End of the Middle Ages,* ed. Thomas. Hoving (New York: Dutton, 1975); J. Huizinga, *The Waning of the Middle Ages* (New York: Anchor, 1954); Christopher Dyer, "Redistribution of Incomes in Fifteenth Century England," in *Peasants, Knights, and Heretics,* ed. R.H. Hilton.

46. Joseph R. Strayer, "The Laicization of French and English Society in the Thirteenth Century," in *Medieval Statecraft and the Perspectives of History,* ed. Joseph R. Strayer (Princeton: Princeton University Press, 1971). This is one of the most important articles on the Middle Ages.

47. Carlo Cipolla, "The Professions: A Long View," *Journal of European Economic History,* 2 (1973).

48. The works of Joseph Strayer are fundamental. A good starting point is *On the Medieval Origins of the Modern State* (Princeton: Princeton University Press, 1970).

49. William Bowsky, *The Finances of the Commune of Siena* (Oxford: Oxford University Press, 1970).

50. Agnolo di Tura del Grasso, *Cronaca senese,* as quoted in William Bowsky, "The Impact of the Black Death upon Sienese Government and Society," *Speculum,* 39 (1964).

51. Edouard Perroy, *The Hundred Years' War* (New York: Capricorn Books, 1965), pp. 121–26.

52. Richard Emery, "The Black Death of 1348 in Perpignan," *Speculum,* 42 (1967).

53. Two works by John Henneman are fundamental: "The Black Death and Royal Taxation in France, 1347–1351," *Speculum,* 43 (1968); *Royal Taxation in Fourteenth Century France* (Princeton: Princeton University Press, 1971). See also: Elizabeth A.R. Brown, "Taxation and Mortality in Thirteenth and Fourteenth Century France," *French Historical Studies* (1973); Joseph Strayer, *The Reign of Philip the Fair* (Princeton: Princeton University Press, 1980).

54. Henneman, *Royal Taxation in Fourteenth Century France,* p. 237.

55. Gottfried, *Bury St. Edmunds and the Urban Crisis, 1290–1539.*

56. Michael Dols, *The Black Death in the Middle East* (Princeton: Princeton University Press, 1977), pp. 185–92.

57. William H. McNeill, *Europe's Steppe Frontier* (Chicago: University of Chicago Press, 1964).

58. William H. McNeill, *Plagues and Peoples* (New York: Doubleday, 1976), pp. 187–91.

59. Ibid., pp. 191–98.

60. F. van Steenberghen, *Aristotle in the West* (New York: Humanities Press, 1970).

61. Heiko Oberman, *The Harvest of Medieval Theology* (Cambridge, Mass.: Harvard University Press, 1963).

62. Robert Lerner, "The Black Death and Western European Eschatological Mentalities," *The American Historical Review,* 86 (1981).

63. Anna Montgomery Campbell, *The Black Death and Men of Learning* (New York: Columbia University Press, 1931.)

64. The total number of universities actually increased in the fourteenth century, especially in the Holy Roman Empire, but many of them were weak foundations and quickly died out.

65. The best information on university collapses and foundations is Hastings Rashdall, *The Universities of Europe in the Middle Ages,* ed. F.M. Powicke & A.B. Emden (Oxford: Oxford University Press, 1936).

66. Campbell, *The Black Death and Men of Learning,* p. 155.
67. Thomas Courtenay, "The Effect of the Black Death on English Higher Education," *Speculum,* 55 (1980).
68. Courtenay suggests that these scholars may not have been in residence.
69. Courtenay, ibid.; Nicholas Orme, *English Schools in the Middle Ages* (London: Methuen, 1973).
70. DuBoulay, *An Age of Ambition,* pp. 160–78; Philippe Wolff, *Western Languages* (New York: McGraw-Hill, 1971), pp. 197–239; Louise Loomis, "Nationality at the Council of Constance: An Anglo-French Dispute," in *Change in Medieval Society,* ed. S.L. Thrupp; Dorothy Kirkland, "The Growth of National Sentiment in France before the Fifteenth Century, *History* (1938).
71. Georges Duby, *The Age of Cathedrals* (Chicago: University of Chicago Press, 1980), pp. 195–220.
72. Robert S. Gottfried, "Population, Plague, and the Sweating Sickness: Demographic Movements in Late Fifteenth Century England," *The Journal of British Studies* (Fall 1977); William H. McNeill, *Plagues and Peoples* (New York: Doubleday, 1976), pp. 199–230.
73. Robert S. Gottfried, "Bury St. Edmunds and the Populations of Late Medieval English Towns," *The Journal of British Studies* (Fall 1980).
74. Édouard Baratier, *La Démographie Provençale du Xiie au XVIe Siècle* (Paris: S.E.V.P.E.N., 1961); Roger Mols, *Introduction à la Démographique Historique des Villes d'Europe du XIVe Siècle,* 3 vols. (Gembloux: J. Duculot, 1954–56).
75. Two additional sources for England are the articles by Paul Slack and Andrew Appleby in *Health, Medicine, and Mortality in the Sixteenth Century,* ed. Charles Webster (Cambridge: Cambridge University Press, 1979).
76. Gottfried, "Population, Plague, and the Sweating Sickness."
77. Aflred W. Crosby, Jr., *The Columbian Exchange: Biological and Cultural Consequences of 1492* (Westport, Conn.: Greenwood Press, 1972), pp. 122–64.
78. Louis Chevalier, "Towards a History of Population," in *Population in History,* ed. D.V. Glass & D.E.C. Eversley (London: Edward Arnold, 1965); E.A. Wrigley, *Population and History* (New York: McGraw-Hill, 1969), pp. 61–106.

## Epilogue

1. *Caveats* are nicely presented by Sylvia L. Thrupp, "Medieval Economic Achievement in Perspective," in *Essays on the Reconstruction of Medie-*

*val History,* ed. Vaclav Murdoch and G.S. Couse (Montreal: McGill–Queen's College University Press, 1974).

2. "The World Upside Down," in *Historical Poems of the Fourteenth and Fifteenth Centuries*, ed. R.H. Robbins (New York: Columbia University Press, 1959), pp. 150–52.

3. Lynn White, "Cultural Climates and Technological Advance in the Middle Ages," *Viator,* 2 (1971).

4. James Westfall Thompson, "The Aftermath of the Black Death and the Aftermath of the Great War," *American Journal of Sociology,* 26 (1920–21).

# A Bibliographical Essay

## General Literature and Sources

The literature on the Black Death is extensive. Two surveys that present the fundamental issues are: G.G. Coultan, *The Black Death* (New York: Macmillan, 1930); Philip Ziegler, *The Black Death* (New York: Harper & Row, 1969). Three studies are fundamental to the study of the Black Death and its effect on civilization: J-N. Biraben, *Les Hommes et la Peste,* 2 vols. (The Hague: Mouton, 1975), considered by many authorities to be the best study of plague; Henry Sigerist, *Civilization and Disease* (Chicago: University of Chicago Press, 1943); William H. McNeill, *Plagues and Peoples* (New York: Doubleday, 1976). Also important is McNeill's *The Human Condition: An Ecological and Historical View* (Princeton: Princeton University Press, 1980).

There are many important thematic approaches to the Black Death. Two are by Yves Renouard: Conséquences et Intérêst Démographiques de la Peste Noire de 1348," *Population,* 3 (1948); "Le Peste Noire de 1348–50," *La Revue de Paris,* 57 (1950). Other fine studies are: Élizabeth Carpentier, "Autour de la Peste Noire," *Annales E.S.C.* (1962); J.D. Chambers, *Population, Economy and Society in Pre-Industrial England* (Oxford: Oxford

187

University Press, 1972); E. LeRoy Ladurie, "Un Concept: L'Unification Microbienne du Monde," *Schweizerische Zeitschrift für Geschichte* (1973); A.R. Bridbury, "The Black Death," *Economic History Review*, 2nd series, 24 (1973). A useful and well-organized survey that presents excerpts from different interpretations of the Black Death is *The Black Death: A Turning Point in History?*, ed. William Bowsky (New York: Holt, Rhinehart and Winston, 1971).

The best way to get a sense of the physical and psychological impact of the Black Death is through contemporary descriptions. The following give narratives of the Black Death and other plagues: Giovanni Boccaccio, *The Decameron* and *The Corbaccio*; Agnolo di Tura del Grasso, *Cronaca senese*; Giovanni Villani, *Cronica*; Gabriel de Mussis, *Historia de Morbo*; Matthew of Neuberg, *Cronica*; Jean de Venette, *The Chronicle*; C.S. Bartsocas, "Two Fourteenth Century Greek Descriptions of the Black Death," *Journal of the History of Medicine*, 21 (1966); Henry Knighton, *Chronicon;* Geoffrey the Baker, *Chronicon*; *The Paston Letters*; Procopius, *History of the Wars*; W.R. Dawson, *A Leechbook or Collection of Medical Recipes of the Fifteenth Century* (London: Macmillan, 1934).

There are a number of good contemporary medical treatments. Excerpts from many of them are printed in D.W. Singer, "Some Plague Tractates in the Fourteenth and Fifteenth Centuries," *Proceedings of the Royal Society of Medicine*, 92 (1916). Important treatises are: *Guy de Chauliac, La Grand Chirurgie*; John of Arderne, *Treatise of Fistula in Ano*; and *De Arte Phisicali et de Cirurgie*; John La Barba, *Treatise on Pestilence*; Bengt Knuttson, *A Little Book ...for...the Pestilence*. Other important, influential medical works include: Avicenna, *Poem on Medicine*; Henry Daniel, *On the Nature of Urines*; John of Gaddesden, *Rosa Medica*; Galen, *On the Parts of Medicine;* Hippocrates, *Diet and Hygiene;* John of Mirfield, *Surgery*; Lanfrank of Milan, *Surgery*; Henri de Mondeville, *La Chirurgie*; and, one of many general guides to health and diet, *The Salerno Regimen*.

## Environment and Society to 1347

Disease, famine, climate, and environment are discussed in a series of works by the eminent German historian, Wilhelm Abel. These works include: *Agarkrisen und Agarkonjunktur in Mitteleuropa* (Hamburg & Berlin: Verlag Paul Parey, 1978); *Die Wüstungen des Ausgehenden Mattelalters* (Stuttgart: Fischer, 1955); *Massenarmut und Hungerkrisen in Vorindustriellen Europe* (Hamburg & Berlin; Verlag Paul Parey, 1974); "Wustungen und Preisfall in Spätmittelalterlichen Europa," *Jahrbuch für Nationalökonomie und Statistik* (1953). Two important general works about disease are: MacFarlane Burnet & David O. White, *Natural History of Infectious Disease* (Cambridge: Cambridge University Press, 1972); *Biology of Man in His-*

*tory,* ed. Robert Forster & Orest Ranum (Baltimore: Johns Hopkins University Press, 1975). The first plague pandemic is discussed in: J.C. Russell, "That Earlier Plague," *Demography,* 5 (1968); J-N. Biraben & J. LeGoff, "The Plague in the Early Middle Ages," in *Biology of Man in History,* ed. Forster & Ranum. Saul N. Brody's *The Disease of the Soul: Leprosy in Medieval Literature* is a model study of a particular disease.

Two summaries of climatology are: E. LeRoy Ladurie, *Times of Feast and Times of Famine: A History of Climate Since the Year 1000* (New York: Doubleday, 1971); and Robert I. Rotberg & Theodore K. Rabb, *Climate and History* (Princeton: Princeton University Press, 1981). Other studies of weather conditions are: J.Z. Titow, "Evidence of Weather in the Account Rolls of the Bishopric of Winchester," *Economic History Review,* 2nd series (1960); and Gustav Utterström, "Climatic Fluctuations and Population Problems in Early Modern History," *Scandinavian Economic Historical Review* (1955).

A fine study of famine is Ian Kershaw, "The Great Famine and Agrarian Crisis in England," in *Peasants, Knights, and Heretics,* ed. R.H. Milton (Cambridge: Cambridge University Press, 1976). Other studies include: É. Carpentier, "Famines et Épidemies dans L'Histoire du XIVᵉ Siècle," *Annales E.S.C.,* 6 (1962); H.W.F. Curschmann, *Hungersnöte in Mittelalter* (Leipzig: B.G. Teubner, 1900); E. Jutikkala & M. Kauppinen, "The Structure of Mortality during Catastrophic Years in a Pre-Industrial Society," *Population Studies,* 25 (1971); M.J. Larenaude, "Les Famines en Languedoc aux XIVᵉ et XVᵉ Siècle," *Annales du Midi* (1952); H.S. Lucas, "The Great European Famine of 1315, 1316, and 1317," *Speculum* (1930); H. van Werdeke, "La Famine del An 1316 en Flandre et dans les Régions Voisines," *Revue du Nord* (1959). A good study of diet is Eli Ashtor, "An Essay on the Diet of the Various Classes in the Medieval Levant," in *Biology of Man in History,* ed. Forster & Ranum.

Europe's development to the thirteenth century is discussed in general social, economic, and cultural terms in the following: M-D. Chenu, *Nature, Man, and Society in the Twelfth Century* (Chicago: University of Chicago Press, 1980); Georges Duby, *The Early Growth of the European Economy* (Ithaca, N.Y.: Cornell University Press, 1974) and *The Three Orders: Feudal Society Imagined* (Chicago: University of Chicago Press, 1980); Robert Lopez, *The Commercial Revolution* (Englewood Cliffs, N.J.: Prentice-Hall, 1971); R.W. Southern, *The Making of the Middle Ages* (New Haven, Conn.: Yale University Press, 1953); Lynn White, Jr., *Medieval Technology and Social Change* (Oxford: Oxford University Press, 1962).

The socioeconomic and cultural developments of thirteenth- and fourteenth-century Europe are covered in: Robert Boutruche, *La Crise d'une société: Seigneurs et Paysans du Bordelais pendant La Guerre de Cent Ans* (Paris: Belles Lettres, 1947); Robert Brenner, "Agrarian Class Structure and Economic Development in Pre-Industrial Europe," *Past and Present,*

70 (1976); Georges Duby, *Medieval Marriage* (Baltimore: Johns Hopkins University Press, 1978) and *Rural Economy and Country Life in the Medieval West* (London: Edward Arnold, 1965); J. Hajnal, "European Marriage Patterns in Perspective," in *Population in History,* ed. D.V. Glass & D.E.C. Eversley, (London: Edward Arnold, 1965); M.M. Postan, *Essays on Medieval Agriculture and General Problems of the Medieval Economy* (Cambridge: Cambridge University Press, 1973); B.H. Slicher van Bath, *Agrarian History of Western Europe* (London: Edward Arnold, 1966); J.Z. Titow, *Winchester Yields: A Study in Medieval Agricultural Productivity* (Cambridge: Cambridge University Press, 1972); E.A. Wrigley, *Population and History* (New York: McGraw-Hill, 1969). Fundamental to an understanding of thirteenth-and fourteenth-century society are the essays in Jacques LeGoff's *Time, Work, and Culture in the Middle Ages* (Chicago: University of Chicago Press, 1980), particularly "Labor Time in the 'Crisis' of the Fourteenth Century."

## The Black Death

It is difficult to provide precise population figures for medieval Europe, but there have been several attempts. Among the more successful are: Edouard Baratier, *La Démographie Provençale du XIIIᵉ au XVIᵉ Siècle* (Paris: S.E.V.P.E.N., 1961); K.J. Beloch, *Bevölkerungsgeschichte Italiens,* 3 vols. (Berlin & Leipzig: De Gruyter, 1961); John Hatcher, *Plague, Population, and the English Economy* (London: Macmillan, 1977); Karl Helleiner, "The Population of Europe from the Black Death to the Eve of the Vital Revolution," in *The Cambridge Economic History of Europe,* IV, ed. E.E. Rich & C.H. Wilson (Cambridge: Cambridge University Press, 1967); David Herlihy & C. Klapish, *Les Toscans et leur Families: Une Étude du Catasto Florentin de 1427* (Paris: Presses de la Fondation Nationales des Sciences Politiques (1978); R. Mols, *Introduction à la Démographie Historique des Villes d'Europe du XIVᵉ au XVIIIᵉ Siècle* (Gembloux: J. Duculot, 1954–56); Zvi Razi, *Life, Marriage, and Death in a Medieval Parish* (Cambridge: Cambridge University Press, 1980); Josiah Cox Russell, *Medieval Regions and their Cities* (Bloomington, Ind.: University of Indiana Press, 1972); A. Hamilton Thompson, "The Pestilences of the Fourteenth Century in the Diocese of York," *Archeological Journal,* 71 (1914) and "Registers of John Gynewell, Bishop of Lincoln, for the Years 1347–50," *Archeological Journal,* 68 (1911).

There are many national and regional studies that show the impact of the Black Death. One of the best is Michael Dols's *The Black Death in the Middle East* (Princeton: Princeton University Press, 1977). Other important studies are: Guy Bois, *Crise du Feodalisme* (Paris: Presses de la Fondation des Sciences Politiques, 1976); C.E. Boucher, "The Black Death in Bristol," *Transactions of the Bristol and Gloucestershire Archeological Society,* 60 (1938); Elizabeth A.R. Brown, "Taxation and Mortality in Thirteenth and Fourteenth Century France," *French Historical Studies* (1973); E. Carpentier, *Une Ville devant la Peste: Orvieto et la Peste Noire de 1348* (Paris: S.E.V.P.E.N., 1962); Charles Creighton, *History of Epidemics in Britain* (Cambridge: Cambridge University Press, 1894); Richard Emery, "The Black Death of 1348 in Perpignan," *Speculum,* 42 (1967); Seraphine Guerchberg, "The Controversy Over the Alleged Sowers of the Black Death," in *Change in Medieval Society,* ed. S.L. Thrupp (New York: Appleton-Century-Crofts, 1964); John Henneman, "The Black Death and Royal Taxation in France, 1347-51," *Speculum,* 43 (1968); William Rees, "The Black Death in Wales," in *Essays in Medieval History,* ed. R.W. Southern (London: Macmillan, 1968); J. Schreiner, *Pest og Prisfall i Sen Middlealderen et Problem i Norsk Historie* (Oslo: J. Dybwad, 1948); J.F.D. Shrewsbury, *A History of the Bubonic Plague in the British Isles* (Cambridge: Cambridge University Press, 1971); H. van Werdeke, *De Zwarte Dood in de Zuidelijke Nederlanden, 1349-57* (Brussels: H. Hayez, 1959); W.P. Blockmans, "Effects of Plague in the Low Countries," *Revue Belgie de Philologie et Histoire,* 58 (1980).

Norman Cohn, *The Pursuit of the Millenium* (Oxford: Oxford University Press, 1957), discusses flagellism and anti-Semitism. The dance of death is discussed by: J. Brossolet, "L'influence de la Peste du Moyen Age sur le Thème de la Danse Macabre," *Pagine di storia della Medicina,* 13 (1969); James M. Clark, *The Dance of Death in the Middle Ages and the Renaissance* (Glasgow: Glasgow University Press, 1950).

Two fine studies of plague in Italy are: William Bowsky, "The Impact of the Black Death upon Sienese Government and Society," *Speculum,* 39 (1964); David Herlihy, "Population, Plague, and Social Change in Rural Pistoia," *Economic History Review,* 2nd series, 18 (1965).

There is an interesting debate about the origins of the Black Death in *The Bulletin of the History of Medicine.* See: Stephan R. Ell, "Interhuman Transmission of Medieval Plague," *BHM* (1980), 54:497-510; John Norris, "East or West: The Geographic Origin of the Black Death," *BHM* (1977), 51:1-24; Michael Dols, "Geographical Origin of the Black Death: Comment," *BHM* (1978), 52:112-113; John Norris, "Response," 114-120.

## Postplague Environment and Society

*The Decameron* and *The Corbaccio* of Giovanni Boccaccio give contrasting perspectives of late medieval attitudes. Other sources which give a sense of late medieval psychology include: Geoffrey Chaucer, *The Cantebury Tales*; Jean Froissart, *Chronicle*; William Langland, *Piers Ploughman*; and François Villon, *Poems*. Modern scholars who have captured the tenor of late medieval life are: Margaret Aston, *The Fifteenth Century: The Prospects of Europe* (New York: Harcourt, Brace, & Jovanovich, 1968); J. Huizinga, *The Waning of the Middle Ages* (New York: Anchor, 1954); F.R.H. DuBoulay, *An Age of Ambition* (New York: Viking, 1970); and Barbara Tuchman, *A Distant Mirror: The Calamitous Fourteenth Century* (New York: Knopf, 1978). *The Secular Spirit: Life and Art at the End of the Middle Ages*, ed. Thomas Hoving (New York: E.P. Dutton, 1975), published for the Metropolitan Museum of Art in New York, is a fine catalogue, with accompanying text, of late medieval art and artifacts; and *Change in Medieval Society*, ed. Sylvia L. Thrupp (New York: Appleton, Century, Crofts, 1964) is a good collection of essays.

The following are excellent guides to the postplague economy: R-H. Bautier, *The Economic Development of Medieval Europe* (New York: Harcourt, Brace, & Jovanovich, 1971); A.R. Bridbury, *Economic Growth* (New York: Barnes & Noble, 1975); Carlo Cipolla, *Before the Industrial Revolution* (New York: Norton, 1976); Robert Lopez & Harry Miskimin, "Economic Depression of the Renaissance," *Economic History Review,* 2nd series, 15 (1962); Harry Miskimin, *Economy of Early Renaissance Europe* (Englewood Cliffs, N.J.: Prentice-Hall, 1969); Douglass C. North & Robert Paul Thomas, *The Rise of the Western World* (Cambridge: Cambridge University Press, 1973); M.M. Postan, *Medieval Trade and Finance* Cambridge: Cambridge University Press, 1973); Sylvia Thrupp, "Medieval Economic Achievement in Perspective," in *Essays on the Reconstruction of Medieval History,* ed. Vaclav Mudroch & G.S. Couse (Montreal: McGill-Queen's College University Press, 1974).

Phillipe Aries, *Western Attitudes to Death* (Baltimore: Johns Hopkins University Press, 1974), describes new attitudes toward death. Maurice Beresford, *Lost Villages of England* (London: Lutterworth, 1954), discusses changes in the landscape, while Alan MacFarlane, *The Origins of English Individualism* (New York: Cambridge University Press, 1978), describes, among other things, changes in inheritance patterns. Changes in standards of living are discussed in: Christopher Dyer, "A Redistribution of Incomes in Fifteenth Century England?" in *Peasants, Knights, and Heretics,* ed. R.H. Hilton (Cambridge: Cambridge University Press, 1976); F. Graus, "The Late Medieval Poor in Town and Countryside" and E. Perroy, "Wage Labour in France in the Later Middle Ages," both in *Change in Medieval Society,* ed. S.L. Thrupp.

Among the many demographic and epidemiological studies of postplague Europe are the following: Louis Chevalier, "Towards a History of Population," in *Population in History,* ed. D.V. Glass & D.E.C. Eversley (London: Edward Arnold, 1965); Alfred Crosby, *The Columbian Exchange* (Westport, Conn.: Greenwood Press, 1972); Robert S. Gottfried, *Epidemic Disease in Fifteenth Century England* (New Brunswick, N.J.: Rutgers University Press, 1978) and "Population, Plague, and the Sweating Sickness in Late Fifteenth Century England," *The Journal of British Studies* (Fall

1976); H. Neveaux, "La Mortalité des Pauvres a Cambrai, 1377–1473," *Annales Demographies Historiques* (1968).

The following are important studies of late medieval rural life, work, and tenure: Jerome Blum, *Lord and Peasant in Russia* (Princeton: Princeton University Press, 1961); F.R.H. DuBoulay, *The Lordship of Canterbury* (London: Nelson, 1966); P.D.A. Harvey, *A Medieval Oxfordshire Village* (Oxford: Oxford University Press, 1965); John Hatcher, *Rural Economy and Society in the Duchy of Cornwall* (Cambridge: Cambridge University Press, 1970); R.H. Hilton, *Bond Men Made Free* (London: Temple-Smith, 1973), *The Decline of Serfdom in Medieval England* (London: Macmillan, 1969), and *The English Peasantry in the Later Middle Ages* (Oxford: Oxford University Press, 1975); G.A. Holmes, *The Estates of the Higher Nobility in Fifteenth Century England* (Cambridge: Cambridge University Press, 1957); Angeliki Laiou, *Peasant Society in the Late Byzantine Empire* (Princeton: Princeton University Press, 1977); Edward Miller, *The Abbey and Bishopric of Ely* (Cambridge: Cambridge University Press, 1969).

The following are studies of late medieval urban life and trade: William Bowsky, *Finances of the Commune of Siena* (Oxford: Oxford University Press, 1970); F.L. Carsten, "Medieval Democracy in the Brandenburg Towns and its Defeat in the Fifteenth Century," in *Change in Medieval Society,* ed. S.L. Thrupp; Phillipe Dollinger, *The German Hansa* (Stanford, Cal.: Stanford University Press, 1970); Robert S. Gottfried, *Bury St. Edmunds and the Urban Crisis, 1290–1539* (Princeton: Princeton University Press, 1982); Jacques Heers, *Gênes au XVᵉ Siècle* (Paris: S.E.V.P.E.N., 1961); Frederic C. Lane, *Venice: A Maritime Republic* (Baltimore: Johns Hopkins University Press, 1973); M. Malowist, "Poland, Russia, and Western Trade in the Fifteenth and Sixteenth Centuries, *Past and Present,* 13 (1958); Gerald Strauss, *Nuremberg in the Sixteenth Century* (New York: Wiley, 1968); Sylvia L. Thrupp, *The Merchant Class of Medieval London* (Chicago: University of Chicago Press, 1948); E.M. Veale, *The English Fur Trade in the Later Middle Ages* (Oxford: Clarendon Press, 1966); H. van der Wee, *The Growth of the Antwerp Market* (The Hague: Mouton, 1963).

Fundamental to an understanding of medieval medicine are: Vern L. Bullough, *The Development of Medicine as a Profession* (New York: Hafner, 1966); Carlo Cipolla, *Public Health in the Medical Profession in the Renaissance* (Cambridge: Cambridge University Press, 1976); Thomas McKeown, *The Role of Medicine* (Princeton: Princeton University Press, 1979); C.H. Talbot, *Medicine in Medieval England* (London: Oldbourne, 1967); and Nancy G. Siraisi, *Taddeo Alderotti and His Pupils* (Princeton: Princeton University Press, 1981). Other important works are: David W. Amundsen, "Medical Deontology and Pestilential Disease in the Late Middle Ages," *Journal of the History of Medicine,* 23 (1977); Carlo Cipolla, "The Professions: A Long View," *The Journal of European Economic History,* 2 (1973); Stephan d'Irsay, "Teachers and Textbooks of Medicine in the Medieval University of Paris," *Annals of Medical History,* 8 (1926); A.M.

Carr-Saunders & P.A. Wilson, *The Professions* (Oxford: Clarendon Press, 1933); C.D. O'Malley, *The History of Medical Education* (Berkeley, Cal.: University of California Press, 1970); and Charles Webster, ed., *Health, Medicine, and Mortality in the Sixteenth Century* (Cambridge: Cambridge University Press, 1979), especially his entry "Medical Practitioners."

Anna Montgomery Campbell, *The Black Death and Men of Learning* (New York: Columbia University Press, 1931), offers a general discussion of the relationship between plague, learning, and culture. Two brilliant studies on art are: Millard Meiss, *Painting in Florence and Siena after the Black Death* (Princeton: Princeton University Press, 1951); Georges Duby, *The Age of the Cathedrals: Art and Society, 980–1420* (Chicago: University of Chicago Press, 1980). Other useful studies include: William J. Courtenay, "The Effect of the Black Death on English Higher Education," *Speculum,* 55 (1980); Gordon Leff, *Heresy in the Later Middle Ages* (Manchester: Manchester University Press, 1967); Robert E. Lerner, "The Black Death and Western European Eschatological Mentalities," *American Historical Review,* 86 (1981); Heiko Oberman, *The Harvest of Medieval Theology* (Cambridge, Mass.: Harvard University Press, 1963); Philippe Wolff, *Western Languages* (New York: McGraw-Hill, 1971).

The works of J.R. Strayer are fundamental to a full understanding of the Middle Ages. Two of his most notable studies are: *On the Medieval Origins of the Modern State* (Princeton: Princeton University Press, 1970); "The Laicization of French and English Society in the Thirteenth Century," in *Medieval Statecraft and the Perspectives of History,* ed. J.R. Strayer (Princeton: Princeton University Press, 1971). Other important works on government, politics, and social class include: Geoffrey Barraclough, ed., *Eastern and Western Europe in the Middle Ages* (London: Thames & Hudson, 1970); John Bellamy, *Crime and Public Order in England in the Later Middle Ages* (London: R.K.P., 1973); John Bell Henneman, *Royal Taxation in Fourteenth Century France* (Princeton: Princeton University Press, 1971); Dorothy Kirkland, "The Growth of National Sentiment in France before the Fifteenth Century," *History* (1938); Louise Loomis, "Nationality at the Council of Constance: An Anglo-French Dispute," in *Change in Medieval Society,* ed. S.L. Thrupp; K.B. McFarlane, *The Nobility of Later Medieval England* (Oxford: Oxford University Press, 1973); Michel Mollat & Philippe Wolff, *Popular Revolt of the Late Middle Ages* (London: Allen, Unwin, 1973).

# Index